ASEN BALIKCI was educated in Switzerland and the Unit... He received his Ph.D. degree in anthropology from ... University in 1962. From 1954 to 1961 he was a staff member of the National Museum of Canada. Since that time he has been on the faculty of the University of Montreal, where he is now Professor of Anthropology, specializing in social organization, cultural ecology, community studies, and ethno-cinematography.

Dr. Balikci has done field work among the Macedonian ethnic group in Toronto (1955); the Great Whale River Eskimos of East Hudson Bay (1957); the Povungnituk Eskimos of East Hudson Bay (1958); the Vunta Kutchin Indians of the Yukon Territory (1961); the Veliko Selo Villagers of Yugoslav Macedonia (1962); the Malinke of Eastern Senegal (1965); the Danakil of Ethiopia (1970); and the Lakenkhel Pakhtuns of Afghanistan (1973-1976). His work among the Eskimos of Pelly Bay began in 1959 and culminated in his direction of nine comprehensive films, complete with natural soundtrack, of the seasonal camps of the Netsilik Eskimos in traditional times. Released in the fall of 1969, the films were made in collaboration with the Education Development Center and the National Film Board of Canada. Presently, Dr. Balikci is chairman of the Commission on Visual Anthropology, International Union of Anthropological and Ethnological Sciences.

Itimangnerk's wife tending seal skins at the spring seal hunting camp in 1964.

Cover photo: Itimangnerk, his wife, and young son at the caribou hunting 몸p in 1964.

THE NETSILIK ESKIMO

Asen Balikci

WAVELAND

PRESS, INC.

Prospect Heights, Illinois

EXTRACTS from *The Netsilik Eskimos,* Reports of the Fifth Thule Expedition, Vol. VIII, by Knud Rasmussen; Copenhagen, 1931; reprinted by permission of the heirs of Knud Rasmussen.

EXTRACTS from *Legal Concepts Among the Netsilik Eskimos of Pelly Bay, N.W.T.,* by Geert van den Steenhoven; Ottawa: Northern Coordination and Research Centre, Department of Northern Affairs and National Resources, 1959, NCRC–59–3; reprinted by permission of the publisher.

To Franz Van de Velde, O.M.I.

For information about this book, write or call:

Waveland Press, Inc.
P.O. Box 400
Prospect Heights, Illinois 60070
(312) 634-0081

CONTENTS

FOREWORD

Margaret Mead, The American Museum of Natural History

This book, written about a contemporary exploration of the ancient ways of a contemporary people, the Netsilik Eskimo, records an unusual and felicitous adventure. The modern anthropologist studies primitive people as they are; if they hunt with guns instead of bows and arrows or build their houses with modern materials, he describes these innovations, however much they mar the aesthetically satisfying picture of an earlier form of life in which every detail had been polished into consistency by a thousand years of use. And so, often enough, especially when he works among a much-studied people who have been in contact with technologically advanced civilizations for a long time, he pays for his fidelity to the way in which the people live today by never seeing, in the flesh, the way they once lived. And yet it is the way in which they once lived, before the introduction of steel and canvas and porcelain and tin, that particularly interests the ethnographer and fascinates the general reader.

Because his mission was unusual, Dr. Balikci has been able to bridge the chasm that separates the Eskimo of Pelly Bay as they once were from the Eskimo as they are today. In addition to the usual type of field work, he had a special mandate—to make films which would demonstrate for today's students and for posterity the way the Eskimo once lived. Those he filmed still lived close enough to their ancient skills so that they could return to them without a sense of loss or unreality. His purpose was one that they could understand. The Netsilik Eskimo are a sturdy people, proud of their abilities, their heads unbowed in the presence of merely superior technology. So he and they and three successive cameramen made a series of nine films. As they did so, he was able to see the past as it unrolled on film—in the camera, and before his eyes. The result is a delightfully vivid story, told now, through the perception of present-day man, in response to questions that are being asked today about how primitive people lived.

To complement this story there are sections based on older records and on memories of old men that keenly point up the difference between a living present, where every member of the group becomes an active and willing participant informant, and the kind of ethnography that we will be driven to in the future, in cases where no films have been made and where everyone has lost his touch with harpoon or snow knife and some of our most precious diversities have completely disappeared without a record.

PREFACE

Most of the data presented in this book were collected
during several field trips among the Arviligjuarmiut of
Pelly Bay between 1959 and 1965. Several papers covering
distinct aspects of Netsilik ethnography were published
following this initial field experience. In 1963, I joined Educational Services, Inc., in order to take charge of an ethnographic film program with the aim of making a detailed
visual record of the daily activities of the Netsilik Eskimos
(Balikci, 1966). In the course of several expeditions to the
Arctic coast enough footage was exposed to produce nearly
ten hours of edited film.

Meanwhile, in Cambridge, Massachusetts, a curriculum
development unit was at work, synthesizing Netsilik anthropological data, film material, and new teaching techniques
in order to prepare an original social science program for
the elementary schools. It was also necessary to prepare a
manual on Netsilik ethnography for the training of the
teachers who were to apply the new program. Such a book
was also intended to help wider audiences understand better the various sequences of the Netsilik films; hence the
idea for the present book.

The first chapter, describing the annual migration cycle
of the Netsilik Eskimos, is closely related to the subject matter of the film series. The rest of the book is a summary of
the published literature with new material added here

and there. I have drawn heavily on Rasmussen's classic *Reports of the Fifth Thule Expedition*. My papers dealing with marriage, suicide, and infanticide among the Netsilik served as additional source material. Substantial portions of my study on Netsilik shamanism are reproduced here with permission of the *Southwestern Journal of Anthropology*. As for the drawings, for reasons of efficiency and economy they were made from the pictures in K. Birket-Smith's *Ethnographical Collections from the Northwest Passage*, although the original artifact collections I assembled for the National Museum of Canada could have been used with similar results.

Dr. Helge Larsen of the Danish National Museum kindly provided the pictures of Netsilik men's and women's fur clothing. Since several of the Eskimo words used here have appeared already in previous publications, no attempt was made to introduce a new spelling of Netsilik names.

Asen Balikci
Département d'Anthropologie
Université de Montréal

The field work upon which this book is based was conducted in the early 1960s. Since then many new developments have taken place in the various Inuit communities along the Arctic Coast of Canada. These transformations affected practically all aspects of Inuit society and culture: settlement pattern, technology and subsistence, community organization, communications and ideology. The primary agent for development and change was the Canadian government with the political intention to establish a balance in living standards between the northern and southern parts of the country. In this context, the Pelly Bay community entered the bureaucratic phase of northern history.

In the fall of 1976, I was invited by WGBH-Boston, a PBS affiliated station, to participate in the making of a documentary film describing the various material and social changes that had taken place recently among the Arviligjuarmiut of Pelly Bay. I welcomed this opportunity to revisit the community which I studied intensively fifteen years earlier. My second visit to Pelly Bay was of short duration. I was able to see many old friends and take notes on the drastic changes that have taken place at Pelly Bay between the early 1960s and the mid-1970s. These notes are summarized in the new epilogue of this book. The epilogue may be useful as background information to the film "The Netsilik Eskimo Today" which is produced and distributed by the National Film Board of Canada.

The first part of this book was written in close harmony with the group of ethnographic films entitled Netsilik Eskimo Film

Series, released in 1969 and internationally distributed by the National Film Board of Canada. Each section of Part I is closely related to a distinct film in the visual ethnography. Written word and film sequence supplement and support each other in order to provide a wider learning experience.

The Netsilik Eskimo Film Series is considered as a major endeavor in the history of visual anthropology. The series is ten and a half hours long and describes in detail various family and subsistence activities in the context of nine seasonal camps distributed along one particular annual migration circuit. This is a visual record of Netsilik ecological adaptation to an extremely harsh environment by linking critical features of environment to specialized technologies, settlement pattern, group formation, and forms of collaboration. The cultural patterns portrayed correspond to the contact-traditional phase. The historical baseline was to be the last year prior to the introduction of rifles in the area, namely, 1919. Understandably, some reconstruction of the film setting was necessary. The extent of our reconstruction efforts is described in a separate article (Balikci, 1975).

This film series became integral part of a new curriculum in the humanities entitled "Man: A Course of Study." MACOS was intended for fifth graders and was distributed during the early 1970s to nearly 3000 schools across the United States. Soon after, a major controversy arose concerning the implicit ideology of the course. The controversy quickly acquired national proportions and was debated in Congress in May 1976 (Nelkin 1976). Meanwhile, various television networks used the Netsilik film archives to produce new films for wider audiences. To date, there have been close to 150 television presentations world-wide of Netsilik film materials in various formats. The controversies surrounding MACOS and the extraordinary success of the Netsilik films have both been related to the vicissitudes of the extremely positive stereotype of the Eskimos held by western peoples (Balikci 1988).

In sum, the Netsilik Eskimo research project led to the completion of a number of multiformat productions: a film archive of 250,000 feet of film, an educational film series, a variety of television programs, several scholarly and popular articles and books, and a highly original curriculum for the upper elementary grades.

Asen Balikci
Commission on Visual Anthropology
Université de Montréal

INTRODUCTION

This is a short ethnographic description of the traditional way of life of the Netsilingmiut, an isolated tribe of Arctic hunters living on the Arctic coast of northern North America. These People of the Seal, referred to below as the Netsilik Eskimos, were primarily seal hunters armed with harpoons, although they relied on other game and other weapons as well in their struggle for survival. They hunted caribou from kayaks with light spears on rivers and narrow lakes; they brought down musk oxen and polar bears with bows and arrows and heavy spears; they fished for salmon trout with crudely-fashioned spears. To protect themselves from the extreme cold in winter, the Netsilik wore tailored clothing of animal fur, and they lived in snow houses heated by soapstone lamps. For travel they possessed a few short sledges made of wood or sealskin, which were pulled by just two or three dogs.

In contrast to this highly specialized and well-adapted technology, the social organization of the Netsilik was relatively simple. They had bilateral families with a strong patrilateral slant, they were generally monogamous, and of course they had personal kindreds. Partnerships and other more or less formal bonds linking two non-relatives were numerous. There were no lineages or clans, no institutionalized chiefs or formal government.

The Netsilik believed in many supernatural beings: hu-

man and animal souls, various ghosts, good and evil spirits,
monsters, and several major deities. Their lives were bur-
dened by innumerable taboos and religious observances.
They believed that any breach of taboo could have dangerous consequences for the individual or society. They
built no graves, and their only religious practitioners were
shamans—half priests, half sorcerers—who could fall into
trance and evoke helpful spirits to cure the sick, aid the
community, or satisfy personal grievances.

Many of these cultural traits were shared by other Eskimo
groups, who cover an area from the eastern tip of Siberia
across Alaska and northern Canada to West and East Greenland—and other of these traits were peculiar to the Netsilik
people. The Southwest Greenlanders lived in stone houses
and were extremely skilled seal hunters in open water, using
kayaks and throwing harpoons. The Polar Eskimos, living at
the northern tip of Greenland, had lost the kayak, the
umiak or large skin boat, and the sled. They did not hunt
caribou nor fish salmon. Meanwhile the Caribou Eskimos
of the Barren Grounds had practically no relations with the
sea. They relied almost exclusively on caribou hunting and
fishing. Their material culture was probably the simplest
and poorest of all known Eskimo technologies.

At the other extreme were the Eskimos living in Alaska.
Timber there was rather abundant, and many Alaskan Eskimos lived in wooden houses. Some groups had elaborate
masks, wore hats in place of hoods, knew how to make
coiled baskets and earthen pots, erected grave monuments,
and had a much more complex social organization comprising strong chieftainships, complicated trading patterns, em-
bryonic clan formations, and warfare activities. Further,
ceremonial life was strongly developed.

Thus, there were substantial cultural differences among
the various Eskimo groups inhabiting the northern end of
the continent and Greenland. Several ethnologists have attempted to establish major groupings for these people living

in such scattered and generally widely separated settlements. Kaj Birket-Smith (1959:233) proposed a subdivision of seventeen distinct units grouped in three major cultural subareas: the Alaskan Eskimos, the Central Eskimos, and the Greenland Eskimos. A. L. Kroeber (1953:27) divided Eskimo culture into two major components: Western or Alaskan, and Central-Eastern (including Greenland). The first was considerably richer and was probably under strong influence from the neighboring Indian tribes. The second was somewhat simpler and more "Eskimo" in general outline.

The Netsilik belonged to the Central branch of the Eskimo family, the igloo dwellers, the seal and the caribou hunters. Their habitat was within the Arctic Circle (100°W. −88°E., 73°N. −68°S.), covering an immense area of nearly 9000 square miles from Committee Bay in the east to Victoria Strait to the west, and to Bellot Strait to the north. This part of the Arctic coast contains huge land masses: King William Island, Boothia and Adelaide peninsulas, the vast hilly region between Sherman Inlet and Pelly Bay, and Simpson Peninsula. The coast is deeply cut by many ocean inlets and lined by innumerable islands. There is every kind of terrain: while Boothia Peninsula and the land just south of it are covered by rocky Pre-Cambrian hills and offer a generally uneven landscape, King William Island and Simpson Peninsula are flat, representative of the typical mossy tundra topography. Countless lakes, ponds, and rivers are found everywhere, but the harsh climate precludes much vegetation. There are no trees; instead, lichens, mosses, and various grass-like plants cover the tundra and hills, sometimes growing with creeping shrubs along the sheltered river beds.

The climate is rigorous. As early as late September, the sea begins to freeze. The sea ice in midwinter is six to seven feet thick and does not disappear until the end of July. Winters are extremely cold. The mean daily temperature in

January falls below −20°F., and often it falls to −40°F. Summers are short, cool, and misty, with a mean daily temperature below 50°F. in the warmest season. Though precipitation is low, the tundra in summer is very wet, mosses acting as sponges full with water. This is due to the solid permafrost beginning just a foot below the surface. Melting snow and rain water remain on the surface, giving to the tundra a marshy appearance.

Certainly this is one of the most desolate environments on earth, particularly inappropriate for human occupation. Yet the Netsilik survived here, their success in adapting to the extreme rigors of the Arctic climate made possible largely by the abundance of certain animals which they used for food, fuel, clothing, and tool materials. The most important of these animals were seal, caribou, and musk oxen. The entire Netsilik society depended on the successful hunting of these animals. Salmon trout, abundant in certain rivers and at particular seasons, were also an indispensable source of food.

There was considerable variation in the seasonal and regional distribution of caribou herds in the Netsilik area. The caribou, essentially a gregarious animal, lived in herds of varying sizes, and in this part of Canada it migrated according to a definite pattern. These herds spent the winter hundreds of miles south of the Netsilik country, in the general area of the tree line, in southern Keewatin or northern Manitoba. In spring they migrated north, the cows reaching the Arctic coast area in mid-April, followed by the bulls a month later. In June, caribou were very common around the large lakes on Boothia Isthmus. The return migration began in September, and only stragglers remained in the country the following month.

In addition to the caribou, there is substantial evidence of the presence of numerous musk oxen in the Netsilik area in traditional times. According to early travelers' accounts, the regions south of Boothia Isthmus, Pelly Bay, and Committee Bay abounded with musk oxen. Polar bears were also present; irregularly distributed, they were usually found near the coast line of the mainland and the major islands.

But of far greater economic importance than musk oxen or polar bears was the ringed seal. Seals could be found in many bays and straits on the Netsilik coast, and were particularly abundant in three areas: the central and northern part of Pelly Bay; the Lord Mayor Bay; and the Shepherd Bay–Rae Strait district. The large bearded seal was much less common and was to be found in a few well-known bays with rather shallow waters.

Salmon trout (or arctic charr) was essential to the diet of the Netsilik. This is a migratory species that swims in large schools down the main rivers to the sea in July and returns to the inland lakes in the middle of August (with local variations in their migratory pattern). But this was by no means the only kind of fish caught by the Netsilik. Many deep-water lakes abounded in lake trout, and arctic cod was also used as emergency food by some of the western Netsilik. Birds were of little importance in Netsilik economy, with only a few ptarmigan caught in the warm season, and some wild fowl taken in their molting period.

Although cut off from the rest of the world by enormous expanses of arctic desert, the Netsilik were not entirely isolated from the other neighboring Eskimo tribes. In fact, intercourse between widely separated groups was a quite common occurrence in the North. Since the Eskimos are known for their great skill as travelers under difficult conditions, it is not surprising that in traditional times (around the end of the last century and the beginning of this), the Netsilik had contact with the Aivilik Eskimos to the east. The Aivilik, who lived near Repulse Bay and belonged culturally to the Igloolik Eskimos, had been in contact with European and American whalers since the last quarter of the past century and thus had the opportunity to acquire firearms. They feared the Netsilik for their allegedly belli-

cose character and also had considerable contempt for their
slovenly manners and coarseness. Relations between the
Netsilik and their southwesterly neighbors, the Utkuhikjalingmiut (Soapstone People) living near Back River,
were better, with many intermarriages taking place between the two groups. This was not the case with the Kitd-
linermiut (Those of the Farther End) of Victoria Island
west of the King William Land, who had an evil reputation
among the Netsilik as murderers and sorcerers.

The Netsilik were a divided and unstable group of people.
They were nomadic hunters who traveled in small bands
from one hunting area to the next. Each band was identified with a particular region where its habitual hunting
grounds were located. A man born and raised in a given
band was identified with it for the rest of his life, even if he
emigrated and settled among another tribelet.

Ethnologists and explorers traveling through the area at
different periods during the last hundred years have given
both different names and sometimes different locations to
these bands. The distribution of Netsilik subgroups I observe here is the one given by Knud Rasmussen based on the
detailed information he obtained from native informants
during his eight months' stay in the area in 1923 as leader of
the Fifth Thule Expedition. The eastern branch of the Netsilik was known as the Arviligjuarmiut (People of the Big
One with the Whale), and they lived around Pelly Bay and
Simpson Peninsula. The Netsilingmiut proper lived around
Boothia Isthmus. They were named for Netsilik Lake, lying
just southeast of Spence Bay, the area the Netsilik considered as their country of origin. The Netsilingmiut occupied one of the richest game areas in the whole country.
Many narrow lakes cut across Boothia Isthmus, and this was
considered excellent caribou hunting country. Further, Lord
Mayor Bay on the eastern side of the isthmus was the best
seal hunting area in this vast region. The northern end of
Boothia Peninsula, near Bellot Strait, was occupied by the

Arvertormiut (People of the Whales) while the eastern and southern parts of King William Island were inhabited by the Qegertarmiut (Island People). Immediately south, on Adelaide Peninsula, lived the Ilivilermiut (People Living at the Place Where There Is Something). They frequently migrated across Simpson Strait to the southern end of King William Island. And in the general area of Shepherd Bay and Murchison River resided the Kungmiut (River People).

Although individuals and families frequently migrated from one group to another for varying lengths of time without losing their group identity, there is historical evidence that the Netsilik as a whole were involved in some westward movement that resulted in their occupying new territory. Explorers from the last century noted, on Adelaide Peninsula and King William Island, the presence of a culturally distinct group called the Ukjulingmiut (People of the Great Bearded Seal); at that time the Netsilik were occupying their traditional hunting grounds on Boothia Isthmus, and there was little apparent intercourse of any consequence between the two groups. Yet when Rasmussen visited the area in 1923, the Ukjulingmiut as a distinct group were practically extinct and their territory was occupied by the western branch of the Netsilik. Elderly informants told Rasmussen what happened in the Ukjulik country:

> Once, the winter was a very severe one, blizzards blowing incessantly over Queen Maud's Sea; famine broke out and the Ukjulingmiut tried to escape from death by starvation by moving to Simpson Strait to fish for arctic cod. A great many people died however: some froze to death, others starved, and the bodies of the dead were eaten by the living—in fact many were killed to provide food, for these poor people were driven almost mad by their sufferings that winter (1931:120).

The survivors of this famine moved south to the rich fishing sites of Back River and mingled with the Utkuhikjalingmiut to form a single group, leaving their traditional country unoccupied. The neighboring Netsilik soon moved in, apparently attracted by the stores of driftwood to be found along the western shores of King William Island and Adelaide Peninsula. Driftwood was precious to the Netsilik, since it was very rarely found in their country.

Despite the remoteness of their habitat the Netsilik were visited by numerous expeditions in the nineteenth century. The main reason behind these expeditions was the search for a northwest passage from the Atlantic to the Pacific oceans that could considerably shorten the route from Europe to East Asia. Sir John Ross was the first to winter with two ships near King William Island in 1830–33. He lost a ship due to heavy ice conditions, thus providing the Eskimos with an enormous supply of wood and iron. In 1833, Sir George Back traveled along the river that carries his name and reached Chantrey inlet from the south, while Sir George Simpson approached the eastern part of the country, reaching what is today Simpson Peninsula. Then in 1847–48 the large expedition of Sir John Franklin arrived near King William Island. Blocked by thick ice, unable to sail, the crew abandoned the ships, and all died of starvation. Subsequently, a number of smaller expeditions came to find out what had happened to Franklin; but none of these various travelers wrote much concerning the Netsilik's customs and manners.

This was not the case with the expedition led by the famous Norwegian explorer Roald Amundsen who wintered in 1903–5 in Gjoa Harbor on the south coast of King William Island and gave a valuable description of Netsilik culture. Then in 1923 came Knud Rasmussen, the Danish ethnographer and folklorist who traveled the entire Arctic coast of North America from Igloolik to western Alaska by dog team. In the eight months he spent with the Netsilik he amassed innumerable data about the subsistence techniques, migration patterns, social organization, and, most important, the intellectual culture of the tribe. Being partly of Greenlandic origin, Rasmussen spoke the Eskimo language fluently and was already well acquainted with Eskimo mentality. This allowed him to view Netsilik culture with considerable insight and interpret it with brilliance and ease.

The Netsilik Rasmussen met were a sturdy people sharing the physical characteristics of most Central Eskimos. They were of medium stature without being short, had abundant head hair which was straight and black, very thin beards among the elderly only, and rather thin eyebrows. Their skin color was light, grayish-yellow in tone. They had relatively large heads with the faces markedly flat. This was due to a narrow forehead, wide and prominent cheekbones, massive jaws, faintly developed brow ridges, and only a slightly protruding and narrow nose. These traits gave the face a peculiar pentagonal form. The teeth of these meat eaters were extraordinarily sound and strong. Together with other Mongoloids, the Netsilik had an abundant deposit of fatty tissue in the region of the eye orbit. In relation to the trunk and general stature, the legs were very long, the arms short, and the hands and feet definitively small.

The language the Netsilik spoke was so similar to the language spoken by all Eskimo groups from Greenland to northwestern Alaska that in his long journey along the Arctic coast, meeting with many different Eskimo groups, Rasmussen never needed an interpreter. He was able to understand each local dialect with ease.

When Rasmussen met the Netsilik in 1923, they numbered 259 people in all and were already in possession of firearms, obtained a few years before from the Aivilik Eskimos. This changed their subsistence activities profoundly. Instead of having to wait in kayaks in order to attack the caribou at special crossing places, they could now chase after herds practically at any season and kill as many caribou as they wanted from a long distance. And with guns, they could also more easily kill seals in winter in open water at the ice edge.

These changes had a great impact. The migration patterns changed and caribou hunting could easily take place in winter. Further, with more food available, larger dog teams could be kept and this increased their mobility. This led to the gradual abandonment of breathing-hole sealing and the associated seal-meat sharing pattern. And a new activity was introduced in the area, namely trapping white foxes. The fox pelts were traded against various imported goods: rifles, ammunition, woolen clothing, canvas tents, tobacco, tea, and canoes that replaced the now useless kayaks.

In the 1930s both Catholic and Protestant missionaries arrived in the area and the Netsilik were rapidly converted to Christianity. They abandoned their various taboos and religious observances together with their use of amulets, and the local shamans stopped their practice. They began to concentrate near three stable settlements: Gjoa Haven on King William Island, Spence Bay, and Kugardjuk on Pelly Bay. Missionaries, traders, and constables of the Royal Canadian Mounted Police radically influenced and transformed Netsilik culture and social life. A rapid acculturation process began, accelerated in the late 1950s by the establishment of government schools and nursing stations. Many young Netsilik boys and girls now speak English, dress in imported clothing, eat imported foods, and dance to Western tunes. The traditional Netsilik culture remains only in the memory of a few elderly persons.

This book is an attempt to describe Netsilik traditional ways prior to the introduction of firearms, elaborate steel tools, imported clothing, and foodstuffs. I will look at the Netsilik essentially as they were when Rasmussen first came upon them nearly fifty years ago.

Part I / MAN AND ENVIRONMENT

1 NETSILIK TECHNOLOGY

The early explorers of the Arctic marveled at the technical competence of the Eskimos, whom they described as remarkable primitive engineers. The Netsilik Eskimos, living in one of the harshest areas of the inhabited North, were able to survive in this cold desert environment because of their efficient and remarkably adapted technology. Their raw materials were few in number: snow, ice, bones of various animals, skins, stones of different kinds, and a small amount of wood. All but the wood were of local origin. By combining these few resources, they produced all that they needed to survive.

Most Netsilik tools had highly specialized functions. The slender harpoon was used for seal hunting in winter, the light spear for caribou hunting from kayaks in late summer, the fishing harpoon for catching lake trout in summer. The bow and arrow, on the other hand, were used in several hunting situations. The arrow's striking power was enough to wound musk ox, polar bear, and caribou, though it was seldom strong enough to kill. The leister, a trident-like spear, was indispensable in fishing for salmon trout, both in summer at the fish traps and in early winter through the thin river ice. Other tools were employed for other specific purposes: the bow drill pierced bone or wood; the small saw cut hard materials; the burin sliced antler. There were only three truly multi-purpose tools: the man's knife (*pilaut*), the snow knife (*pana*), and the woman's knife (*ulu*). They were used for cutting, scraping, and piercing many different materials in varied situations.

Netsilik technology was successful because of its efficiency. A snowhouse that offered adequate protection from storms and cold could be built in less than an hour from material obtainable almost everywhere. The sealskin tent was waterproof and so light that it could be carried by a dog during summer migrations. A kayak could easily be carried across land for miles, and its slender shape allowed the Netsilik to pursue and kill swimming caribou at crossing places. Caribou skin was ideally suited for clothing in the Arctic, trapping a thick layer of warm air against the body that was excellent insulation against extreme cold. Sled runners were lashed to the crossbars with sealskin so that the sled was pliable and would not break when it was pulled over rough ice.

Netsilik technology was almost entirely utilitarian in character. Aesthetic manifestations were limited to tattoos on the women's faces and limbs, long hair sticks, and white fur decorations on the outer coats. An artifact was made because it was indispensable, not because it was pleasing to the senses. The difficulties of travel in the tundra did not allow people to carry useless articles. Every Netsilik Eskimo had to look after his own equipment, make new weapons, and repair the old ones. Despite the complexity of articles such as the kayak and the composite bow, every man had the skills and the tools to be technologically self-sufficient. This was an absolute necessity in the Arctic.

During the long migrations or on hunts, when tools were broken, lost, or worn beyond usefulness, substitutes and alternatives were found. Here the Netsilik showed great ingenuity and resourcefulness. If a spear broke, it was repaired quickly by lashing a snow knife to the shaft; if there was no stick to support the drying rack above the lamp in the igloo, a leister was used; when the soapstone lamp was not there, a shallow stone would do. In adversity the Netsilik was quick to improvise with what he had on hand.

Netsilik material culture can be subdivided into four major technological complexes based on the raw materials used: *the snow complex*, including the use of ice; *the skin complex*, based on sealskin and caribou fur, and less frequently including musk-ox fur and polar-bear skin; *the bone complex,* including driftwood and iron; and *the stone complex,* referring mainly to the use of soapstone.

THE SNOW COMPLEX

Snow and ice were enormously important to the wandering Netsilik Eskimos, as they were an almost constant part of the Netsilik environment and largely determined how they lived, hunted, and traveled. When a strong wind had packed the snow, the dogs could pull a sled with ease. In spring, however, when the snow was melting, pulling the sled was an exhausting task, because the runners sank in the soft snow, losing first their ice and then their peat shoeing. Under pack ice no seals could be found. The seals kept breathing holes open only through fresh, smooth ice. To express the great importance of these elements to their lives, the Netsilik had an extensive vocabulary for different kinds of snow, depending on its state, and ice, depending on whether it was smooth, rough, drifting, old, or young.

Snow was most important in architecture. Because of its insulative properties, it made a warm winter dwelling for the Netsilik. Igloos, their porches, and their narrow entrances were all made of snow blocks. So were the beds and kitchen tables inside, and the doors. Outside the igloo was a high meat stand of snow and a snow shelter for the sealskin sled. Windbreaks of snow blocks protected the sealer and fisherman in stormy weather. Fathers made animal figures of snow for their children, and bowmen practiced target shooting at snow men.

The *pana,* or snow knife, was the tool used in working snow. Usually it was of a single piece of caribou antler, and only rarely was it over fifteen inches in length. The handle was indented so that it could be gripped securely. When a long piece of antler was not available, a long blade was secured to a separate handle with bone rivets and sinew thread. When iron was introduced into the area, blades of iron became common and were attached to wooden handles.

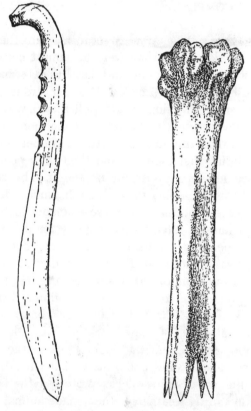

Figure 1   *Snow Knife*   Figure 2   *Fur Comb*

The slender snow knife made it easy to cut the snow into large, rectangular blocks. As the snow blocks were placed on top of each other, they were trimmed with the *pana* to fit tightly to one another. The *pana* was a man's knife, and each man always carried his own *pana* with him.

Though the snow complex was primarily a field of male activity, women helped with snow work. As an igloo was being built by her husband, the Netsilik wife covered the outer walls with a thick layer of snow, using her snow shovel, *poalrit.* The Netsilik snow shovel had a frame of antler to which a piece of sealskin was fastened with sinew thread. (In other areas snow shovels were made of wood with bone handle.) Men used the snow shovel inside the igloo to give a final shape to the bed and the kitchen table.

The Netsilik also used snow in other less important ways. After butchering a seal a Netsilik woman might clean her hands and knife with wet snow. If there was not enough water in a seal-meat soup boiling over the stone lamp, she could scrape some snow from the igloo wall to put in the pot.

Ice does not have the insulating properties of snow, but in architecture it was sometimes used similarly. There were periods in the autumn before the snow was deep enough to build an igloo, but when it was too cold to live comfortably in a sealskin tent, the Netsilik built rectangular icehouses with skin roofs. The ice slabs for the walls were cut from relatively thin river ice. The ice chisel used was a simple tool made in earlier times of hard bear bone fastened with skin thongs to a long wooden shaft. Later, iron spikes replaced the bone points.

With the ice chisel the Eskimos made holes through the river and lake ice to get drinking water or to fish. They used an ice scoop to remove the ice fragments cut with the chisel, working alternately with chisel and scoop down to the water level. The ice scoop was a ladle of musk-ox horn or caribou antler attached to a wooden or bone shaft.

Ice slabs were used in late autumn to make fish caches in areas where good-size stones were not available. A thin slab of fresh-water ice made a window in the igloo roof. Many children's toys were made of ice. For drinking water the Netsilik melted old sea ice in their soapstone pots. (Sea ice

loses most of its salt content after a year.) Most important
of all, ice formed the runners of the sleds.

As with snow, most of the work with ice was done by the
men, who owned the ice chisels and scoops. Women did little with ice but cut old sea ice near the camp to be melted
for drinking water.

THE SKIN COMPLEX

The skin complex much more actively involved the Netsilik women, who were quite skilled as seamstresses. Two
kinds of skin were used almost exclusively: caribou skin for
the warmth of its fur, and sealskin for its durability.

Caribou-fur clothing was ideally suited for a hunting life
in the Arctic. The skin was light and soft, with dense, upright
hair. Each hair was hollow, making the fur an ideal insulation against extreme cold. Caribou clothing enabled the
Netsilik to spend long periods of time outdoors in bad
weather. Despite its thickness, this skin allowed the body
considerable freedom of movement because of its light
weight and softness.

Preparing caribou skins for use was a long and tedious
job. First, the animals were skinned—always by men. While
the skins were fresh, the women laid them out to dry,
spreading (but not stretching) them on the ground with the
hair down and anchoring them around the edges with small
stones. Were the skins stretched while wet, they would become stiff and unsuitable for clothing.

The skins were cured later in the season by either of two
methods. If fine, soft skins were needed, the men and
women covered themselves with the raw skins at night in
their igloo with the flesh side next to their naked bodies.
Over these they laid their regular caribou sleeping skins.
By morning their body warmth had softened each raw skin,
and it was ready to be scraped. The scraper was a blunt tool

of stone or bone, usually a caribou scapula or a sharpened tubular bone. With it the woman softened and stretched the hide. After she scraped and stretched it, she slightly moistened the hide and put it out in the cold to freeze for a day or two. In the last phase of curing she removed the subcutaneous tissue by using a sharp scraper. In recent times, sharp scrapers have been made of slightly curved iron blades fitted into bone or wooden handles; before metal was introduced, bone implements with sharp edges were used. As a final softening process, the men thinned the skin by vigorous scraping, arduous work that only men could do successfully. Caribou skins cured this way were well suited for inner coats and trousers.

For outer garments and sleeping bags, for which soft skin was not needed, the curing process was somewhat simpler. The night-warming process was omitted, and the women scraped air-dried skins directly with both blunt and sharp scrapers. This helped to make the skins snowproof and easier to dry, qualities necessary for outer clothing.

Skins for other purposes were treated differently. Some were not cured at all. They were just stretched and dried in the sun, and when they were thoroughly dry they were used as mattresses. Other skins intended for clothing had fur that was so long and thick that it had to be thinned for the skin to be useful. These skins were either from spring caribou that still had some loose winter hair or from late autumn caribou with hair already too long. Women removed the excess hair by vigorously scrubbing the fur with a fur comb, which was a coarse, short-toothed comb made from a tubular bone. When depilation was necessary, they first dried the skin and then scraped it with their knives. Before it could be used, the shaved skin had to be moistened with water.

Different kinds of caribou skins, cured in different ways, were used for a variety of purposes. Children's garments were made from the skins of the very young caribou. The

heavy, thick hides of caribou killed in late autumn were best
suited for bedding material. The animals hunted in early
autumn had the best fur for inner and outer clothing. The
short-haired skin from the legs was used for making boots
and mitts, because it was particularly resistant to wear. The
white fur from the caribou's stomach was used for women's
clothing or hair decorations or shaman's paraphernalia.
Drums and long lines of thong were made from depilated
caribou skin. Thong was used to build kayaks, to tie various
objects, to lace boots, and to make drying racks.

Sealskin was almost as valuable as caribou skin to the
Netsilik. Sealskin was considerably stronger and more durable than caribou skin, and it was particularly useful during
the summer wet season because it was quite waterproof.

Women did all the work to prepare a seal for use. They
cut it up into the prescribed number of parts, removed the
bones, blubber, and skin, and cured the latter. Various uses
for sealskins required different curing processes. The preparation of skins for kayak covers was particularly elaborate.
This took place in the igloo in late winter or spring. The
skins of adult female seals were preferred. The housewife
first laid the skin on a wooden scraping board or a flat stone
and used her ulu to scrape most of the blubber from the inside of the skin. The skin had to be completely free of fat
to reduce the weight of the kayak, so after she scraped it
she chewed the skin thoroughly until the last particle of fat
was sucked out. She then rolled the skins in bundles, hairy
side out, and placed them on the drying rack over the gentle
heat of her soapstone lamp. Several days later when the hair
began to rot, she could scrape it off easily. Finally, she buried
the clean skins in the snow to prevent further rotting, and
there they stayed until the time came to move camp and
begin work on the kayaks.

The unshaved skins of young seals were preferred for
coats and trousers. First, the fleshy membrane on the inside of the skin was removed, then the skin was washed

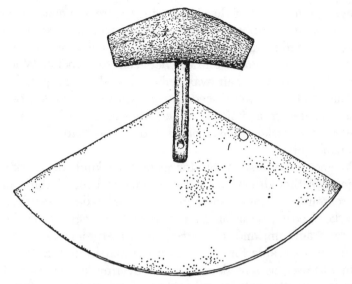

Figure 3   Woman's Knife (Ulu)

vigorously with water and snow. The skin was then stretched to dry, held taut by wooden pegs driven into the snow or ground, and pegged in such a way that it was a few inches above the ground to allow air to circulate. Once dry, the skin had to be softened with blunt scrapers before it could be sewn.

Sealskins to be used for waterproof summer boots required very careful scraping of the hair. To do this a woman spread the cold, wet skin over her bare thigh and went to work with a sharp ulu. When the hair had been removed, she turned the skin over and removed the blubber. After the skin had been thoroughly scraped, she stretched and dried it on the snow. Skins cured this way were waterproof but very hard. Before they could be sewn they had to be thoroughly chewed and softened.

Boot soles and heavy thongs were made from the thick skin of the great bearded seal. To make thongs, the skin of this large mammal was cut first into a number of rings roughly ten inches wide. These rings were removed from the body, the blubber scraped, and the hair washed. Each ring was cut spirally into long thongs, which were then stretched under great tension between two rocks. When they were dry, the hair was removed with a sharp knife. If thinner thongs were needed, the skin of the ringed seal was prepared in a similar manner. Men occasionally helped the women make thongs, but for the most part it was a woman's job.

Women were responsible for making all kinds of sealskin objects. Although caribou fur was preferred for clothing in all seasons, in summer some clothing was made of sealskin: kayakers' coats; occasionally a pair of trousers; mittens for work in autumn; and, of course, the waterproof boots that were indispensable for walking on the marshy tundra. Sealskin was used as tent skins and for covering kayaks, as roof sheets for late autumn or spring snowhouses (*karmaq*), and to make sled runners. Many other items were made wholly or partially of sealskins as well: e.g., shamans' belts and masks, oil and water containers, packs carried by dogs, snow shovels, and dog shoes. Sealskin thongs were used for dog whips, dog-harness lines, harpoon lines, fish-drying racks, slings, tent lines, packing lines, and ropes for athletic games. Sled runners were lashed to crossbars with sealskin thongs. Sections of some tools and weapons were lashed together by fine sealskin thongs; the iron blade of the adze and the bone or steel points of ice chisels and lances were strongly tied to their shafts with sealskin thongs. To be able to use thong in so many ways required the making of many special knots—a skill in which the Netsilik excelled.

Although the Netsilik used the skins of other animals as well, they were only substitutes for the vitally important caribou and sealskin, with the exception of bearskin. When no wooden or sealskin sled was available, a bearskin was loaded with equipment and dragged on the snow as a sledge, the hairy side down, because the fur did not absorb moisture. It was for this reason that bearskin was employed in the icing and polishing of sledge runners. Bearskins were also used occasionally as *karmaq* covers and mattresses. The hair of the bearskin had the peculiar ability to attract lice and was consequently used to make louse catchers. Clothing was rarely manufactured of bearskin because of its great weight. Musk-ox skins were also too heavy to use for clothing. Early travelers in the western Netsilik area reported whole families dressed in musk-ox skins, but this was probably due to a poor caribou hunting season. If they were used at all, musk-ox skins were usually used as bedding material.

Other animals were used only occasionally. Trousers could be made from white foxskin, wolf, wolverine, and dog-skins because these skins repelled frost; they were also highly valued for hood trimmings. Properly dried duck skins were turned into containers for wick moss. The skin of the salmon trout was an ideal container for a man's small tools—its long, slim shape was suited admirably for carrying the long bow drill, crooked knife, and various burins.

The Netsilik women had to be skilled seamstresses to make such extensive use of a variety of skins. Needles and sinew thread were their main tools. Before iron tools were known, needles were made of bone, usually the strong wing bones of birds or bear bone. These bone needles broke frequently, to the annoyance of the seamstress, and they were quickly and gladly replaced by needles of metal when metal came into use.

Caribou sinew was important to the Netsilik both as thread and for cord. When the caribou were butchered, the sinews from the caribou's back muscles were removed with great care. The women spread the sinew flat on the scraping board and, with their semilunar knives, cleaned it of flesh. After washing it thoroughly, they flattened it on the tent sheet to dry in the sun.

Sinew thread was used to sew clothing, boots, kayak

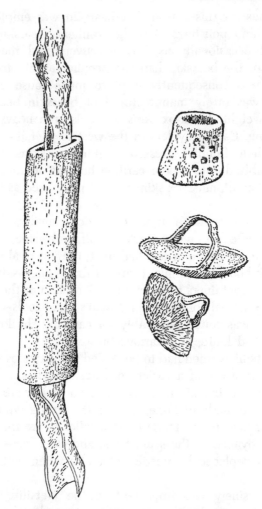

Figure 4   Needle Case and Thimbles

covers, and tent sheets. A simple overcast stitch was used
for sewing fur clothing, a blind stitch passing only halfway
through the skin made waterproof seams, and a running
stitch attached soles to boots. Kayak covers required a
double stitching: a running stitch on the inside and a similar

stitch on the outside. Netsilik women also braided sinew into cord of various thicknesses. Braided sinew cord was used for bow strings and reinforcements, running strings in clothing, fishing lines, and toys.

Thimbles consisted of a semicircular piece of depilated sealskin. Bodkins for piercing thick skin were made of bear bone or antler. Precious needles were kept in cylindrical needlecases of antler, stuck in the skin cord running through the bone case. At the lower end of the needlecase a carved thimble holder supported the thimble. The seamstress wore her needlecase hanging on her chest, fastened to the drawstring of her coat.

THE BONE COMPLEX

Because driftwood was so scarce in the Netsilik area and iron was not known, in traditional times most tools and weapons were made of bone. Bone was extremely important in Netsilik technology, and the men were skillful in adapting the qualities of bone to specific uses. The important characteristics were, first, size, then hardness and elasticity. Bear bone was the hardest; and musk-ox horn was highly valued for its elastic pliability; but caribou antler was the basic raw material of the bone complex. It was hard yet resilient and relatively easy to work. Holes could be drilled through it without much effort. It could be bent into various shapes, and several pieces could be assembled to form larger articles.

All bonework was done by men using very few tools, tipped with iron points and edges. (In years past, before the Netsilik knew of iron, they used flint for tools, weapon points, and knife blades.) A hunter's tool bag contained several simple but ingenious implements. A *bow drill* was a composite device consisting of a bow, a mouthpiece, and a drill. The bow was a caribou or bear rib strung with seal-

skin thong. The mouthpiece was a caribou anklebone, and
the drill had a sharp iron point set into a wooden shaft. (A
well-supplied tool kit included drills with points of varying
sizes.) The bow drill could perforate any kind of bone or
wood object. An *adze* had a narrow iron blade fastened to
an antler handle with skin thongs. It was used to thin down
antler or, less often, wood. A *whittling knife* had a small,
pointed iron blade with a curved edge. The blade was riveted to a very long handle of antler. The lower end of the
whittling knife rested under the man's arm as he drew the
blade toward his body. Special implements were used for
splitting and incising antler. They consisted of short and
sturdy blades—either slightly curved, ribbon-shaped with a
transverse edge, or beak-shaped—inserted into a bone
handle.

Although the saw was not an Eskimo implement, the Netsilik Eskimos made and cut antler with small saws patterned after the European saws of the early explorers. The

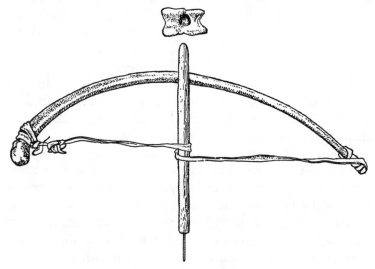

Figure 5   Bow Drill

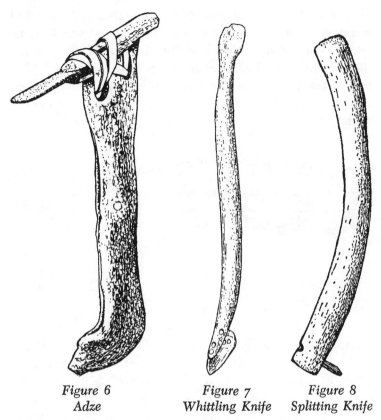

Figure 6
Adze

Figure 7
Whittling Knife

Figure 8
Splitting Knife

Netsilik saws consisted of small, rectangular pieces of sheet metal inserted into antler handles. The teeth of the saw were regularly recut and sharpened with the adze.

These few implements were all the tools needed for working caribou antler. To prepare antler for use, first the lateral branches of the antler were cut off with the saw, then the main antler trunk was split into two or more long pieces by making a longitudinal groove with the splitting knife and gradually deepening it while at the same time applying pressure downward. The sharp edges of the resulting slabs were rounded with the adze and smoothed with the little scraping knife. If the antler had to be straightened, it was first warmed to make it more pliable, then one end was inserted into one of the holes of an antler straightener. This was a thick piece of antler through which large holes had been bored. The warmed and softened antler could then be bent into any shape desired, held firmly at its base by the antler straightener.

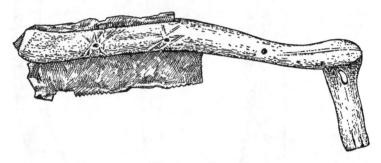

Figure 9   Saw

Other bone was worked with similar techniques. Musk-ox horn was softer than caribou antler and considerably easier to work. Before it was split, however, it had to be well heated in hot water or over the lamp. Bear bone could not be split; it had to be laboriously thinned and sharpened with an adze and various knives. Often when men were not carrying their tool bags on hunting trips but needed to sharpen the bone heads of their weapons, they did so by rubbing the bone points on any flat stone.

To make large weapons—harpoons and bows, for example —several pieces of antler were joined together. This was done by riveting and lashing. To rivet two pieces of bone together, both pieces were pierced with the bow drill and antler rivets inserted. More recently, copper or iron rivets were used when a strong joint was needed. Often a riveted joint was further strengthened with a solid lashing. For small objects, caribou sinew was used for lashing; for larger tools, sealskin thong.

To make wooden poles, small lengths of wood were glued together, using blood for glue. (Dried blood was dissolved in the mouth, then applied.) The blood-glued joints were so strong that they did not need any additional lashing. The use of glue was an important technique in an area where wood was scarce and usually found only in small pieces, as it was often the only way possible to make poles long enough to be useful as tent poles, drying racks, and weapon handles.

Many artifacts were made from bone and antler: hunt-

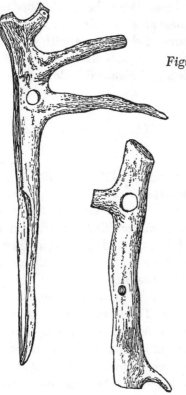

Figure 10   Antler Straighteners

ing and fishing implements (seal-hunting harpoons and their accessories, fishing harpoons with detachable points, double-pronged leisters, bows, hunting spears, ice picks); furnishings and tools (frames for drying rack and snow shovel, snow beaters, meat forks, blubber pounders, marrow extractors, ladles, snow knives, handles for tools, needle-cases); and various toys and sacred objects. Wood was used for spear handles, tent poles, meat trays, pegs for drying skins, parts of sled, and, most importantly, kayak frames.

Even this partial list of vital artifacts shows how important bone technology was to the material culture of the Net-silik Eskimos. It determined how well the other technolog-ical complexes functioned, because many tools for work on snow and skin were made of bone. With the availability of iron and wood from outside their area, the Netsilik replaced many of their tools and weapons made of bone with similar tools of iron and wood, but the new tools were closely pat-terned on the traditional models and changed little in either form or function.

THE STONE COMPLEX

Soapstone was a valuable material to the Netsilik, since they made their lamps and pots from it. The stone was avail-able in the eastern part of the Netsilik land in an area southwest of Pelly Bay. In the winter, sled drivers could reach the quarry with little difficulty, and they went there to cut out soapstone blocks of considerable size. In the area of the western Netsilik, where soapstone was not easily found, pots and lamps were obtained through trade.

Soapstone lamps varied in size. Travelers or hunters usu-ally carried small lamps twelve to fifteen inches long to use for light in their small overnight igloos. In more perma-nent family igloos larger lamps were used, ranging between twenty and thirty inches in length. Only occasionally in large ceremonial igloos were lamps forty inches long found.

The usual soapstone lamp was a shallow, flat-bottomed, oval-shaped vessel with nearly perpendicular sides, the back more convex than the front. Long, narrow lamps were occasionally imported from the Netsilik's western neighbors. Broken lamps were not discarded but were repaired by lashing a piece of wood to the soapstone lamp as a kind of splint. Otherwise, women generally used a naturally hollow slab of stone as a makeshift substitute.

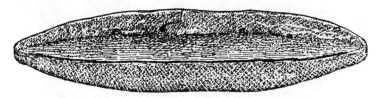

Figure 11   Soapstone Lamp

Netsilik cooking pots were carved out of a single block of soapstone. A typical pot was rectangular with slightly convex sides and straight inside walls. At the top corners there were holes for suspension cords. Pots varied in length from twelve to twenty-four inches. If a pot broke, the fracture was cemented and the parts tied together with sinew lashings.

Soapstone (talc chlorite schist) is so soft that it can be scratched with a fingernail. Despite its softness, however, working soapstone with flint tools was a long and arduous task. With iron-tipped tools, carving soapstone into useful objects took several hours. Blocks were quarried out with the ice pick, then shaped with the adze. To hollow out the pot, numerous holes were bored close to each other into the solid block with the bow drill. Then the thin walls between the holes were crushed with the adze. Working soapstone was a man's job, but when he finished the pot or lamp, he gave it to his wife and it became her permanent property.

Figure 12   Cooking Pot

The four technological complexes were subject to seasonal variations. The snow-ice complex, quite clearly, was restricted to the winter season. The skin complex varied from season to season: sealskin was used little in winter but was important in summer; caribou fur was vital for survival in the winter and less important in the summer. In summer, the soapstone lamp was not used, so soapstone was of lesser importance. Only antler was equally important in all seasons.

With these basic materials and their accompanying techniques, the Netsilik Eskimos were able to survive and adapt to one of the harshest environments known to man. Again, it should be emphasized how few their material resources were, and how carefully these materials' qualities were put to advantage. With the exception of occasional uses for wood and vegetation, the Netsilik got everything they needed from stone, the animals they killed, and the snow that surrounded them.

2 SUBSISTENCE ACTIVITIES AND CAMP LIFE

The Netsilik faced severe difficulties in hunting the animals essential to their survival. One of their most menacing problems was a mobile and irregular game supply. The large caribou herds on which the Netsilik depended for much of their clothing migrated north early in spring, spending only the summer along the Arctic coast, then in autumn returning south to the tree line. This meant the caribou was available for hunting only during the summer months. Likewise the salmon trout migrated seasonally, swimming down the river to the sea each spring, returning upstream to the lakes in the fall. To catch these fish, the Netsilik had to be waiting at the rivers at just the right time.

Technological factors also imposed seasonal limitations on hunting. The seal, for instance, was not a migrating animal, yet the Netsilik could hunt seals only in the winter. This was because the Netsilik had no techniques for hunting seals from the water, and so had to wait until the winter when they could get out on the ice directly above the seals for a kill.

These seasonable variabilities of game and hunting techniques meant that the Netsilik Eskimos, like their food supply, were always on the move. These migrations were not random in character. On the contrary, the annual migration cycle of the Netsilik followed a basic, predictable pattern. This nomadic movement had two phases, which reflected the two main seasonal changes in the Arctic. First, there was a short *summer phase* characterized by migrations inland, accompanied by fishing for salmon trout and hunting for caribou. Second, there was a longer *winter phase* during which the Netsilik hunted seals on the sea ice. The summer phase represented a land adaptation; the winter phase, a marine adaptation.

To these two types of ecological adaptation corresponded not only marked changes in technology but also different kinds of social morphology. Winter camps on the sea ice were conspicuously large, bringing together a number of extended families for the purpose of hunting seals collectively. At the center of the igloo encampment a large ceremonial snowhouse allowed all camp fellows to assemble to watch drum dances and shamanistic séances. The presence of so many people in one settlement encouraged communication, markedly intensifying social life. Summer camps inland were much smaller. Concentration of people there was restricted to a few families, mostly related by ties of blood or marriage. Visiting, playing, and eating together took place daily during the warm season, yet few major festivities occurred at the summer caribou hunting grounds. The annual migration cycle will be presented in greater detail later on.

SUMMER FISHING AT THE STONE WEIR

In the Arctic at the beginning of July the sea ice begins to melt very rapidly. Dangerous cracks form in all directions, and the ice becomes covered with water, making sledge travel increasingly difficult and dangerous. On land many flat areas rapidly lose their snow cover and mosses and shrubs appear. Soon whole carpets of brightly colored flowers will cover the tundra, though in shady places, along riverbanks and behind rocks and boulders, large patches of deep snow still remain. The ice cover of the many rivers flowing into the sea breaks at this period, and ice blocks of many shapes and sizes are carried downstream. Melting lake ice also forms cracks and widening channels.

Soon many waterfowl will be swimming in the open lakes.

The birds and other animals of the tundra change their appearance. Rabbits, owls, and ptarmigan lose their white protective covering and acquire their brownish summer garb, which is better adapted to the colors of the tundra. The migrating caribou from the south, arriving in the area in early spring, disperse into small herds, searching for food in the valleys and plateaus. This is the season when the caribou change hair, replacing their thick winter coats with short-haired fur.

Salmon trout and lake trout were particularly important to Eskimo subsistence at this time of year. The salmon trout, soon after the ice starts to break up, assembles in large schools and migrates downstream to the sea from the large lakes where they have spent the winter. The lake trout during that season congregate under the widening cracks breaking the solid ice cover of the many lakes. The Netsilik took advantage of these concentrations and directed their migrations from the winter sea ice accordingly.

To get ready for the move back to land for spring fishing, the Netsilik made certain necessary preparations. These tasks took place at the close of the late spring sealing season, and the new sealskins were used to sew new sealskin tents and to re-cover the kayaks. Then, at the beginning of July, before the breakup of the sea ice, the Netsilik engaged in the final sledge migration, abandoning their seal-hunting grounds and moving to the shore with all their properties, including their accumulated seal oil.

With the establishment of the first summer camps on the mainland coast or King William Island, usually near some promising fishing spot, a number of bulky items, mostly winter equipment, became unnecessary for summer life and had to be safely stored where they could be found again the following autumn. To accomplish this purpose, the Netsilik built storage rooms, or caches, in which they put wooden sleds, dog harnesses and whips, drying racks, soapstone lamps, some unnecessary clothing, and sealskin bags

filled with seal oil from the spring hunts. These caches were
erected on high cliffs, out of reach of foxes, or, better still,
on small offshore islands, surrounded by open water which
predators could not cross.

Once on the mainland, preparations for summer life proceeded in haste. Women gave their first attention to the
family tents. Most families had old skin tents from the previous spring sealing camps, but these often needed repairs.
Other families had to make entire new tents, and consequently additional tent skins were needed. Some tent skins
came from the skin top covers of the fast melting igloos in
spring, others from the now broken runners of the skin
sledges. But the recently killed seals provided most of the
fresh skins needed for summer tents. Busy seamstresses repaired old tents, brought together old skins, or used fresh
skins to make new tents, depending on the needs and resources of each family.

At the beginning of this century the Netsilik knew of at
least two types of tents. The traditional Netsilik model
was round at the base and supported by a single tent pole.
A later type was borrowed from the eastern neighbors of the
Netsilik who lived along the northwest shore of Hudson Bay.
It was somewhat elongated and had a small H-shaped beam
placed on top of the pole, widening the ceiling and giving
a roundish appearance to the roof. The traditional Netsilik
tent was conical and in general smaller. The tent was constructed by first placing large, squarish stones in a ring, thus
marking out the floor size of the tent. Then a tent pole
was erected in the middle of this circle, resting on a flat
stone. At the upper end of the pole a number of sealskin
thongs were attached, strongly fastened at the other ends
to the heaviest of the ring stones. This constituted the frame
of the tent, over which a sealskin tent sheet was stretched.
The bottom part of the sheet was pulled tight and held
solidly under the stone ring. Often additional stones were
placed inside, leaning heavily on the outer ring and pro-

viding more stability to the tent. All these precautions were necessary for the small tent to withstand the pressure of strong winds and gales. Most of this work, and essentially the carrying and placing of the heavy stones, was accomplished by the men with some help from their women (see plate 1).

When it came to arranging the furnishings inside, women were free to act as they wished. First the housewife placed a line of flat stones all across the floor space, separating the sleeping area behind from the kitchen and work area in front, near the opening of the tent. She covered the sleeping section with thick caribou furs to protect her people from the humidity of the soil, which was usually marshy. Old clothing was thrown around the sleeping area in a disorderly manner. In one corner she placed her husband's tool bag and his bow and arrows.

Though some women preferred to have their fireplace (two or three stones supporting the soapstone pot) just inside the door, usually the fireplace was located outside in order to avoid the discomfort of smoke filling the tent. Near the fireplace the housewife kept a heap of heather for the fire. She always kept some food, mostly fish at this season, in the kitchen compartment beside the sealskin water containers, dog packs, and other items of summer equipment. The tent was built to face away from the prevailing winds. The door was a large opening covered by a loose, hanging sealskin. Right at the opening there were usually two or three large stones, which were used as chairs, since the tent was too small to allow visitors to sit inside. Inside the tent the housewife sat at one extremity of the sleeping area while her husband occupied the middle.

While the women in camp were busy with their daily chores and their work on the tents, the men hunted for food. Although small herds of caribou could be seen here and there, these animals were very lean in this season and their fur was unsuitable for most purposes, but they were

hunted occasionally. In addition the camp had stored seal
meat to eat. But the staple food of the Netsilik in July was
fish, and it was fishing that took up most of the men's time.

As mentioned, the salmon trout formed schools and swam
down the river to the ocean's coastal waters soon after breakup in July. To take advantage of this yearly migration, the
Netsilik had long before built stone weirs, which were a
kind of dam, across the rivers. They used these weirs to trap
the trout, which they then caught with their leisters. These
stone weirs were preferably located near the sea. Fishing
for salmon trout during the downstream migration in July
very seldom produced substantial catches. Much more important were the fishing activities at the stone weirs (*saputit*) in August.

A second method of fishing was related to a peculiar
seasonal characteristic of the lake trout. In late spring, when
the lake ice started breaking up in large chunks and channels of open water appeared, the lake trout congregated
in the freed areas in large numbers. Once such a concentration was located, it was easy for men standing on the
ice to spear the assembled lake trout in large numbers with
their leisters.

The third fishing method was more difficult, as it necessitated considerable skill in the handling of a special
weapon, namely the fishing harpoon with detachable head.
This weapon consisted of a long wooden shaft terminating
with a bone tenon, or projection, to which a long barbed
head was attached. Head and shaft were held together by
a sealskin thong. The fishing harpoon was used throughout
the summer in fishing for large lake trout swimming near
rocky shores. The hunters stood high on the shore for better
vision. The difficulty lay in the refraction angle—the harpoon
always had to be thrown a little below the fish as perceived
by the hunter. The weapon was retrieved by a long sealskin
line attached to it. There were also certain river mouths
where salmon trout could be secured with the fishing har-

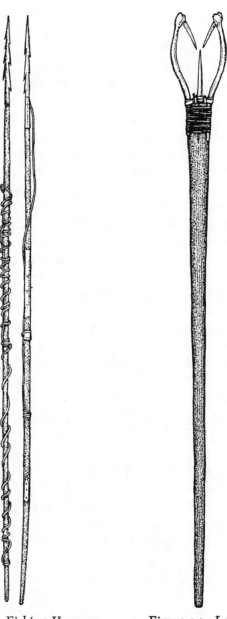

Figure 13   Fishing Harpoon   *Figure 14   Leister*

poon, usually in shallow estuaries subject to the action of tides. The flat shores of these tidal estuaries were covered with water each high tide, allowing the salmon trout to swim freely over them. When the tide withdrew, occasionally salmon trout were trapped in the tidal pools left behind. It was then relatively easy to spear them with the fishing harpoon. Fishing lake trout under the spring ice with the leister, and catching salmon trout with the wooden harpoon were both individualistic techniques; unlike fishing at the stone weirs, they did not involve any collaborative activities.

Fishing was thus the main subsistence activity of the Netsilik Eskimos during the month of July. Most of the fish were eaten raw, although some were cooked in the soapstone pot while still others were dried. In the event that spring fishing had been particularly successful, as might have been the case at the stone weir, large amounts of cleaned salmon trout were hung to dry on thongs and then cached. Dried fish was considered a great delicacy in winter when the diet consisted almost exclusively of seal meat, and it was relished by children.

Besides fishing, the people were busy with several other activities, all related to the forthcoming journey inland. The women had to make dog packs and waterproof sealskin boots while the men repaired kayak frames and made new leisters. Great care was given to all work connected with the kayak, as this, together with the wooden sledge, was one of the most valuable possessions of a Netsilik, and would be used extensively in inland travel and in hunting the caribou. The kayak was cached each autumn near the caribou hunting grounds, stripped of its skin cover, and placed high on stones. It was fetched with the sled to the early summer camp in spring, when snow still covered the tundra, to prepare it for the summer's use. The various parts of the kayak frame were checked, some ribs replaced, some joints sewn anew, and the whole kayak covered with a fresh sealskin cover. While all repair work connected with wood and bone was done by men, covering the kayak with fresh skins was the task of the women.

Finally, the beginning of August, when all preparations were completed, the people started traveling inland toward the stone weirs with all their summer belongings. They hastened to arrive at the fishing sites early enough to have time to repair the stone weirs before the first runs of the salmon trout reached them. Some weirs were just a few miles from the shore and could be reached in a day, others were deep inland and required camping en route. On these inland migrations the men who owned kayaks paddled them upstream, by no means an easy way to travel. The kayaks were heavily laden with various equipment hidden below deck, and had to be handled expertly. When rapids were reached, the kayak had to be portaged and a second trip made for the surplus load. Meandering bends of the river were also shortened by portaging. Women and children, together with the men who did not own kayaks, followed on foot. Often, however, the kayak owners accompanied their families across the tundra and walked back to fetch their kayaks after camp was established at the stone weir (see plate 2).

On these travels inland both men and women were heavily laden, carrying on their backs sleeping skins, spare clothing, various tools, and food. The leisters were kept at hand. Small children were put on their fathers' backs. Dogs were used as pack animals in this season, each dog carrying two large and heavy pouches on either side (see plate 3). Dogs also carried each family's carefully folded tent and heavy soapstone pot. Walking inland was a strenuous exercise, as men and dogs sank several inches into the marshy tundra with each step. The balance between the two pouches hanging on the dog's back was difficult to keep and had to be constantly adjusted. All this made for frequent stops to allow men and beasts to rest.

As usual, the first task awaiting the people on reaching
a camp site was to set up the tents and get settled. The men
then entered the river in order to examine the state of the
stone weir. During breakup the upper part of the stone weir
was usually carried away by the floating ice, resulting in
damage that had to be assessed. The following day repair
work on the stone weir began. This was a long and laborious
task which usually took two or three days, depending on
the number of men participating. Up to their waists in the
ice-cold water, half naked, the workers piled stones for
hours, taking occasional breaks to warm up and eat. Work
proceeded quickly, since everything had to be ready in time
for the first run of salmon returning from the sea around
the first or second week of August.

The stone weir was a relatively large dam, its size depending on the width of the river, which it spanned from
one shore to the other. The best sites for a stone weir were
the relatively shallow river beds covered with rocks with
which the dam was to be built. The dam itself consisted
of a stone wall rising a foot or two above the water. The
end parts of the wall, touching on the shores, pointed upstream, leading the fish to an enclosed and round central
basin where the spearing was done. The stone walls of
the central basin were somewhat higher, in order to prevent the fish from jumping over them, except for the entrance of the central basin to which the lateral parts of the
dam led. There was a narrow opening through which the
fish entered the central basin. Once in the basin the salmon
trout had no way to escape (instinctively they swam only
upstream and never turned back) and were securely locked
in the central basin, becoming easy prey for the Eskimos'
leisters. In conjunction with the stone weir, traps were also
employed. These were built around the upper end of the
central basin, with openings toward it. Fish traps were simple constructions, narrowing underwater tunnels made of
stones. Searching for an escape, the fish entered the trap

from the central basin, desperately trying to swim upstream and of course remaining inside until a man opened the trap by removing a stone and caught them with his bare hands.

The stone weir was repaired by the first men to arrive at the fishing site. After the completion of the dam and the arrival of the first fish runs, additional families usually joined the initial group. The composition of these summer camps varied greatly. Frequently two or three extended families, about twenty to thirty people including children, camped together. Often, however, only a single extended family exploited a given stone weir. Each individual family had its own tent, located near the tents of close relations in a cluster. It was important for the camp to be right near the stone weir so that people could keep a constant watch on the central basin from the tents and check on the fish runs.

All fishing at the stone weir was conducted with the double-pronged leister. This was a highly valuable instrument used not only at the stone weir but also during other seasons whenever salmon trout had to be speared. It consisted of a long wooden shaft, at the end of which were two prongs of musk-ox horn, tightly attached with plaited sinews and thongs. This material was preferred to caribou antler because of its greater elasticity. In the two prongs were inserted two small hooks of bear bone, and in between the prongs was fastened a sharp point, also of bear bone, directly at the end of the wooden shaft. In recent times, both the central point and the two little hooks were made of iron. In use, the leister's needle-like point would sink into the fish, the two hooks then grasped it and retained it from escaping. This was a simple and ingenious tool that could be employed with great speed and efficiency. At the stone weir the leister was employed in conjunction with the fishing needle. This was a strong needle about a foot long made of hard bear bone with a very sharp pointed end.

To the other end of the needle a long sealskin thong was attached. It served to string the fish caught with the leister.

Despite certain hardships involved, such as walking half naked in the cold river water, fishing at the stone weir was a joyous activity. Most of the fishing took place early in the morning before dawn and later in the afternoon. The stone weir was under constant watch—though always from a distance, so as not to scare the fish. When a school of trout was spotted heading for the weir's central basin, men and women hastily prepared for the catch. The men removed their trousers while the women put on old clothes, if such were available. All kept on their coats and their sealskin boots, which were strongly tied around the leg just below the knee in order to keep the water that entered the boot inside as insulation against the colder water outside. Then all fishermen assembled in front of the tent of the local "superintendent of fisheries," who was the oldest capable man in the camp and most frequently the head of the largest extended family.

An atmosphere of anxious expectation prevailed, accompanied by much excited talk and laughter. All eyes were centered on the central basin. When the whole school of fish entered the basin, the headman gave the signal for the attack. A wild melee ensued, everybody rushing to the shore where the leisters lay on the ground, grabbing the weapons, and hastily proceeding to the central basin.

The women, some of them with small babies on their backs, followed closely. The first man who reached the central basin, usually the headman, closed the entrance with a large stone. Then all the men entered the basin and the spearing of the fish began. There was no orderly work pattern. This was an extremely rapid and competitive activity, every fisherman trying to catch as many fish as he could, as rapidly as possible, spearing in any direction the bewildered fish might go. While the men occupied the middle of the basin, up to their waists in the cold water, the women and boys stood higher up on the stone walls in a peripheral position. The fishing needles were held in the fishers' mouths to allow more freedom in the manipulation of the leister. As soon as a fish was speared it was pulled out of the water, the two prongs bent in order to release their hold on the fish. The jerky fish was then skewered with the bone needle behind the gills. This broke its spine, killing it instantly, and strung it securely on the thong. All these operations were performed with great speed and dexterity, and in less than an hour over fifty fish could be caught.

Fish that had entered the stone traps were not forgotten. A trap belonged to the man who built it—often an elderly or handicapped man who could not handle the leister efficiently. Any fish caught in these traps became the property of the trap owner.

Once the spearing was over, the people slowly left the central basin, numbed by the cold, dragging their long lines of fish behind them. The fish were pulled to the riverbanks and spread near each fisherman's tent. There the women busied themselves with cleaning the fish, expertly slitting them with their sharp ulu, removing the intestines, and setting aside the white bellies, rich in fat. Substantial amounts of fish were hung to dry. Boys played with little leisters, spearing the fish on the ground and closely imitating their fathers' gestures. This was probably the happiest season of the Netsilik year—food was plentiful, the weather was warm, and there was no immediate cause for anxiety. Despite the fact that there was plenty of work to be done, there was also time for games, laughter, and communal eating. The fish were passed from hand to hand, mostly eaten raw, each bite being cut off with a knife just in front of the mouth.

On sunny days, women collected mosses or dryas and cooked the fish in the soapstone pots. (Fire was made by striking pyrites against a piece of iron and letting the sparks fall on some dry moss or arctic cotton.) Or it could be made by rubbing two pieces of dry wood together. To make fire by this method, a flat board with a socket was placed on the ground. One man pressed a round stick on it vertically. A second man with a thong wrapped around the stick made it rotate as fast as he could, pulling at the two ends of the thong. It worked like a bow drill and created considerable friction and heat. As soon as smoke appeared, a piece of arctic cotton was placed at the point of friction, which ignited as the heat built up, and finally caught fire.

It usually took several hours to cook enough fish for the whole camp. For the communal meal two groups were formed, women and small children eating separately from the men. Large pieces of cooked fish were passed around the group, each individual having a bite and handing it over to the next person.

Many other activities took place at the stone weir camp. Leisters needed frequent repair, and sewing had to be done occasionally. But it was strictly forbidden for such work to be done right at the fishing site. The *saputit*, like most other hunting and fishing sites of importance, was considered a holy place, and numerous work taboos had to be observed. For such work the people had to go to a special place, called *sannavik*, or the "working place." The men and women frequently congregated there during daytime, busily occupied with their leisters and boots and chatting happily.

Frequently the people took walks around camp, the women to gather heather, the men just to look around. Sometimes flocks of ptarmigan were encountered during such trips. The ptarmigan, a low-flying bird resembling the partridge, is not migratory and remains in the Arctic area through the winter. Though ptarmigan meat was considered very tasty and a welcome change in diet, the Netsilik were not in the habit of organizing special ptarmigan-hunting expeditions. Nonetheless, if a flock of ptarmigan was encountered during a journey inland, the birds were inevitably chased and many were killed by just throwing stones at them. The bow and special blunt arrows were also used in ptarmigan hunting. This was a favorite occupation of boys.

Toward the end of August, the fish runs began to slow down and the time came to close up camp. This was done in haste, since by this time the people were weary of the constant fish diet and eagerly looked forward to the forthcoming caribou hunts. Women started piling up the dried fish while the men busily built large caches to which they would return during the winter. These oval-shaped caches were made of large boulders, and it took two or three men working together to build one. First the floor was covered with a layer of gravel, then the fish were piled inside, all laid in one direction. Once full, the cache was covered with stones, heavily pressing down on the fish. This covering was done with care, lest some space be left open for a fox to get in. Predators such as foxes and polar bears were greatly feared, since there were numerous cases of cache destruction.

There was considerable variation in the amount of fish that could be caught from year to year. Usually a family could fill three to five large caches containing up to 500 pounds of fat fish each. These stores were to be used in winter as a welcome change from seal meat and of course as dog feed. Before the end of August, all fishing and caching were completed. The tents were pulled down, and once again, people and dogs were on the trek, all carrying heavy loads.

AT THE CARIBOU CROSSING PLACE

The first herds of migrating caribou, mostly cows, reached the Netsilik area from the south as early as mid-April. The bulls followed later, forming the rear guard of the migration. These large formations traveled along habitual paths. Although numerous caribou spread for the summer over

Boothia Peninsula and King William Island, the preferred summer grounds of the caribou were the eastern part of Boothia Isthmus and the area north of the three largest local water masses: Lady Melville Lake, Netsilik Lake, and Willersted Inlet. Simpson Peninsula and the region lying south of it attracted relatively few caribou. For summer grazing the caribou spread over vast areas in small herds, from a half dozen up to twenty or thirty individuals, with stragglers scattered here and there. In September the larger herds formed again and the southbound migration began. This was the time for the great caribou hunts. During this season the caribou were particularly fat, and their new hair was still relatively short and very well suited for clothing. It was essential for the Netsilik to kill as many caribou as they could precisely in this season, as the results of this hunting period would have to be enough to last them for a year. Occasionally some caribou hunting with the bow and arrow and even with the kayak took place during July and August, but the Eskimo did not rely to any great extent on these marginal hunts.

The Netsilik used a number of caribou-hunting techniques which can be grouped into two main categories: caribou hunting with the bow and arrow, and caribou hunting from the kayak.

The choice of hunting method depended on many factors: the nature of the topography, including the presence or absence of suitable crossing places, flat plains, lakes, or narrow valleys; the availability of game and the size of the herds; the climate and resulting snow and ice conditions; the number of hunters and supporting personnel; and so on.

The bow was used in hunting a number of different animals, such as polar bears, musk oxen, ptarmigan, and occasionally waterfowl. Yet it was in caribou hunting that it was most important to the Netsilik. The usual Netsilik bow was a composite weapon, about three feet long, and consisted of several elements of antler and musk-ox horn held together with sinew strings. The bowstave was generally reflex. The middle part or handle was of musk-ox horn for better pliability, while the two thinner limbs were of antler. At the back of the stave, between the joints of handle and limbs, there were thin antler splits, while thicker blocks of antler were adjusted on the other side. Several hitches of plaited sinew joined splints and blocks. The bow was reinforced with a backing of plaited sinew usually running all the length of the stave and secured to it by means of numerous hitches; the bow string was also of plaited sinew. The arrows had wooden shafts with long bone points, mostly barbless. The bow and arrows were kept together in a sealskin quiver. The Netsilik employed the Mediterranean type of arrow release. The preferred posture for shooting was half kneeling, the left leg straight and the right knee a little above ground.

The simplest method for catching caribou was to dig pits in deep mounds of snow at the paths caribou habitually follow in early winter. Knives were planted in the bottom and often snow and moss were used to cover the pitfall. Some urine was spread nearby to attract the caribou. This method for trapping caribou, though simple, was infrequently used, however, since it seldom gave any appreciable results.

Stalking the caribou with the bow and arrow was much more difficult, requiring great patience and endurance together with considerable skill. It was preferably carried out by two hunters, the first serving as a blind for the second. The strategy adopted depended on the nature of the terrain. As the caribou have an excellent sense of smell, the hunters would first examine the wind direction. If the terrain was uneven, they took advantage of every rock, swamp, or tuft of grass, crawling circuitously toward the game and lying flat whenever the animal could see them. The hunters might lie concealed like this for hours with the expectation that the caribou would draw near them and come within shoot-

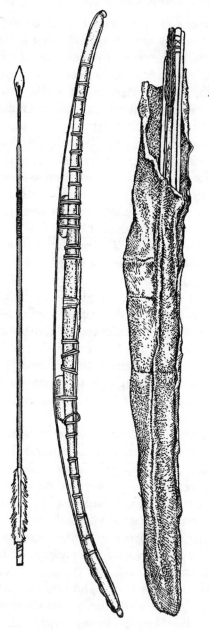

Figure 15   Bow, Quiver,
and Arrows

ing range. If the ground offered no cover, the hunters stood up and imitated the gait of the caribou, their bodies bent forward with their hoods covering their heads, their bows and sticks held upright like antlers. The hunters might wander around pretending they were grazing, getting nearer and nearer until the time was right to suddenly straighten and release an arrow. Sometimes the caribou itself, pushed by curiosity, walked toward the hunters. There was no rigidly established strategy in stalking, the hunters constantly having to make *ad hoc* decisions and adapt to rapidly changing circumstances.

Certain narrow valleys habitually crossed by small, wandering caribou herds were well known for the hunting opportunities they provided. As soon as the hunter spotted the moving caribou from the top of a hill, he ran quickly to the narrow end of the valley and hid himself, often placing a few stones in front of him for better concealment. As the unsuspecting caribou came by, the hunter lifted his bow as quickly as possible and shot one or two arrows. He seldom had time for more shots, as the terrified animal would bolt away as soon as he saw the hunter. This was an individualistic technique with many variations, and seldom was the single hunter able to kill more than one caribou this way.

A somewhat more complicated and productive method of hunting caribou with the bow and arrow involved the co-operation of "beaters" and "archers." Stone cairns designed to frighten the caribou were erected in a row on top of a ridge leading to a lake. At the end of the line of cairns and near the lake the archers lay in ambush, concealed behind low piles of stones. The beaters, using wolf cries, drove the caribou down the line of cairns toward the concealed archers, who then attacked the caribou with a barrage of arrows. Several caribou could be killed in this manner.

On the straits separating King William Island from the mainland and on certain lakes on Boothia Isthmus habitu-

ally crossed by the caribou, the Netsilik sometimes used an
interesting but dangerous method to hunt caribou that
involved the frailty of thin autumn ice. When crossing a
strait, lake, or river, the caribou herds followed promon-
tories, peninsulas, and narrows, looking for the shortest distance between the two shores. When the Eskimos spotted
a herd moving toward such a peninsula in preparation for
crossing, they would hide by the shore and wait until the
herd began its walk over the thin ice. Then the hunters would
suddenly run out, shouting and waving, driving the herd
toward the most central part of the lake, where the ice was
thinnest and most treacherous. Under the weight of the
galloping caribou, the ice broke and continued to break
after every attempt was made by the animals to climb out.
The exhausted animals were then shot with arrows or
speared and dragged out of the water by the hunters. This
was a dangerous way to hunt, however, since the ice could
break under the feet of the hunters themselves, and such
accidents did indeed occur from time to time.

The bow and arrow, then, was used as part of several
different strategies under a great variety of changing circumstances. Although it occasionally gave rise to some collaborative forms of activity, it was especially well suited for
individual hunting, and that was where its value rested. It
enabled the individual hunter to take advantage of spontaneous opportunities and, in hard times, it gave him the
means to get by on his own.

The Netsilik were not very good archers. "A record of ten
archers showed that scarcely any one of them could hit the
mark with anything like certainty at a range of about sixty
feet, and it is difficult to get so near to caribou" (Rasmussen 1931:170). Netsilik archers therefore did not kill
many caribou, except when a large migrating herd was encountered in spring. When in large formations, the caribou
seemed less fearful and were easier to approach. Unfortunately, the caribou is lean and its fur unsuitable for clothing.

Whatever meat was brought to camp did not last very long. The autumn caribou hunts thus acquired vital importance, and the most productive hunting was conducted from the kayak.

The Netsilik kayak was sheathed in sealskins and was practically never used on the sea. The average length of a kayak was about twenty-two feet with a round cockpit and a narrow stem and stern for easier handling. The frame was made of driftwood, and its ribs most commonly of willow branches. Only lashings were used on the kayak, never nails. Two or three thongs were stretched just forward of the manhole, holding an antler buckle on which the paddle rested. The kayak was outfitted with two long spears—each consisting of a wooden shaft and a long, barbless point of antler. Right at the head of the flat deck were attached two semicircular buckles of antler. These spears were held firmly on the deck by the thongs behind and two antler buckles attached to the deck's front. The kayaker had a piece of bearskin to sit on and a long sealskin thong which he used to drag caribou killed in the water back by the antlers.

Caribou hunting from kayaks in late summer was conducted according to two major patterns: at the natural crossing places without the collaboration of beaters, and at the "artificial" crossing places with the help of beaters. The first method was somewhat more productive and was applied mainly on the several narrow lakes on the east side of Boothia Peninsula, which were habitually crossed by the southbound caribou herds. Camp was pitched on the southern shore of the lake, just in front of the crossing place and at some distance from the shore, in order not to scare the animals. Camp sites were usually elevated places from which the approaches to the northern shore were easily visible. The hunters gathered in front of the camp site, concealing themselves and watching the movements of the herds on the other side of the lake. As soon as a herd began entering the water, the eldest hunter gave the signal for the hunt to start.

The men carefully crawled to their kayaks lying on the shore, pushed them into the water, jumped inside, and paddled out for the chase.

Figure 16   Kayak

Every man hunted for himself, as in the fishing at the stone weir. Speed in paddling was essential. The few fast kayakers were quick in reaching the frightened herd and began spearing the swimming animals one after the other. The slow kayakers followed behind, trying to reach the caribou that had gone astray. The spearers aimed primarily at the buttocks or the kidney region. Some caribou were killed, some wounded, while still others managed to reach the shore and tried to escape. At the beginning of the chase, women and children had deployed all along the coast with pieces of skins in their hands. Now, as the caribou tried to escape the hunters by making for shore, the women and children started howling and screaming, imitating the cry of the wolf and waving the skins high in their hands. When menaced by wolves, the instinctual reaction of the caribou is to take to the water, and so the frightened caribou turned back from the shore—only to face the kayakers once again. This method made for a very large kill. At the end of the hunt, each man collected the animals he had killed, tying them together by the antlers with his thong and slowly dragging them to the shore. If there were too many, they were left in the water for favorable winds to push them near camp.

The second hunting method at the "artificial" crossing places was considerably more elaborate. It was employed primarily in areas where the caribou did not have well-defined migration paths, and natural crossing places did not exist. Simpson Peninsula, at the eastern end of the Netsilik country, seems to have been such an area. There it was impossible to hunt caribou with any hope of substantial success without the collaboration of beaters, because it was impossible to tell where the herds might decide to cross the lakes. The topographic characteristics here were similar to the previous case: a long lake with a peninsula on the northern shore creating a narrow neck of water, a camp on a hill on the southern shore opposite the peninsula and from which the movements of the herds could be observed. The novel feature here was the use of "beaters." These were primarily young men capable of running over great distances. They spread in the tundra north of the lake, then surprised the caribou herds from behind. Howling like wolves, they then drove the animals to the desired "artificial" crossing place. Often they covered many miles during such drives, with the herd moving frequently in the wrong direction. Once the herd was in the water, the hunt proceeded as it did at the natural crossing places. Depending, of course, on the size of the herd, these hunts could result in very good returns. It was not uncommon for a fast kayaker to kill up to ten caribou during a single hunt.

All butchering of caribou was done by the men with their short knives, right at the shore and immediately after the hunt. Only occasionally were the young calves carried to camp to be cut up beside the tents. Great care was given to skinning the animals and to the removal of the precious sinew. Both skins and sinew were handed to the women, who put them to dry near the camp. The thigh- and shinbones, the fillets and tongues were also brought home. Children avidly ate the eyes of the caribou on the spot, while men and women gulped raw meat. Then the carcasses were cached under piles of stones for later consumption.

Later the camp people gorged themselves with meat cooked in their soapstone pots. Breaking the bones and eating the marrow was highly appreciated, together with the green contents of the stomach. As was the case at the stone weir, most meals were communal affairs, carried over for many hours among much laughter and merrymaking. Men had plenty of leisure time for gossiping and playing games. Though the caribou crossing places were considered "holy" and all sewing work was rigorously forbidden, the women had much else to do, such as drying caribou meat by hanging it on long lines and gathering heather for fire making.

This was the season when the arctic berries became ripe, and almost everybody could be seen crawling around camp in search of them. Berry picking was the favorite pastime for children, as was the snaring of sea gulls. To catch gulls, a piece of caribou liver was placed on a stone and a round snare below it. A child would lie patiently a few yards away, holding the end of the snare. As soon as a gull cautiously approached the bait and put a foot in the snare, the child pulled vigorously and the thong trapped the bird. Children then played with the gull for many hours, letting it fly and pulling it back and throwing stones at it, all under the approving eyes of the parents.

Gorges were used for catching both gulls and fish. The gorge was a simple bone needle pointed at both ends with a hole in the middle through which a long line of plaited sinew was attached. For catching lake trout, a piece of meat from the caribou leg was attached all around it. The gorge was then thrown into the lake with the end of the line fastened to a heavy stone. It was left there for several hours, until a fat lake trout came along and swallowed both bait and gorge. All that remained then was to pull him out. Gorges were also employed to catch sea gulls, with caribou liver as bait. Some harpoon fishing also took place, but none of these activities was of any real importance, and none was allowed to interfere in any way with the vitally important caribou hunts. It was essential indeed that at least the minimal number of necessary fur skins be obtained in the brief time they had for hunting. And there were about thirty needed for a family of four: seven skins for the winter clothing of an adult man, six for a woman, and three or four per child. The rest were used as mattresses and sleeping skins. In a good year, the better hunters working at the natural crossing places could accumulate a sufficient number of skins to satisfy the needs of their families without any real trouble. But not all hunters were good hunters, not all years were good years, and the pursuit of a migratory game was hazardous at best. Consequently, in spite of the Netsilik's best efforts, there were winters when bearskins or even musk-ox skins had to be used as a substitute for caribou fur.

Around the end of September, caribou hunting came to an end. Lakes and rivers had frozen over, the big herds had left the country and migrated south. There were a few resident caribou who remained all winter through in the Netsilik area, but creaking snow under the hunter's feet made them very difficult to approach. And so the Eskimos had to leave the caribou hunting ground, look for other game, and begin preparations for the long winter to come. The kayaks were placed high on tall piles of stones, the tents pulled down, and the small bands of Netsilik were on the move once more.

AUTUMN FISHING THROUGH THE THIN RIVER ICE

The late fall season was primarily a transitional period between the autumn caribou hunts and the winter sealing activities. The weather was cold, with strong northwesterly winds. Lakes, rivers, and sea arms were covered with ice. The marshy tundra became hard from the frost, but there was still not very much snow on the ground. For subsistence during this period, the Netsilik depended primarily on their cached fish and caribou meat, on river or lake fishing, and occasionally on musk-ox hunting. In general, it was only

when the summer caches were emptied, or nearly so, that
seal hunting would begin.

Since neither salmon trout nor lake trout were to be found
in great concentrations at that season, the bands of twenty
or thirty people that camped together at the caribou hunting
sites had to disperse themselves in smaller units of just a few
families and try their luck at several fishing spots. Since the
snow was not deep enough to allow for the building of igloos, the people had to remain in their cold sealskin tents,
which offered scant protection from the strong gales. Occasionally, when sufficient snow was available, snow walls
were built around the tents as brakes against the wind.

But the most ingenious type of house that was used during
this period was built with several slabs of ice cut from a river
or lake. At this season, lake ice was about six or seven inches
thick. Two or three men armed with ice picks collaborated
to cut the blocks needed. A number of holes were made in
the ice along the intended outline of the rectangular slab,
about five by three feet in size. The slab was detached by
pressure. A little hole was then made at the corner, a sealskin thong passed through, and the heavy slab dragged to
the building site. Eight to ten slabs were sufficient for an ice
hut. The slabs were bound with a mortar of snow and water,
then the tent skins were stretched over the ice wall to make
a roof and a doorway was cut at the joint between two slabs.
For that particular season this was a very commodious shelter, though as soon as enough snow was packed on the slope
of hills, both tents and ice huts were abandoned and igloos
erected (see plate 7).

Because of the shortage of driftwood, wooden sledges
were very rare. Some hunters, primarily among the eastern
Netsilik, were obliged to make sledges out of sealskins as a
substitute for wood. These were most ingeniously built out
of the tent sheets that had been used that summer. The tent
was cut in half, each half rolled up, and the rolls lowered
into the river waters through a hole in the ice. When

thoroughly wet and soft, the skins were pulled out again and spread out. Then fish were laid along one side of each of the tent halves, shingle-fashion. Then the two skins were rolled up again with the fish inside, this time very tightly, bound all around with sealskin thongs and left to freeze after being flattened with their ends turned up. The end result was sufficiently thick with the addition of the fish sections inside. For crossbars, caribou antlers were employed, bound tightly to the runners with sealskin thongs. For the preparation of shoeing, some moss was pulverized and mixed with snow and water in a bowl cut in the river ice. This sludge was applied to the underside of the runners in a thick coating, hand smoothed, left to freeze, and smoothed again with a knife. Then an ice glazing was spread over the peat shoeing. The Eskimo took mouthfuls of river water, spewed them into a piece of polar-bear fur, and gently rubbed the wet fur over the coarse peat cover. This produced a hard and very resistant coat of thin ice that allowed the sled to run smoothly over the snow-covered surfaces and protected the skin runners themselves. The sledge was then ready for the dogs to be harnessed to it (see plate 8).

Though an occasional caribou could still be found and killed with the bow and arrow, most energies now were concentrated on autumn fishing. In this activity, the Arviligjuarmiut of Pelly Bay were most fortunate. The Kellett River, which ran into Pelly Bay, abounded in salmon trout in that season. The people knew where the best fishing places were located along the river and set up small camps nearby to fish under the thin autumn ice. To prepare for ice fishing, the fisherman had to cut a round hole in the river ice, which at that season was less than ten inches thick. This he did with the ice pick. Then he removed all the floating ice particles with the antler scoop. In the hole thus cleared he plunged his lure, a figure of a small ivory fish

Figure 18   Scraper

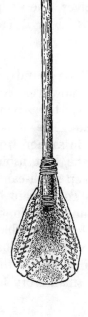

Figure 17   Ice Scoop

about two inches long hanging on a line of plaited sinew from an antler handle.

Sometimes two freely suspended pieces of ivory, a small piece of skin, and a soapstone sinker were attached near the figure. Usually a sharp bone needle was inserted at the end of the lure handle for killing the landed fish. The fish decoy was held in the left hand with a constant jigging movement while the leister was held in the right hand. The fisherman knelt in front of the fishing hole and kept his eyes close to the water in order to see approaching fish. When he spotted one he quickly thrust his leister, impaled the fish, and pulled it out. This method was used with considerable success throughout October and up until November, when the river ice became too thick and decoy fishing had to be abandoned. Not only could enough fish for daily subsistence be secured this way, but quite a few caches could likewise be filled. These caches were made of ice slabs, put together in very much the same way as the ice huts were.

The eastern Netsilik were fortunate in another respect. They had land near the only area where musk oxen could be profitably hunted. Small herds of these large, meaty animals roamed the hilly country lying west, south, and southwest of Pelly Bay. In late fall and early winter small parties of Arviligjuarmiut traveled over that vast area in search of musk oxen. Dogs played an indispensable part in these hunts. When faced with danger, the musk oxen form a defensive circle with the females and the young ones in the middle, while the bulls point their horns outwards. Only rarely would the musk oxen charge. The dogs kept the musk oxen at bay while the Eskimos shot arrows at a particular animal. The wounded and infuriated animal finally charged, but was again surrounded by the dogs. The hunters then moved in and killed him with a heavy spear. A similar strategy was followed when a single musk ox was encountered inland: dogs kept it at bay while the hunter shot his arrows until the opportunity came for a final thrust with the spear. This heavy spear had a strong wooden shaft and a large point of bear bone. If a musk ox was found grazing near the top of a cliff or steep hill, it was pushed over the precipice by the hunter and his dogs. After butchering, the meat was cached and the skins brought to the igloos to serve as sleeping mattresses.

But musk oxen did not frequent the lands of the northern Netsilik, and fishing salmon trout through the thin autumn ice there was a less rewarding activity than south at Pelly Bay. Accordingly the northern people relied on lake-trout fishing during the fall. Their caribou-meat caches were also much more substantial than was the case with the Arvilig-juarmiut, and so they had these to rely on as well for the many weeks in the dark season spent waiting for the seal hunts to begin.

Late fall was the women's busiest time, as it was only during this season that they made the new fur clothing. Men's clothing consisted of an inner and outer layer for the coat, trousers, stockings, and boots. The hair of the inner layer was turned toward the wearer's body, while the hair on the outer layer faced the outside. The inner coat was made generally of a finer fur skin with shorter hair. It had a hood and was slit on the sides, making for two flaps. The back flap usually was much longer, and the whole of the lower edge was fringed. The outer coat was similar in cut, but the hair was somewhat longer and thicker and the whole coat was bulkier. It also had a sewn-in hood, in this case usually with dog-fur trimming, a longer back, and fringes along the lower edges. White borders and decorative inserts were common. The trousers were large and hung on the hips, reaching below the knee. Usually the outer pair of trousers had a white strip at the bottom. Stockings were made of the finest caribou fur, and sometimes much shorter socks were worn on top of the stockings. For boots the caribou leg skin was preferred, with the fur outside. Finally a pair of shoes was worn, fur inside. These shoes were short, had draw cords, and were usually fitted with an extra sole with the hair side out. The feet were thus protected by four layers of caribou fur, a necessity during travel under intense cold. Mittens were short, the hair side out, and they, too, were made of the highly resistant caribou leg skin with very short hair. The outer and heavier garments were worn only when traveling or hunting, as they were generally heavy and restrictive. Around camp the inner coats and trousers constituted sufficient protection. This applied also to women's and children's clothing (see plates 9-A and 9-B).

Though women's clothing was similar to the men's in that it consisted also of two layers of fur, its appearance was different. Both inner and outer coats had extremely large hoods and shoulder pieces, necessary to give a mother the shoulder room she needed to handle her baby, which was carried in a pouch on the back of her coat. The front flap was usually narrower and the back flap longer than those of the men's coats. There were borders and trimmings of white fur from the caribou's abdomen. Women usually wore only one pair of trousers, with the hair on the outside, decorated with white stripes running down each side. And women's boots were of an extraordinary shape. They were long legging-boots with the hair outside that came well above the knee and were fastened to the belt. Their peculiarity consisted of their baggy appearance, which resulted from a large fullness on the outer side below the knee. The stockings were also baggy, only they were worn with the hair turned inside. The foot part of the legging-boot, in contrast to the upper portion, had the hair inside. Women's mittens were the same as those of the men. Over the outer coats the women wore a skin belt that passed under the arms, across the back, and was held tight with one wooden button. This belt helped support the infant (see plate 10).

Small infants carried in their mother's pouches were usually naked, but wore small hoods. As soon as they began to walk and until the age of five or six, girls and boys wore

Figure 19 Child's Combination Suit   *Figure 20 Snow Probe*

combination suits, preferably made of caribou-calf skin. The hood, jacket, trousers, and footwear were all made in one piece with an opening on the chest through which the child slid in. There was a slit behind to allow elimination. Short boots were worn with this garment.

A very rigorous taboo was observed while the sewing work was in progress: no hunting whatsoever could be undertaken. Most if not all the work connected with new clothing was customarily carried out at special camp sites, usually located on the seacoast. These settlements were somewhat larger than the previous ones and constituted a transition between the summer, inland phase and the winter, marine phase of the annual migration cycle. While the seamstresses were busy with the skins, the men traveled back and forth between camp and caches, bringing in supplies of caribou meat and fish. There were many other things to do as well in preparation for the forthcoming winter season. Besides the repair and building of sledges, they had to put in good order the numerous tools and weapons needed for sealing and bear hunting, check on the dog harnesses and lines, etc. Most evenings were passed in song fests and communal meals.

The distribution of activities and the duration of this transitional phase seem to have varied greatly among the different Netsilik subgroups from year to year. The Arviligjuarmiut fished intensely during the first part of October and made most of their new clothing immediately afterwards at their special sewing place on the southern shore of Pelly Bay. The occasional musk-ox hunts were done only after the completion of all skin work. Among the northern Netsilik the preparation of the new clothing followed the caribou hunts more closely. Determination of the time when sealing was to begin depended essentially on how much stored food there was. In lean years, people had to move to the sea ice by the end of November, but if there were plenty of cached supplies, the move could be postponed until the

end of February or even the beginning of March. In most
normal years, the Netsilik congregated in their large winter
camps on the flat sea ice by January.

SEAL HUNTING IN MIDWINTER

Midwinter in the Arctic regions is the darkest and coldest
season of the year. At its highest point, the sun barely shows
above the horizon and twilight reigns for the rest of the
short day. Land and sea are frozen hard, with the sea ice
over seven feet thick. The tundra looks more barren and
desolate than ever, with nearly all caribou and migrating
birds gone south, and lemmings, marmots, and hares bury-
ing themselves under the snow. Frequent winds sweep
the snow, making it drift and piling it high and hard under
slopes and hills. Blizzards and snowstorms greatly reduce
visibility.

It was through this frozen desert that the Netsilik had to
travel to reach the seal-hunting areas, taking with them
their women and children, their sledges loaded high and
heavy with all the necessities of life. The Netsilik had very
little food to spare for their dogs and consequently could
afford to keep an average of only one or two dogs per family. This meant that the men had to help the dogs to move
the heavy sledges while at the same time guiding the dogs
with the whip and directing the sledge between all the
crevices and pits in the broken ice that the caravans had to
cross. The wives usually led the dogs, walking in front of
them at a distance of five to ten yards, turning frequently
and shouting the signal cries. Sometimes, however, the
women had to join the men in dragging the sledges. Only
small children incapable of walking over long distances were
allowed to sit on the sledges. As for the older people, they
dragged themselves behind the caravan, painfully stumbling
over the protruding ice, moving their feet with difficulty

through the thick snow, and falling farther and farther behind the caravan. Often the main part of the group had reached its destination and completely set up camp before the older people caught up.

Seals were to be found in many bays and straits of the Netsilik coast; they were especially plentiful at Pelly Bay, Shepherd Bay and Rae Strait, and Lord Mayor Bay. Many factors influenced the choice of a particular camp site within a general marine area, but the most important was the presence of clusters of seal breathing holes, an unmistakable indication of seal availability. The sealing area also had to be well covered with snow. The seal could easily hear the hunter's steps on the ice if there was no layer of snow to dampen the noise. But the snow cover could not be too thick or soft, as then the breathing holes were extremely difficult to find. It was also essential for the settlement to be located near a pile of old, broken ice imprisoned in the fresh and smooth ice sheet. Old sea ice has the characteristic of losing most of its salinity after a year, and it was necessary that old sea ice be available in order for the camp to have a supply of drinking water.

Hunting seals at the breathing holes was the main subsistence activity of the Netsilik from January until the end of May. It was essentially a group activity requiring the collaboration of numerous hunters, which is easy to understand when the winter habits of the seal are taken into consideration. The seal is an air-breathing mammal, and he has to come to the surface of the sea every fifteen or twenty minutes and breathe prolongedly. This is easy enough in summer, but in the winter, when the sea is covered with a continuous sheet of ice, the seal has to breathe through a hole in the ice. This hole the seal makes himself, right after ice formation in autumn, by scratching the lower part of the sea ice with his sharp claws. This creates a small air-filled ice dome which is gradually covered with snow. As the sea ice thickens to six or seven feet through the win-

ter, the seal keeps his breathing hole open by continuously
destroying any new ice that forms in it, until his breathing
hole has taken on the form of a tall funnel with a small air
chamber on top. The warm air from the seal's breath makes
a small hole through the snow cover.

Since a seal has to move over a considerable area in his
search for food and cannot return constantly to the same
breathing hole, he generally uses a number of breathing
holes over a wide area. This makes it very difficult for a
single hunter to catch a seal, since he could not possibly
watch all the breathing holes that a seal might be using. If,
however, a group of hunters attends a number of breathing
holes lying in proximity, their chances of catching a seal
speedily will be considerably increased; thus the Netsilik
joined in large winter camps so that a maximum number of
hunters could collaborate.

The size of these winter settlements varied considerably
from large camps containing up to one hundred persons to
the more common camps of fifty to sixty people. The hunters, including the boys capable of contributing to seal hunting, constituted about one third of the population. Thus
there were at least fifteen hunters in most sealing stations,
though there were also some camps only about half that size.

Numerous factors influenced settlement dimensions. One
was seal availability. Under decreased ecological pressure,
the necessity for large groups of people to hunt and stay
together decreased and sections of the big community
might break away. As soon as the seal returns became
less regular, the tendency toward larger group formation re-
asserted itself. Camps sometimes broke up into smaller
groups toward the end of the winter sealing season in order
to get nearer to their spring sealing areas. And sometimes
smaller winter camps could be located near each other with
frequent intercommunication. Obviously, purely social factors influenced the fusion of the camps, as well as hunting
necessities. Winter camps rarely remained for over a month

in one locality. After the seal resources of an area were considered exhausted, the people moved to another hunting place, constantly in search of better opportunities. Winter life was one of frequent migrations, though the distance between old and new camps rarely exceeded ten miles.

The first task that faced men and women upon arrival at a sealing area was the construction of snowhouses and the setting up of camp. This was doubly tiresome, since it took place at the end of an exhausting journey. The selection of an appropriate site was made with the help of a special tool, the snow probe, a long, thin rod of antler, three to four feet long, with an ovoid ferrule at one end and a small handle at the other. The igloo builder pushed the snow probe gently through the snow in various places in order to find a building material of the right consistency. A sizable snow bank is always made up of several layers of snow, frequently of unequal thickness and density. The snow probe could go down through the top layer of soft snow and help to find a good layer, thick and hard enough so that snow blocks could be cut in it.

Once the proper sort of building snow had been found, the igloo builder went to work. The thin top covering of soft snow was removed quickly with the snow shovel, an ingenious tool illustrating the Eskimo's ability to employ substitute materials for hard-to-find wood. The frame was made of split antler, four or five pieces held strongly together with plaited sinew threads, to which a piece of depilated sealskin was tightly fastened. It was held very low, almost horizontal to the snow surface, by an antler handle and was operated with short quick thrusts.

The soft snow thus removed, a large circle was drawn with a snow knife on the harder snow surface, representing exactly the dimensions of the igloo. Then the cutting of the rectangular snow blocks proceeded quickly. These were about twenty inches wide, twenty-five inches long, and four inches thick. Usually the building site within the drawn

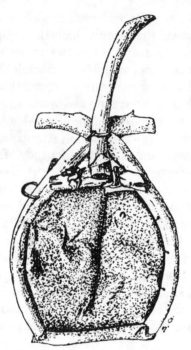

Figure 21   Snow Shovel

circle provided all the material needed for the construction.
After each few snow blocks were cut, they were placed on
the circular wall, one beside the other, in a spiral manner,
with each ascending row extending a little further inwards.
This, of course, created the igloo's characteristic beehive
shape. To ensure that the blocks fit closely together, each
new block was gently pressed against the preceding one with
a slight stroke. Chinks were eliminated with the snow knife
and the sides of the snow blocks were smoothed and
straightened. As blocks were cut out of the snow for the
walls, the igloo floor was cleared downwards. The last blocks
for the igloo were cut and shaped with particular care. They
were smaller, and when set in place they completed the
roof of the snowhouse.

All this construction work was carried out by the man, standing inside the igloo. As he built up the walls, his wife stood outside, using the snow shovel to plaster over the outside of the igloo with fine, soft snow which concealed the outlines of the blocks and filled in all the holes. The completed igloo consequently looked something like a snow heap.

The snow furnishings inside were constructed next. First a hole was cut through the igloo wall at the level of the sleeping counter, two or three feet above the floor. It was through this hole that all excess snow was thrown out and people's belongings moved in. To build the sleeping counter, a row of snow blocks was placed at its front limit and all the snow lying on the floor space was piled up behind them with the snow shovel, then the irregular surface was packed hard and smoothed with the snow shovel. At one corner of the floor adjoining the wall, the "kitchen table" was similarly erected. It was of the same height as the sleeping counter. A small block of snow was placed between the kitchen compartment and the sleeping area for the housewife to rest her feet on.

The main part of the igloo was now almost complete and ready for the housewife to move in. At this point the sled was unloaded and all household furnishings thrown in through the wall opening. This opening was then closed, and while the woman put away their belongings, the man built the porch and the doorway. The round porch stood at the entrance of the igloo and had the same semispherical shape, although it was much smaller. The entrance hole connecting the igloo itself to this porch was very low, rarely higher than two feet, and it had a rounded top. To the porch he added the doorway, a long, low, and narrow corridor with straight walls and flat roof consisting of a single row of snow blocks. The entrance from the long doorway to the porch was somewhat bigger than the entrance to the igloo itself. The long doorway functioned as a windbreak, since it could be moved to the left or right in order to keep the prevailing winds from blowing directly into the igloo. A shifting doorway was a necessity, since the igloo's entrance was never closed during the daytime. Finally a ventilation hole two to three inches wide was cut through the igloo's ceiling, which caused a constant circulation of fresh, cold air throughout the igloo (see plate 11).

The following day, or even later, a window was placed in the wall, most frequently above the entrance. This was a large panel of fresh-water ice (always clearer than sea ice), rectangular in shape with rounded corners, about three inches thick. First a square hole was cut in the wall, somewhat smaller than the window. Then the ice panel was placed over it from outside and the joints were trimmed with the snow knife until the window fit tightly into the wall. The window faced east or south, and frequently a snow block was placed on the outer wall nearby to function as a reflector. The ice window was carried along during the migrations, as there was no fresh water available with which to make a replacement.

There were many variations of this basic building pattern. Very often two related families shared the same igloo, as was the case when a recently married son resided with his father. In this case, kitchen tables were set up in front of both ends of the sleeping counter, with two lamps. Or sometimes an adjoining igloo was erected, sharing a common porch with an older igloo. Extensions of an existing igloo also could be added to accommodate a friend or a relative. And up to four igloos could be joined to provide support for one communal dance house.

The dance house was a very large structure erected several days after camp had been set and requiring a joint effort. Usually the four foundation igloos had already been built in the necessary circle, facing each other, with an eye to the forthcoming construction of the festive hall. To build the dance house, snow blocks were laid in a circle that included the front halves of the four base igloos. As the dance-house walls rose, they came together in the typical beehive shape, topping the four base igloos at a height just below where their ice windows were placed. After the completion of the large building, the snow walls of the base igloos now inside the new, bigger structure were knocked down. Through these large openings one could easily observe the neighboring families. The whole architectural complex sheltered a social unit.

In size as well as complexity the igloos varied greatly. There were very small igloos built by travelers for an overnight stay and designed to provide shelter for one or two men. The usual family igloos may have ranged from nine to fifteen feet in diameter and slightly over six feet in height. In these the sleeping platform was twenty to thirty inches high and extended in depth to nearly two thirds of the igloo. The doorway was less than three feet high. Among neighboring tribes the Netsilik were highly regarded for their igloo-building abilities. When working at full speed, a man helped by his wife could erect a family-size igloo in slightly more than a hour.

Arranging the furnishings inside an igloo was mainly the woman's task. After all the family's possessions had been thrown inside on the sleeping platform and the opening in the wall closed, the woman lit her soapstone lamp. She placed this lamp on the kitchen table, making it stand flat with three antler or wooden sticks stuck vertically in the snow table. The lamp was placed with the inner edge of the crescent turned toward the interior of the hut. To provide fuel for the lamp, she extracted a piece of frozen blubber from the blubber bag and beat it with the blubber pounder on a board until it became soft and the oil liquefied. (The blubber pounder was a common tool made of the distal end of a musk-ox horn with several incisions serving as a handle.) The woman then threw this dripping piece of blubber on the lamp. From a round sealskin container she

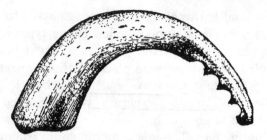

Figure 22   Blubber Pounder

then took some finely chopped wick moss soaked with oil
and skillfully laid it all along the outer edge of the lamp. It
was essential that the lamp be lighted to its maximal capacity.

Then the housewife either made fire herself with pyrites
and a piece of iron or went out to bring fire from a neighboring igloo, in which case she carried a flaming piece of
moss in her hands, under her coat. She lit the long lampwick,
and soon the entire length of moss would be burning. As the
burning wick heated the lamp, the blubber melted completely and the lamp was fully operative. The housewife
controlled the wick with a stone wick trimmer, which she
used to sharpen the upper edge of the wick to eliminate
smoke; and underneath the lamp she put an oval sealskin
container to catch any oil that might drip through the porous
stone. The heat generated by the fully lit lamp led to a
slight melting of the inner surface of the igloo, which helped
the blocks settle down and caused a thin crust of ice to be
formed which welded the blocks together and increased the
strength of the ceiling. Her lamp lit, the wife then set about
ordering her household.

In order to set the drying rack above the lamp, three long
sticks were necessary. The first usually came from the leister's shaft. It was stuck vertically in the floor, right at the
outer corner of the kitchen platform. It supported the ends
of the other two sticks, which were horizontally stuck into

the igloo wall. These sticks provided the support for the drying rack, which was indispensable for the drying of wet clothing.

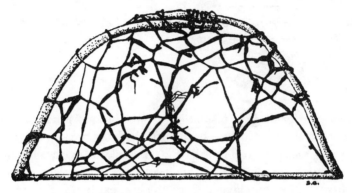

Figure 23   Drying Rack

The drying rack itself consisted of a rectangular frame of antler over which a net of thin caribou-skin thongs was hung. One of the supporting sticks was arranged so that it was parallel to the lamp's axis, and it was from this stick that the soapstone pot was suspended on thongs, right above the lamp wick.

Meat sticks and soup ladles were usually placed on the kitchen platform. The soup ladle was made of the proximal end of a musk-ox horn, with a small handle at the back. Many cuts of meat were also thrown on the kitchen platform, behind the lamp. Near the drying rack a piece of antler was driven into the wall for hanging various dippers and sealskin containers, which were used mostly for water carrying.

Once her kitchen was in order, the wife looked after the bedding. She placed the tent pole at the edge of the sleeping platform, to provide additional resistance to the friction caused by constant climbing and sitting at the platform edge. The sleeping skins were never laid directly on the

Figure 24   Soup Ladle

snow platform. For insulation from the moisture of the snow, caribou ribs were frequently laid down first, aligned in rows, or the waterproof kayak skins might be used for the same purpose. On top of the insulating material came the mattress skins, two layers of the thickest caribou fur, the hair of the lower layer facing downwards and the hair of the upper layer upwards. Then came the blanket or sleeping skins, sewn together. The Netsilik did not use sleeping bags. In addition to their bedding, they threw old clothing at the back of the sleeping platform.

They neglectfully stored extra skins, various amounts of meat and blubber, and all the weapons and tools on the floor at the opposite corner of the kitchen platform and in the snow porch. Small pups were usually kept on the igloo floor. Harpoons and spears were stuck in the outside igloo wall near the entrance, and the snow beater was stuck into the wall on the inside.

There were several snow constructions outside, nearby the igloos. Dog feed was kept high on an elevated snow platform, out of reach of the dogs. For the sealskin sledge a special shelter was dug out in the snow and well covered with snow blocks. Finally, a small toilet room was built near the igloo settlement. It was a small, round shelter constructed of snow blocks, sufficient for protection from the drifting snow.

Figure 25   Sealskin Container

After camp was set, seal hunting began. During the winter, the Netsilik practiced the breathing-hole method of sealing, called *maursurniq*, almost exclusively. Among the Netsilik Eskimos seal hunting at the breathing holes was an elaborate and demanding artful technique requiring prolonged training, enormous endurance, and patience. Many ingenious and delicately carved tools were necessary for this method of hunting.

The ice-hunting harpoon was the most important weapon. It was made almost entirely of antler, and was about four and a half feet long. The shaft was round and strong.

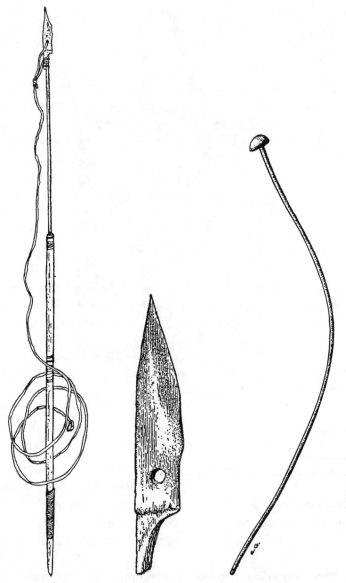

Figure 26
Ice-Hunting Harpoon

Figure 27
Harpoon Head

Figure 28
Breathing-Hole Searcher

At one end was inserted a long and thin foreshaft, also of caribou antler, while at the other end a strong blade of hard bear bone was fixed, used as an ice pick. Various kinds of harpoon heads were utilized, originally with chipped flint blades, then during the historic period with iron blades. Often harpoon heads were made entirely of bear bone with no separate blades inserted. All harpoon heads were barbless, with sharpened stems. Thongs of bearded sealskin or plaited sinew were used as harpoon lines, the latter preferred in midwinter.

The snow probe was also taken along and used to locate the breathing hole. Another important tool was the breathing-hole searcher, a long and slender piece of caribou antler, curved in the middle, with a knob-like handle on one end. With this searcher inserted in the seal's breathing hole and turned around, the hunter could test its exact contours. This was necessary, since some breathing holes had irregular shapes. The seal, in keeping his hole free of ice, might scratch one side of the hole's wall more than the others, thus giving it a somewhat curved shape. The hunter had to be informed of this in order to strike down in the hole in the proper direction to kill his seal.

Out on the flat ice, the harpoon without the head, the snow probe, and the searcher were held in the hunter's left hand while the dog was held on leash in the right hand. All the other tools were kept in the hunting bag, which the hunter carried on his back. The squarish hunting bag was made of caribou fur, foxskin, or fetus-seal skin. Besides using the bag as a tool container, the hunter stood on it during the long motionless watch at the breathing hole, even sometimes putting his feet inside it. This was done not only for additional protection against the intense cold, but for reducing any possible foot noises on the snow, to which the seals were highly sensitive.

Figure 29   Game Bag

Inside the bag he kept a harpoon head and line, one of two kinds of indicators, a wound pin, the two harpoon rests, a horn scoop, the breathing-hole protector, and a short thong with a toggle to drag the seal home.

The indicator was a device used to signal the arrival of the seal at a breathing hole. The down indicator was the most commonly used. It was an extremely delicate device, consisting mainly of a piece of hard caribou leg sinew, split so as to resemble a small spider with two claws. A bit of swan's-down was attached to this by a sinew thread. The horn indicator was much simpler, consisting of two very thin

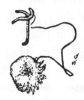

Figure 30   Down Indicator

antler rods of unequal length connected by a cord. The longer rod, about twenty inches in length, had a bone knob at the end.

As for the two harpoon rests, they were made either of wood or of antler, pointed at the bottom and with a fur skin-lined notch in the upper edge. This addition of skin was necessary to reduce any possible noise that might be pro-

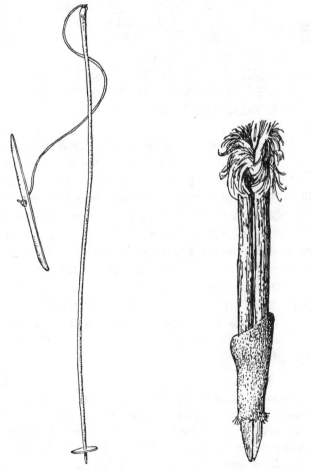

Figure 31   Bone Indicator   *Figure 32   Harpoon Rest*

duced when the harpoon was lifted from its rests at the
crucial moment before the strike. The breathing-hole scoop
was a musk-ox horn, with a narrow, deep bowl and a straight
handle. These tools and the indispensable snow knife made
up the complete equipment of the seal hunter.

The decision where to hunt was taken after much discussion and deliberation. The hunters concentrated their attention on the areas consisting entirely of fresh flat ice, since
seals avoided all old broken ice. After each hunt, long comments were made on the seal availability in particular areas.
These discussions were sometimes continued in the morning
before preparations for the new hunting expedition had
started. The say of the elderly hunters naturally carried
greater weight, although the younger men freely expressed
their views.

Each winter camp had a leader, usually the eldest of the
capable hunters, and it was up to him finally to decide when
and where to hunt. The hunters started their preparations
early in the morning. A good meal before departure was indispensable, since that was often all the food the sealers
would eat on a hunting day, at least until their return in the
evening. After the meal they put on their outer clothing and
thick footwear, then checked and assembled the various instruments to be used during the hunt. The dogs were put
on leash, the harpoons were tested for strength, and everywhere there was an atmosphere of general excitement. As
Amundsen, who watched the departure of a large sealing
party, skillfully observed:

> They have a great deal to talk about. One would think
> they were living in a world of stirring events, and offer-
> ing a variety of topics for conversation and discussion,
> and not here in an ice field, which has been lying silent
> and desolate for aeons, and where life from day to day,
> yea, from century to century, has gone on in changeless
> monotony (1908:30).

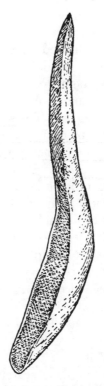

Figure 33   Breathing-Hole Scoop

The group set off together toward the selected hunting area, which was not too far, usually within walking distance from camp. Once there, the group split up and the hunters moved individually in different directions, led by their dogs. The role of the dog was of crucial importance in winter sealing. Since there was no sign on the snow surface that might indicate the presence of a breathing hole below, the hunters relied on their dogs' sense of smell to find them. As soon as the dog smelled a breathing hole he stopped and either turned around at the same place or lay down. Not all dogs were good at this task, so a dog with a good smell for

breathing holes was highly prized for his usefulness in
sealing.

Once his dog had indicated that a breathing hole was
nearby, the hunter announced the discovery with a loud
cry. Other hunters searching close by then rushed to the
scene and thrust their snow probes into the snow, trying to
find the narrow breathing hole. The hunter who first actually
hit the hole became its "owner" and remained there, though
he was not always the one whose dog had initially discov-
ered the presence of the hole. This custom of course, was
not observed by those other hunters who were out of ear-
shot or who had already found their own holes.

Having found a breathing hole, the hunter then prepared
for the watch. First he removed his dog from the hunting
place and tied him to a block of snow. Then he cut away
the upper layer of snow covering the breathing hole with
the snow knife and leaned down to see and smell whether
the breathing hole was still in use or whether it was abandoned and frozen. If the hole was a good one, he broke the
hard, ice-like snow on top with the ice pick fixed on this
harpoon and removed it with the ice scoop. Then he took
his long, curved breathing-hole searcher and examined the
contours inside and the curvature of the hole in order to
determine the direction in which the harpoon should be
thrust. After this the hunter again covered the breathing
hole with snow, holding the snow probe straight in the middle of this snow heap, right above the hole and in the proper
striking direction. When he lifted the snow probe out, a tiny
dark hole of about half an inch remained below in the
snow. The down indicator was then prepared for use. With
a little saliva, a single piece of down was attached to the
claws of the hard sinew so that the swan's-down appeared
like a barely visible, curved thread between them. The indicator then was placed on the snow, with the single piece
of bright down resting exactly above the dark little hole. In
case there was drifting snow that might cover the hole, the

breathing-hole protector, a small cylinder of translucid seal-skin, was placed right on top. The agitation of the water below following the arrival of the seal sent an air movement through the tiny hole which made the swan's-down vibrate. This was the signal for the strike.

Some hunters preferred the horn indicator. The shorter antler rod was stuck in the snow near the hole, while the longer rod was inserted in the water in a breathing hole. When the seal came to breathe, the rod either fell down or came up. In both cases the harpoon strike had to come fast.

After setting the indicator the hunter stuck the two harpoon rests in the snow and placed the ready harpoon on them. He put the furry hunting bag under his feet, pushed his hands in his sleeves to keep them warm, and began his watch, his knees slightly bent and the body leaning forward. This may have lasted several hours, depending on numerous conditions. As Rasmussen writes, "the hunter stands as motionless as a statue . . . eyes fixed intently on the swans-down. . . . Hour after hour goes by, and I realize what a fund of patience and hardiness is required when this hunting has to be pursued in a storm and in a temperature of about −50° Celsius" (1931:153). (Rasmussen's party of fifteen hunters kept watch for eleven hours and caught one seal.)

The actual harpooning came immediately after a positive signal from the indicator. The hunter seized the harpoon with his right hand while holding the coiled line with his left. The thrust was given with the whole strength and weight of the hunter's body. With the harpoon head sunk deeply into the seal, the hunter quickly withdrew the harpoon shaft and let some of the line go. The seal pulled down with all its strength while the hunter kept the lines firmly in hand. After a short struggle, the seal generally lost strength and the hunter was free to enlarge the ceiling of the breathing hole with his ice pick and pull the seal out.

This was the signal for all the hunters to assemble and

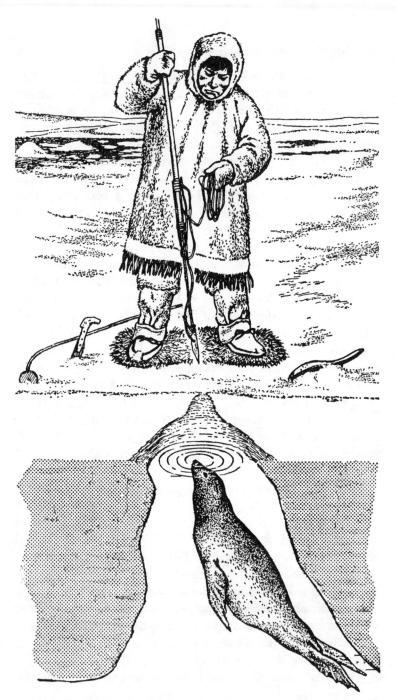

Figure 34   A Seal Hunter Prepares to Strike

partake of a minor feast. An incision was made on the seal's belly, the liver and some blubber removed, and these parts shared and eaten by the gathered hunters on the spot. The incision was then stitched with the wound pin and the seal strapped to the dogs to be dragged to camp. Once in the igloo it was laid on fresh snow and butchered by the wife of the lucky hunter. (Meat and blubber were shared throughout camp according to complex rules to be described later.)

This was the principal sealing technique of the Netsilik in winter. Only in Tuat, on the east coast of Boothia Isthmus, was a method of sealing different from the breathing-hole method just described in practice. This other method was called *itertalerineq* and was related to the ice cracks formed by sea currents in that region. As soon as such cracks occurred in the ice, the seals abandoned their breathing holes and came to breathe freely along the cracks. Taking advantage of this concentration of seals, the hunter built a snowhouse over one of these open cracks, closing the door with skins so that the interior should be as dark as possible. Inside his house he made an "artificial" breathing hole. A piece of ice with a hole in the middle resembling the seal's natural breathing hole was carved and placed over the ice crack in the igloo's floor. The seals swimming below were particularly attracted by this little hole, came up to breathe, and became easy prey to the hunter's harpoon. It was essential for the seal to be removed from under the ice very quickly in order to keep the crack clean from blood and leave it ready for another strike. This method of individualistic hunting was considered highly rewarding later in spring. It was also comparatively comfortable, since the igloo protected the hunter from storms and cold.

Occasionally bearded seals were caught in some areas, such as the northeastern part of Pelly Bay and the area around Ukjulik. The large bearded seal was killed in exactly the same manner as the ordinary ringed seal, but being a much larger animal, it offered considerably more resistance

[margin note: exception of hole sealing method]

and could drag the unwary hunter right down into the opening of the breathing hole. Letting a bearded seal go was
considered very shameful, and usually the hunter struggled
to the last. "No wonder that one often sees stiff and mis-
shapen fingers as memorials of these bearded-seal hunts"
(Rasmussen 1931:162).

Polar bear encounters ✳

Occasionally traveling or hunting the Netsilik came across
polar bears, or their tracks. These bears were almost always pursued, and ferocious battles followed. First they let
loose the dogs, who rushed madly at the bear, attacking it
from all sides. The bear clawed viciously at the dogs, but
they were quick enough to avoid his attacks and were able
to keep the bear at bay until the arrival of the hunters. The
hunting strategy depended on the number of hunters and
the nature of the weapons. Generally the Eskimos carried
with them a special barbless harpoon head, specifically designed for bear hunting. If heavier spears such as those used
for musk-ox hunting were not available, the bear was attacked at close quarters with the sealing harpoon armed
with the special head. It was a dangerous fight, and often
the hunters suffered many scars and wounds, but the Netsilik never withdrew from a bear hunt. Bear meat was highly
valued and was shared by all the hunters, while the man
who gave the bear the fatal thrust kept the skin.

While the men hunted on the flat ice, domestic routines
followed their usual slow rhythm in the igloos. The house-
wives tended their lamps, adding fresh blubber as needed,
trimming the moss wicks. Old sea ice for drinking water had
to be chopped in small pieces with the ice pick, brought
home in the sealskin pail, and put in the soapstone pot to
melt. Unused clothing and boots had to be put to dry on the
drying rack. Both kitchen table and igloo floor had to be
scraped clean from time to time with the ulu. Some boots
had to be softened by chewing, and the children had to be
fed and looked after.

While boys over the age of twelve were hunting seals already with the men, smaller children stayed in the camp and played outside, oblivious of the cold. Off and on they would duck inside for a bite of meat or a drink of water, or they might move their games into the dance house, filling the air with laughter. Older girls and even married women, after having watched the younger ones for some time, would suddenly jump and excitedly join the play, only to withdraw later just as abruptly and resume their work. Relatively small girls around the age of ten actively helped their mothers, some even carrying babies on their backs. Women abstained from sewing. As long as the sun was low, there was a taboo forbidding all sewing work. Around March, however, the sun moved high enough for the taboo to be relaxed, and the women were able to repair some clothing at the camp.

While the hunters were sealing, a great deal of visiting went on in camp. The large winter settlements united people who were separated the rest of the year, and were the ideal place for endless chatting and gossip. Visiting took place informally. The women, often accompanied by their small children, walked in and out of the igloos, visiting several households in succession and spending much time in each one. This went on all day until, in the evening, somebody spotted the returning hunters on the horizon and gave the call. Then the whole community came out of their igloos to scan the horizon for the hunters, trying to guess about their success.

Lively conversation greeted the hunters on their arrival. The exhausted men removed their outer clothing together with their caribou fur boots. Coats, trousers, and boots were carefully beaten with the snow beater to remove any snow remaining on the fur, then the clothing was spread to dry on top of the drying rack while the men put on short sealskin boots sufficient for walking around camp.

The evening meal followed quickly. All members of an extended family usually ate together, men and boys on one

side, women, girls, and small children on the other. Then
came the men's turn to do some visiting. Informal gatherings
took place here and there, all the events of the day were discussed, and plans for future hunts were worked out. Then,
one by one, the men withdrew to their igloos and prepared
for sleep.

During the night the igloo door was closed with a snow
block functioning as a door. When bedtime came, people
undressed completely, quickly jumped under the sleeping
skins, and slept naked with their heads toward the entrance.
The housewife was the last to go to bed, for she had to turn
down the flame on the lamp, leaving a very small flame
burning all night, and to place the *korvik*, a long chamber
pot of sealskin, on the floor within easy reach.

CAMP LIFE IN SPRING

As winter went along, gradual changes began to take
place in the environment. The days became longer, the sun
brighter and higher in the sky, so that the warmth of its
rays could be felt on the face at midday. New activities
were added to seal hunting at the breathing holes. The end
of March was the time when the seals gave birth. They did
this by digging their way through one of their breathing
holes to come onto the ice, where they opened a round little
cavern in the thick snow cover. There, beside their mother's
breathing hole, the baby seals were born, and they became
easy prey for the Netsilik hunters. Since these young seals
had not yet learned to swim, the hunters could capture them
by hand.

Some trapping of white foxes took place in the early
spring. Among the traditional Netsilik this was very much a
secondary activity, not necessarily restricted to the spring
season. The intensity of trapping generally varied with the
need for clothing skins. Although the Netsilik were ac-

quainted with several trapping techniques, they relied mostly on the stone trap, a rectangular structure of flat stones. A piece of bait was placed so as to lure the fox inside the trap, at which point the trap door was knocked into place and the animal was caught. Spring was also a good time to catch ground squirrels, and there were excellent places for catching them throughout the Netsilik country. A thin snare was hung on a short stick just over the squirrel's burrow. The hunter, lying concealed a few yards away, held the end of the line. As soon as the squirrel appeared, the hunter pulled the line and the small animal was caught by the neck.

By early May, the igloos began to be somewhat uncomfortable. With the warming up of the weather there was sporadic dripping from the ceiling. Dampness inside the igloo increased, making the sleeping skins wet. As new igloos were built later in the season, their domes were made progressively higher and more pointed to prevent them from collapsing. Most families finally did away with the ceilings altogether and covered their igloo walls with a sealskin tent sheet. This structure, half igloo-half tent, was called a *karmaq*. Although it eliminated dripping, it was dark and remained somewhat damp.

As the weather warmed up and the snow began to melt, sledge travel became more difficult. The ice patina on the runners did not last long enough, and the peat shoeing began to wear away, leaving dark traces on the snow. The sledges sank in the softening snow, and dragging them forward required exhausting efforts. Under these conditions, the Netsilik sometimes added ice "skis" to the runners. Long blocks of fresh-water ice were cut and trimmed down to a suitable size and thickness and then glued to the runners with wet snow. This was done on cold nights and allowed for smoother sledging for a day or so. Then the sealskin runners gave out and started melting. At this point, sledging had to be abandoned altogether. Bearskins or the skins of

the large bearded seal with the hair outside were loaded
with material, folded up all around, and tied up with thongs
on top and were pulled by dogs and men to replace the
sledges.

Around the end of May or beginning of June the people
abandoned their *karmaq* on the sea ice and moved onto
firm land, setting tent camps either on the mainland coast
or on the islands. The days now were very long and the sun
practically never set beneath the horizon. The snow cover
was melting very fast and patches of bare tundra began to
appear. Gradually the sea ice became covered with shallow
ponds of melted snow and ice. Long cracks of varying width
cut across the ice. The seals' breathing holes were now laid
bare and the water accumulating on top of the melting ice
passed through them in a whirl. The migratory caribou and
sea gulls came, and hares, lemmings, and ground squirrels
ran about in the open, basking in the sun. Now the seals
came out onto the ice through their breathing holes early
in the morning and lay there for most of the long day.

This was the season of the most intensive and profitable
seal hunting. The increased game returns reduced the necessity of large winter concentrations of seal hunters. The
winter settlements broke up into smaller groups of twenty
to fifty people, scattered over wide areas, with each group
moving in the direction of its summer fishing and hunting
grounds. From these coastal camps the hunters could span
a large hunting territory.

Spring sealing, called *maulerktoq*, differed in several ways
from midwinter hunting. It was still conducted collectively
at the breathing holes with harpoons, but in a much simpler
fashion. Without the snow cover, the large open breathing
holes were easily visible and neither dogs nor seal indicators
were necessary. Women and children armed with sticks
came out to help the hunters, stationing themselves at those
breathing holes that the hunters could not cover. When a
seal came to breathe at a hole watched by a woman or child,

it would be chased back under water. Since the seal was unable to stay under the ice indefinitely, it had to surface at another hole nearby, where a sealer's harpoon was likely to be waiting for it. The seal was then pulled out and quickly dispatched with a fist blow on its skull. After several seals had been killed at one cluster of breathing holes, the party, including women and children, moved to another hunting area and repeated the operation. The small number of hunters was compensated for by the participation of women and children. Since breathing holes were easily found and the days were long and the weather mild, spring sealing could be conducted with relatively little hardship for long periods.

Two other seal-hunting techniques were employed in spring. *Sivuliksiroq* was an individualistic variant of the collective spring sealing technique. It took place at night, in the twilight of the never-setting sun, and exploited a peculiar habit of the seal. Shortly before midnight the seal slipped through his breathing hole into the water, then always returned to the ice through the same hole early the next morning. Taking advantage of this never-changing habit, the hunter searched the ice late in the evening for a seal lying near his breathing hole. When the seal went into the water, the hunter moved to the breathing hole, spread a piece of bearskin to lie on, and waited for the relatively certain emergence of the seal. When the animal arrived early in the morning, he was waiting. He harpooned it and dragged it out.

Auktoq, or stalking the seal, was also an individualistic seal-hunting technique. It was a difficult method requiring special skills and was not practiced extensively by the Netsilik, except by some hunters who were very good at it. The hunter first spotted a seal basking in the sun, and from a safe distance, usually behind some broken shore ice, prepared for the hunt. Under his arm and left buttock he attached pieces of polar-bear skin to protect him from the melting ice he was to lie on. On his right arm he carried the harpoon and the snow knife, while his eyes were protected from the reflections of the glaring sun or snow and ice by snow goggles.

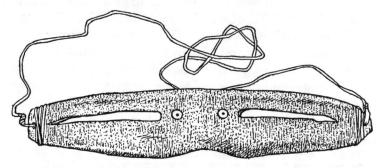

Figure 35   Snow Goggles

After having tested the wind direction, the hunter started his approach, first crouching low and then lying flat on his left side. He slowly dragged himself toward the seal, trying to look like another seal by imitating its movements and sounds. The seal took short naps (a minute or so), after which he lifted up his head, looked around, and occasionally moved his back flippers. The hunter watched every movement of the seal. As soon as the seal put his head down to sleep the hunter crawled a few feet ahead. When the seal's head came up, the hunter at first lay motionless, his head down, pretending he was asleep. Then he raised his head and lifted his right leg, in imitation of the seal's hind flippers. With the snow knife he scratched the ice as if a seal's claws were making the noise and skillfully imitated the deep cry of the seal. Then he advanced a few more feet.

This was a long process taking over an hour, during which the hunter could easily get soaking wet. It was essential that the ice be firm for this kind of hunting, since overly wet ice was too difficult to cross without good waterproof clothing. Also a few inches of water over the thick sea ice sometimes froze during the cold nights with a thin crust of ice. Breaking this layer of ice was very annoying, since it both aroused the suspicion of the seal and hampered the advance of the hunters (see plate 12).

With good ice and wind conditions the expert hunter could get to a distance of fifteen to twenty feet from the seal. Then he suddenly jumped and with raised harpoon ran as fast as he could to the seal and thrust his weapon. This was the crucial period when seconds counted. Unless the hunter was very fast and sure of his shot, the seal might manage to escape through its breathing hole in time.

A curious method for catching the large bearded seal was practiced occasionally by the western Netsilik at Queen Maud's sea. This was a collective hunt and involved bewildering the animal as it lay on the ice. A number of hunters approached the big seal cautiously, as if preparing to stalk it. But at a distance of a hundred yards or less they all jumped and screamed wildly and rushed at the seal, which was generally so stupefied and terrified by the noise that it could not move but remained paralyzed on the ice until harpooned.

Spring sealing generally yielded an abundant catch of seals. This was one of the most productive seasons for the Netsilik. With the exception of the bones, the whole of the seal was utilized. The skins were dressed by the women for various purposes, the meat was eaten and the blood drunk, the intestines were plaited in long lines, hung up to dry, and eaten as a delicacy. Almost all of the blubber was saved and cached for use the following winter. It was stored in a sealskin that was specially prepared for the purpose. The whole of a large sealskin was carefully removed from the seal as if the animal were being undressed. The skin was then turned inside out, and the few holes in it neatly sewn up. This sealskin bag with the hair inside was filled with blubber, tied strongly with a thong, and cached under a heap of stones. Slowly the blubber melted inside and changed into oil, ready for use in the soapstone lamp the following year. Often a family would fill four or five such bags in the spring.

In certain areas some other subsistence activities took place, preceding or co-existing with spring sealing. Among the western Netsilik cod fishing was sometimes an important occupation, though not necessarily restricted to the spring season. In case of failure in the winter seal hunts, cod were fished as emergency food. Holes were dug through the sea ice at places known to be good for cod fishing, and jigging was carried on with a large barbless hook inserted in a bone sinker. A small decoy was sometimes added, but bait was never used. The fishing line was of plaited sinew fastened to a curved reel of antler. In late spring when narrow cracks cut through the sea ice, little boys were often to be seen jigging for cod near camp.

Another subsistence activity was catching sea gulls and

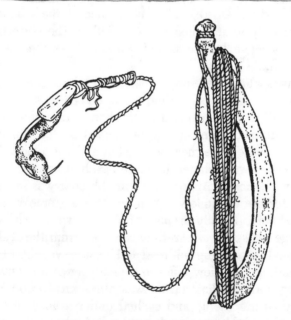

Figure 36   Fish Hook with Reel

collecting their eggs. This took place only at certain localities where the sea gulls were in the habit of nesting. These nests were hidden high in the crags of vertical cliffs, out of reach of predators. The hunters were very skillful in climbing these cliffs, and in a short time were able to fill their coats' hoods with eggs.

For catching the sea gulls themselves, two devices were used: short gorges (which have been already described), and little igloo-like constructions that were set near the nesting cliffs. These sea gull traps were round, made of snow blocks, and high enough for a man to sit inside in a crouched position. The center of the ceiling was particularly thin, and over it the hunter placed some seal liver as bait. Whenever a sea gull came to gulp the bait, the trapper below pushed his hand through the ceiling and grabbed the gull by the legs. The operation could be repeated many times. Both eggs and sea gulls were boiled in the pot over a heather fire and then eaten.

After a long winter season the people became weary of their constant seal-meat diet and occasionally some families would decide to fish inland for lake trout. They did this prior to the intensive spring sealing. Their belongings were packed in a bearskin and dragged slowly behind them to their destination, where a karmaq was erected, and fishing began early the following day. The good, promising spots were well known, and it was there that holes were dug through the thick lake ice. This was a man's task, performed with his ice pick and the long-handled ice scoop. All the ice chips cut with the ice pick were removed with the scoop until the water level was reached. Then, after building a small windbreak out of snow blocks, they started digging. The iron hook used for this was barbless and small, and a bait of fishskin and meat was used. Since the hook was barbless, it had to be pulled up quickly when a trout came along and took the bait. Both men and women jigged actively, oblivious to changing weather and snowstorms. Such fishing expeditions lasted usually a few days only and were often very rewarding.

At the beginning of July, sealing came to an end and the people who were staying on the islands moved hastily to the mainland before the wet sea ice broke up. This terminated the winter phase of the annual migration cycle and marked the beginning of the transitional period of preparation for the summer life inland, which was described at the beginning of the chapter.

It can be seen that, though the annual migration cycle of the Netsilik was based on two primary phases—the winter on the sea ice hunting seals, the summer inland fishing and hunting caribou—transitions between the marine and the inland phases were not abrupt. The passage from one to the other was accomplished gradually, with many technological characteristics of one season's activities being carried over to the next with some modifications and additions. Spring sealing is a case in point. Hunting seals with harpoons at the breathing holes was a characteristic midwinter activity associated with igloo life on the sea ice. In spring a much simplified harpooning of seals still took place, but from tent settlements established on the firm land. The seal-hunting complex was thus carried over into spring, when it became associated with some summer elements. Furthermore, there were traits specific to the transitional phases: karmaq, ice-houses, bearskins used for sledging, etc.; but the existence of these transitional forms did not blur the basic marine-inland dichotomy of the Netsilik annual cycle.

Game, both migratory and resident, was somewhat unevenly distributed throughout the Netsilik area. Musk oxen were hunted profitably only by the eastern Netsilik. Cod was abundant primarily in the western bays and straits of the country, while caribou availability was maximal in the area of Boothia Isthmus. As for salmon trout fishing, the Pelly Bay Eskimos were in the best location. This indicates that even within a single tribal area such as the Netsilik one, each subgroup exploring the resources of a particular region must have evolved specific and somewhat differentiated patterns of ecological adaptation. It is probable that the people around Boothia Isthmus acquired over 50 per cent of their subsistence from hunting caribou and seals, with fishing correspondingly less important, while the reverse was true for the people of Pelly Bay.

After studying the Netsilik hunters, one might think that their constant and intensive efforts, involving the use of so many ingenious hunting techniques and adaptive strategies, would result in abundant and regular game returns, but this was hardly the case. At the winter settlement of Kuggup Pamiut in Shepherd Bay, Rasmussen conducted a detailed survey of the local sealing results. This village of thirty-one persons counted twelve hunters who, for the whole of the winter season, had caught about 150 seals. Assuming that winter hunting started in January and ended in May, for a period of five months the yield was one seal a day. A ringed seal in those regions weighs on the average sixty pounds. With bones and skin amounting to over ten pounds, about fifty pounds consisting of meat, blubber, blood, and intestines could be considered food. Thus there was a share of slightly less than two pounds of edible seal meat per person per day. With about one third of the community consisting of children, the share of the adults was correspondingly larger, but on the other hand, substantial amounts of blubber were used in the lamp, and the thirty dogs in the community had to be fed out of the seal as well. "As the result of a whole winter's hunting in all kinds of weather this may well be said to have been dearly bought food . . ." (Rasmussen 1931:153).

Rasmussen's data on caribou returns are much less reliable, since the great caribou hunts he observed at the southern tip of King William Island were carried out with guns. But judging from the drawings of Eskimos made during Ross's journey across Boothia Felix, a number of people

used bear and fox skins as substitutes for caribou fur clothing, clearly indicating that the Netsilik were not always able
to kill enough caribou to cover even their elementary needs
for winter clothing.

The Netsilik, then, were far from living in a land of plenty.
The migratory life described in this chapter was a very harsh
one, requiring tremendous adaptive abilities on the part of
these people to stay alive at all. Probably all the technological and ecological adaptive patterns described so far would
not have been enough to ensure the Netsilik's survival without a similar evolution of adaptive social forms, and these
forms are the subject that we will consider next.

Part II / MAN AND SOCIETY:

Social Collaboration

3 KINSHIP AND THE NUCLEAR FAMILY

Reconstructing the past social life of the Netsilik Eskimos is a considerably more arduous task than reconstructing their annual migration cycle and its related activities. It is obvious that the explorers and travelers who associated intimately with the igloo dwellers were not trained to observe and record in detailed manner either the repetitive character or the more fluid aspects of everyday interpersonal relations. They conceived of the daily routines of the Eskimos as a succession of work tasks different for men and women. This perspective naturally stressed the relationship between humans and objects and neglected the relations existing among the people themselves. But, as was common for European travelers in exotic countries, curious social patterns and extraordinary events such as wife exchange and polygyny, murders and fights, inevitably did attract their attention and were described in some detail in their travelogues. Any reader of these works should be aware of this lure of the sensational which often distorted the real social situation existing among the Netsilik.

Judicious analysis of much of this case material actually reveals patterns of relatively normal behavior. Furthermore, elderly informants today vividly remember the various customs which ruled interpersonal relations within and outside the family. And when biographical material of major informants is added to this verbal information recently recorded in the field, a general, accurate picture of Netsilik social organization can be pieced together. This is presented in Parts II and III. Part II describes the various social forms and alignments, often supported by precise rules, which had integrative functions and contributed to social cohesion. Kinship, of course, constituted a vitally important network of ties, giving rise to familial units and more extended alignments. But unlike some other primitive societies, it would be wrong to consider kinship as the sole or even principal basis of social organization among the Netsilik.

Transcending kinship and collaboration, the functioning of a number of patterned dyadic relationships may be considered an important supplementary network of social bonds, made especially valuable since Netsilik society lacked unilineal descent features. These formal relationships involved two persons either in isolation or in clusters of pairs and entered into many spheres of social life: meat-sharing partnership involving food distribution, wife lending in connection with the circulation of women, song partnerships expressive of sociability, wrestling partnerships linked to the prestige structure within society, etc. There are thus three main factors: kinship, collaboration in the field of subsistence, and patterned dyadic relationships, which brought people together and integrated society.

In chapters 3, 4, and 5, I shall describe the Netsilik kinship system as well as their basic kinship units. In doing so, I shall consider only their normative aspects, as if all their mechanisms functioned properly and no deviations ever took place. In other words I shall first portray the Netsilik as they ought "ideally" to have related toward their kinsmen and not as they actually did.

In the analysis of kinship systems, two complementary lines of investigation are generally followed. The first analyzes the various terms relatives use to identify each other. This is the kinship terminology. These linguistic usages are essential for understanding the social relations between kinsmen. The second line of investigation traces the actual patterns of behavior exhibited by close or distant relatives in contact with each other. The acting out of kinship roles is such a vast and important subject that an effort will be made here to emphasize this topic over purely formal analysis of kinship nomenclature.

Because of a peculiarly Netsilik preference for marrying

relatives and the resulting high degree of inbreeding, there was a considerable overlapping of kin categories (two relatives might be connected in various ways and thus name each other differently). (Further, the habit of marrying relatives, particularly cousins, led to the superimposition of affinal terms (denoting relations by marriage) to certain consanguines (blood relatives).) The existence of these double relationships can be particularly confusing to the field worker. Netsilik kinship terminology is highly complex. A detailed analysis of the terminology, therefore, was not attempted. Instead, only an outline of the general features of this system appears below.

The following pattern will serve to show the variations of kin terminology applicable to consanguinity (blood relationships) and to affinity (marriage relationships). In referring to consanguineal relatives, the speaker (ego) may distinguish those who are his contemporaries from those who are of an earlier generation (ascending generation) and those of a later generation (descending generation). It is well to note that if ego (the speaker) is female, there are significant variations. Similarly there is a wide variation in terminology for relationships acquired through marriage. The range accentuates the widespread character of the varied degrees of kindred.

CONSANGUINEAL RELATIVES

Ego's generation	*Male speaking*
elder brother	*angayoq*
younger brother	*nuka*
older sister	*aliga, naya*

Aliga is used among the western Netsilik, *Naya* seems preferred in the eastern area.

younger sister	*naya*
cousin in general	*idloq*

More specifically, *Idloq* applies to
cousins of the same sex. For cousins of
the opposite sex, sibling terms are
listed. Among the eastern Netsilik
cousins can also be named according
to the sex of their parents. The
children, male and female, of two
brothers were called *angutekattigeq*,
while the children, male and female,
of two sisters were known as
arnakattigeq.

Ego's generation	*Female speaking*
elder brother	*ani*
younger brother	*ani*
elder sister	*angayoq*
younger sister	*nuka*

Cousin terms similar to those used
by male speakers.

First ascending generation	*Both sexes*
father	*atata*
mother	*anana*
father's brother, father's sister's husband	*akka*
father's sister, father's brother's wife, mother's brother's wife	*atsa*
mother's brother, mother's sister's husband	*anga*
mother's sister	*arnarviq*

The terms for both parents' siblings
may be extended to collaterals of the
same generation.

Second ascending generation	*Both sexes*
father's father, mother's father	*iktoq*
father's mother, mother's mother	*ningio*

Both terms are extended to their siblings.

Third ascending generation	*Both sexes*
all ancestors of that generation, regardless of sex	*amaoq*
First descending generation	*Both sexes*
son	*irnik*
daughter	*panik*
	Male speaking
brother's children, regardless of sex	*kangia*
sister's children, regardless of sex	*uyoroq*
	Female speaking
brother's children, regardless of sex	*anga*
sister's children, regardless of sex	*norrak*
Second descending generation	*Both sexes*
all grandchildren, regardless of sex *irngutak* can be extended to descendants of nephews.	*irngutak*
Third descending generation	*Both sexes*
all great grandchildren, regardless of sex	*amaoq*

AFFINAL KIN

	Male speaking
wife	*nuliak*
wife's sister, brother's wife, cousin's wife, and, in general, an affinally related female of ego's generation	*ai*
sister's husband, daughter's husband,	

cousin's husband and, in general, an affinally related male	*ningao*
wife's brother	*sakia*
wife's father and mother	*saki*
wife's younger sister's husband	*nukangor*
wife's elder sister's husband	*angayungoq*
son's wife	*ukua*

	Female speaking
husband	*ui*
husband's brother, sister's husband, cousin's husband and, in general, affinally related male of ego's generation	*ai*
brother's wife, cousin's wife, son's wife and, in general, an affinally related female	*ukua*
husband's sister	*sakia*

The terms *sakia, nukangoq,* and *angayungoq* were used similarly as for male speaking only for the opposite sex. Terms for more distant affines carried the suffix wa, thus the siblings of a husband's parents were called *sakiwa,* a niece's husband became *ningauwa,* etc.

Let us now examine whether this system of kinship terms can be related to some essential features of Netsilik social organization. The items to be examined in this connection are: the great importance of both the nuclear and extended families as basic kinship units, the prevalence of patrilocal residence, age as a factor determining superordinate-subordinate relations, the solidarity of persons of the same sex, and the preference for marrying cousins.

Specific kinship terms were applied to the different members of the nuclear family, which was thus terminologically distinguished from the wider circle of relatives. Individual kinship terms, reflecting the factors of age and sex, were applied to siblings. The terms for mother and father, daughter and son were never extended to collateral kin, with one important exception being the extension of sibling names to cousins of the opposite sex, girls calling male cousins "brother" and boys calling female cousins "sister."

Though terminological differentiation was maximal within the nuclear family, it also applied to the extended family, notably at the first ascending generation where paternal and maternal uncles and aunts were distinguished from each other. This particular feature is expressive of the considerable importance of the uncle-nephew relationship. ✳ Normally, under patrilocal residence, a boy lived with his father and father's brother, the two forming the core of an extended family. The boy, by virtue of common residence, had ample opportunity to develop a very close relationship with his paternal uncle. It was not surprising then for the nephew to call his paternal uncle by a distinct kinship term, thus recognizing his social importance.

The Netsilik pattern of residence however was flexible, and for a variety of reasons, including environmental uncertainty, a young man could establish residence with his maternal uncle or stay with any one of his aunts. These were very close relatives of his and he could rightfully expect help from them. These vital bonds were reflected in the kinship terminology by the existence of distinct kinship terms for uncles and aunts.

✳ Age was another factor which structured behavior between kinsmen. Within the extended family a hierarchy of domination and subordination was maintained, and older True persons were accorded obedience and respect. Again this in was reflected in the kinship terminology by separate terms many being given to blood relatives of different generations. It Cultures was similarly recognized at the sibling level, where an important distinction was made between elder brother and

sister and younger brother and sister. Age also determined
the naming of people related through marriage. This was
especially true for individuals married to siblings of an individual's spouse who were ranked according to the age of
the siblings themselves (within the same generation). Thus
a wife of one brother referred to the wife of an older brother
as *angayungoq,* while calling the wife of a younger brother
nukangor. These two terms were similarly used by male
speakers only for the opposite sex. Whether a wife lived
with her husband's relatives, as was normally the case, or
whether occasionally a husband joined his wife's camp, the
system incorporated the individual into the extended family, relating him specifically to other affines of the same
generation living in the kinship unit.

Sex influenced terminology in many ways, one of which
affected the classification of parallel cousins (descendants
of same-sexed siblings). Ties between brothers were very
close, as were those between sisters. Descendants of the
latter, whether boys, boys and girls, or only girls, were
called together *arnakattigeq,* while similarly descendants of
brothers were termed *angutekattigeq.*

Sex was equally as important in naming affines or additions to the family by marriage. Most people who married
into an extended family were classified simply into one of
two categories: *ningao* for the man, *ai* for the woman (male
speaking); *ai* for the man, *ukua* for the woman (female
speaking). This lumping together of several affines separated the sphere of affinity from the sphere of consanguinity,
which was characterized by its greater differentiation of kin.

The Netsilik preference for marrying cousins, including
first cousins, was not reflected in the kinship terminology.
All cousins were considered relatives, and although some
were closer than others, none was excluded from the sphere
of consanguines. In most other Eskimo groups cousin marriage was forbidden as incestuous. The Netsilik were almost
unique in this respect. This was the only case of dishar-

mony between the kinship terminology and a basic feature of Netsilik social organization, resulting in a curious overlapping of names. Thus a female cousin who was named "sister" following the extension of sibling terms to a cross-sexed cousin was called either "wife" or "sister" after marriage.

A few additional comments should be made concerning the extension of kinship terms on a broader basis. At the third ascending and descending generations considerable lumping together took place. This can be explained by the fact that at the period when an individual reached adulthood, few of his grandfather's generation were living. Therefore there was no social reason to differentiate among such a restricted class of relatives. Similarly as for the grandchildren, all stood in identical social relationship to their grandfather so that he had no reason to distinguish among them.

Finally we must ask why certain kinship terms such as those for aunts and uncles were extended to collaterals, and why distant relatives were considered as cousins. The answer is found in the nomadic habits of the Netsilik. Frequently a man or his family had to take long trips and risk meeting strange people in distant settlements. Since travelers were thought to be dangerous, possibly carrying evil spirits, they were often at the mercy of their hosts. The best way for a traveler to secure the co-operation of the community was for him to establish kinship links with one of the people. Under such circumstances, kinship extensions were invaluable, for in a hostile land they widened the area of social security of the individual.

THE NUCLEAR FAMILY

 The nuclear family, consisting of the father, mother, and children, was the most important social unit among the Netsilik Eskimos. It was characterized by continuous co-residence, sexual division of labor between the spouses in various technological activities, sexual intimacy between husband and wife, and child rearing. The nuclear family was not completely independent in the accomplishment of many of these important functions, but had to align itself continuously with other families, closely or distantly related, to become part of larger social groupings. Sometimes such wider alignments were determined by the inexorable necessity of collaboration in hunting. On other occasions the interplay of personal preferences and interests brought people together or separated them; but only very rarely was the unity of the nuclear family threatened by such shifting alignments.

The husband-wife bond was the basic relationship upon which the nuclear family was founded. Girls married at an early age, at fourteen or fifteen years. Traditionally it was a rare occurrence to see single girls past that age. Boys married later, usually around the age of twenty, when they were able to support a wife. This involved not only the acquisition of the varied hunting techniques but, more important, a knowledge of the habits and distribution of the game in the varied areas they inhabited. A long apprenticeship was necessary for these purposes.

A very necessary tradition — Traditionally after marriage the young wife would move to her husband's house and remain there permanently. Patrilocality was motivated by factors specific to the hunting way of life. It was essential for the young man to remain near the hunting grounds he was intimately acquainted with and where his hunting companions resided. For him to move to another more distant community would have meant undergoing a new period of apprenticeship in a different hunting area, and this was not considered necessary at his age. There were, however, accepted alternatives to the rule of patrilocality. In cases where a father had only daughters and badly needed a young helper and collaborator in his household, the young husband was permitted to take matrilocal residence. Orphans and "poor" boys often found themselves in such situations, and came to rely heavily on their father-in-law for instruction and help.

No particular marriage ceremony existed among the Netsilik. The girl simply took her belongings and moved to her husband's household. From then on co-residence was practically continuous, interrupted temporarily only by the hunter's longer expeditions and occasional wife-exchange practices. In time, numerous factors contributed to the emergence of a strong bond of affection and interdependence between the spouses. One was the importance of sex. Although intercourse was permitted outside of marriage, it was usually within marriage that adults most frequently found sexual enjoyment. There were no prohibitions against the exercise of marital sexuality, except during a brief period following childbirth, nor were there limits on the frequency of intercourse.

Another factor which strengthened the marital bond was co-operation through division of labor. The marital alignment was the basic collaborative unit in Netsilik society. The husband hunted and fished, brought the food home, made all the weapons and tools, including his wife's, constructed the snowhouse, fed the dogs, butchered the caribou, etc. Occasionally he helped his wife with the heavy task of scraping the caribou skins. Generally any work connected with snow and ice, bone and antler, wood and stone was done by the husband. But in relation to the subsistence activities which took place away in the hunting grounds, the technical tasks performed by the man within or near the household took relatively little of his time.

The woman worked at home: she butchered seals, cleaned fish, cooked the meat, cared for the wick fire, and was responsible for all kitchen activities, including the melting of ice for drinking water. She helped her husband with the construction of the igloo by laying over it a thick snow

cover with her shovel, or by loading the sledge and harness-
ing the dogs. On the migration trail she showed the way to
the dogs and pulled the sledge whenever necessary. But it
was her skin work that was most helpful to her husband.
She scraped, cut, dried, cleaned, and washed the various
kinds of skins, sewed all clothes and boots, made tents and
skin containers, covered kayaks. She softened the boots,
dried the clothes, and looked after the sleeping skins.
Clearly the wife's work was as essential to the well-being
and survival of the family as was the husband's.

It is in relation to this sexual division of labor that the
ownership of material possessions can best be understood.
The wife owned all the tools and utensils she used: the
semilunar knife, various skin scrapers and combs, the needlecase, and the precious soapstone lamp and pot. The
husband had his own snow knife, cutting knife, tool kit,
hunting weapons, fishing gear, and kayak. The male and female technical tasks were so rigorously complementary,
however, that these ownership rights, albeit individual, had
meaning only when they were functioning together as one
economic unit.

The marital bond was of course further strengthened by
the presence of offspring. Like all other Eskimo tribes, the
Netsilik were extremely devoted to their children. Family
life or, better, adulthood, acquired a deeper meaning only
in reference to procreation. It would be wrong to assume
that children—especially boys—were desired only as future
helpers of their aged parents. On the contrary, children at
all ages were an endless source of joy to their parents, despite the sacrifices that their rearing entailed.

Until his young son or daughter reached the age of five or
six, the behavior of a father was identical toward them.
When a newborn infant was in the mother's *amautaq* the
father played fondly with it, holding its arms and caressing
its cheeks while gently talking and teasing the infant with
the hope of provoking a smile. Sometimes the father would

hold the baby himself. After the age of three or four body contact gradually diminished, while the playful relationship involving slight teasing continued. The father made some of the toys his children played with, such as ice toys or spinning toys of bone.

After the age of four or five the father-son relationship grew more intense. The boy watched his father at work, patiently and silently, observing each gesture. The father continued to make various toys, often miniature models of weapons and other articles of the material culture like sleds. With these the boy actively imitated the adult hunter's postures. A father might even set up sea gull snares for his small son in order for him to play with the bird. Learning proceeded exclusively through observation and imitation; no formal teaching whatsoever took place.

By the time he was ten or eleven, the boy had become his father's helper. On the migration track, he no longer sat on the sledge, but tried to push and pull with the others. He accompanied his father on hunting and fishing trips, performing various light but useful tasks. He rarely asked questions. Instead his father would briefly instruct him before or after a task, when necessary. This always took place in context and in reference to the particular situation at hand. During adolescence the authority of the father remained very strong, and the boy undertook no hunting trips on his own or without his father's approval. His attitude was one of complete submissiveness. It was only very gradually that the son acquired autonomy of action.

Relations between father and daughter lacked this intimacy and, of course, engaged in none of the collaborative aspects of the father-son tie. Female infants were treated by their fathers very much like their male siblings of similar age. The same playful interaction occurred, followed by respectful submissiveness and reserve, bordering on avoidance. At all times girls past eight or nine years of age tried to be helpful to their fathers in small matters such as hand-

ing over an object to the father when asked to do so, etc.
The mother-daughter relationship was much more significant.

The mother had the primary responsibility for the rearing
of her children. She generally breast fed them, although she
also used the mouth-to-mouth technique whenever necessary. Infants were fed whenever they were restless, crying,
or otherwise seemed to desire food. Feeding was not necessarily prolonged, but it was quite frequent and was provoked by the infant. The baby was deftly manipulated
under the mother's large coat. The mother toilet-trained the
child, using a piece of old fur skin or dry moss. The child
remained most of the day in the mother's *amautaq*, and at
night it slept on the bed right beside the mother. Contact
with the mother's body was practically uninterrupted during the first two years, the infant benefiting by constant attention and affection.

As the offspring grew up and became capable of performing some useful functions, a marked difference in behavior
separated boy and girl in their relations with their mother.
In some cases, notably when the five- or six-year-old son
was the last offspring of a middle-aged couple, he took extraordinary liberties with his mother. In his informal play-
acting he frequently disturbed his mother's work by pulling
her hair or climbing on her back when she was in a sitting
position, or falling on her lap despite her being busy with
some handwork. Such playful behavior, although obviously
distracting or annoying, provoked practically no repri-
mand. Occasionally the boy acted similarly with his father,
although with more restraint. The parents' permissiveness,
marked by lack of bodily punishment or even scolding, was
very characteristic. The small boy behaved like an all-
powerful being, doing as he pleased. The parents' anger
was provoked only when valuable objects were broken.
Occasionally, however, they engaged in teasing and slightly

deriding the boy, and mocking came increasingly to be a disciplinary strategy.

No such freedom of behavior was allowed young girls. Already at the age of seven or eight a girl began to interrupt her play in order to participate in her mother's activities. First she collaborated with the mother, accompanying her while cutting fresh ice, getting water, or gathering moss. Gradually she began to perform many of the women's tasks by herself whenever asked to do so by her mother. Soon her functions as household helper became very important. Often young girls were seen carrying infant siblings on their backs. Sewing and skin work were learned somewhat later. After a girl reached the age of eleven or twelve, just as father and son began to collaborate closely, so mother and daughter worked on similar tasks.

Relations between young brothers were characterized by restrained affection and respect. However if age did not separate them greatly, they played together without displaying much competitiveness or jealousy. If they belonged to different age groups they associated more rarely, preferring to play with their age mates. As they grew, they increasingly collaborated and worked together, either with their father or by themselves. A patterned division of tasks existed during such co-operation, the older brother assuming initiative and decision-making, and the younger respectfully obeying.

Relations between young sisters were much more intimate and playful. They talked much more freely to each other, giggling and joking, and were very expressive of their affection. This closeness of sisters was expressed both at play and at work.

In contrast, relations between siblings of the opposite sex were marked by considerable respect, reserve, and distance. As was mentioned previously, older sisters fondled their infant brothers and took motherly care of them. Yet when they reached puberty and adolescence they avoided each

other somewhat, even though their different spheres of activity and interests separated them naturally.

Adoption was a common practice among the Netsilik,
motivated by several complex demographic factors to be
discussed later. Let us note here, however, that within the
family the position of adopted children, boys or girls, was
exactly that of natural children. Parents called adopted
children *tiguak*, while the latter addressed their adoptive
father as *angutiksak* and the adoptive mother as *arnuaksak*.
For all the other relatives, whether consanguineal or affinal,
adopted children used the usual terminology, only adding
the suffix *sak*. Adopted infants were acquired for a variable
price soon after birth, the mother having no interest in nursing a child she was to give away. If the adoptive mother
had no milk, mouth-to-mouth feeding of caribou or seal
soup was practiced. Parents behaved toward an adopted
child exactly in the same manner as toward their own
offspring, giving him the same care and affection. Consequently in later years, although an adopted child recognized his genitors, his loyalty was almost exclusively
directed toward his adoptive parents.

In sum, the presence of children, whether natural or
adopted, united parents closely and further strengthened
the marital bond. The children were never separated from
their parents for any length of time. They grew up in close
association with the adult world, free to observe and imitate
their parents. They became conscious of the respective roles
of each parent early, as adult activities were easily visible
and there was nothing hidden in the igloo.

The upbringing of small children was characterized by
consistent permissiveness, yet there was one activity which
was rigidly controlled, and that was feeding. Children did
not help themselves directly to food. Of course whenever
they asked for some they were always gratified, yet it was
their mother who had to hand them the actual food itself.
If a child was given some food in a neighboring igloo, he

had first to bring it to his mother and then take it only from her. Thus at an early age the child learned that meat was an important thing he could not have access to directly, that others had to intervene in its distribution, and that food was a vital matter of collective concern.

These brief descriptions of interpersonal relations reveal certain patterns of authority within the family. The father was the recognized head of the family, responsible for all major decisions, essentially those involving family location and movement. He did not interfere in his wife's sphere of activity; there she enjoyed considerable autonomy. And there are cases, to be described later on, indicating that a wife could successfully influence her husband in practically any decision. A husband very often took notice of his wife's desires. Personality factors were highly important in the decision-making process and the application of authority or influence. The authority patterns within the nuclear family expressed sex and age factors: the husband was in a superordinate position in relation to his wife, and younger siblings were submissive to the older ones.

[margin handwriting: Patriarchal society!]

4 THE EXTENDED FAMILY AND THE PERSONAL KINDRED

THE EXTENDED FAMILY

Under no circumstances could the Netsilik nuclear family survive for prolonged periods isolated by itself among the rigors of the Arctic wilderness. Doubtless there were many situations when the nuclear family labored alone, such as traveling from one camp to another, but such situations were short lived.[1] The nuclear family was always part of a larger kinship group or else contained some additional relatives. For lack of a better term, such a kinship alignment is called the *extended family*. This term is usually applied to two or more consanguineally related (blood-related) nuclear families living together as a unit. Although many similar cases could be found among the Netsilik, some extended kinship units did not correspond to this alignment of multiple nuclear families. There was great variation in the composition of extended families. Rasmussen's survey is of no great help here, because his census considers the household as the unit of analysis, without describing kinship relations between members of different households. Further, Rasmussen has not recorded any genealogical data from which the formation of extended families could be abstracted. Despite these shortcomings, the composition of some households from Rasmussen's table is presented below for illustrative purposes.

At Pelly Bay one igloo sheltered a grandfather with his wife, their married son with his spouse, and their two children. This was clearly an extended family consisting of two

---

[1] In the distribution table of the Netsilik compiled in the spring of 1923 by Rasmussen, there is not a single example of a settlement consisting solely of one family.

nuclear families with the father-son bond as the central binding link.

At Ilivileq (Adelaide Peninsula) a similar although larger alignment was found: a grandfather with his wife, with their four sons of whom two were married (one had two children, the second, one) and two single sons: eleven people altogether. Also at Ilivileq another igloo contained a husband with his wife and their daughter, together with the husband's mother and an adopted girl of hers. Here again members of three generations lived together, yet there was only a single nuclear family. We may assume that in this case it was the marital relation that constituted the basic bond. Again at Ilivileq a widower lived with his son and daughter and his elderly mother, who had adopted two boys. In this case there was no marital relation and, ignoring the age of the boys, it is impossible to make any guesses as to the internal structure of this extended family.

These examples illustrate the great variation in the composition of extended families as recorded by Rasmussen. Some of my elderly informants added the following. In the early 1920s Kringorn, a hunter from Pelly Bay, recognized as being part of his extended family: his adoptive father (in this case his paternal grandfather); his adoptive grandmother; his father and mother; four married brothers and their children; and his sister, married to an Aivilik Eskimo, who used to live in the Repulse Bay area with her husband and came to Pelly Bay occasionally. Asked to define this circle of close relatives, Kringorn answered: "These are related people who may go away but come back and then share food, help each other, and stay together."

Such a close-knit group the Netsilik call *ilagiit nang-minariit*, or my "own relatives in proper," the term *ilagiit* corresponding to the circle of relatives. Let us first briefly describe the formation process of the true extended family and then consider the variations from this basic pattern.

Preferred patrilocal residence was the main factor influencing the developmental cycle of the extended family. As a hunter's sons grew up and married, they brought their wives to stay with them. If a father had several such married sons, it was naturally impractical for all of them to reside together under the same roof. Usually only the younger married son stayed with his parents, while the older ones camped nearby in separate dwellings. An extended family thus usually occupied a cluster of snowhouses or tents and included relatives of three generations. Of course in many activities father and adult sons co-operated closely, the basic structural feature of such a closely knit kinship group being the strong link between father and sons. But as the father grew older and senile and the grandchildren were more numerous, this basic link was gradually replaced by the brother-brother bond, the elder brother acting as the functioning head of the extended family. In many cases such a horizontal bond proved to be very durable and the brothers continued to stay together, co-operate, and share.

As time went by, divisive forces of various kinds started to operate, which resulted in the splitting of this extended alignment: the death of the grandparents, personality conflicts either between the brothers or between their wives, lack of leadership qualities of the eldest brother, the determination of one of the brothers to move to a different area with allegedly better hunting prospects or where some of his wife's relatives might reside, or simply the growth of the brothers' own sons with whom they began to co-operate. Thus the brother-brother bond was replaced gradually by a new father-son link and slowly gave birth to the emergence of a new extended family. Under the rule of patrilocality, the brothers' sisters resided elsewhere with their husbands, although they might visit their brothers from time to time. A sister was always considered part of the *ilagiit nangminariit,* despite the fact that she rarely resided with her consanguineal relatives.

Although in many cases this pattern was followed closely,

there were nevertheless innumerable variations. Some fathers had only daughters and were eager to attach adult young men to their establishment as sons-in-law. These became matrilocally extended families. Some young hunters joined the families of their uncles, matrilateral or patrilateral, the nepotic bond becoming the bases of such alignments. There were also men who associated with their cousins. Thus collateral ties were preferred. Or a widower might reside with his mother and her adopted sons.

While there was a prevalent tendency for the nuclear family to associate with consanguineal relatives and in so doing to favor patrilateral extended alignments, there were occasional alternative arrangements. One important alternative was for two brothers-in-law, married to two sisters, to reside together. Brothers-in-law called each other *angayungoq-nukangor;* these were specific terms underlining the importance of the relationship. The core of such a residential unit was not the two sisters, but rather the two affinally related men. They were the providers and collaborators and they hunted and shared together. In this alignment, an affinal bond was exploited and preferred to the usual consanguineal relations.[2] A similar situation prevailed in matrilocal households where a son-in-law resided with his father-in-law, this in the absence of sons.

Co-residence was a major characteristic of the *ilagiit nangminariit.* But this was only a tendency, and there were many exceptions. At almost any season a segment of this large domestic group could separate for a variable length of time. A young wife might wish to visit her relatives in a distant area and spend some time with them, resulting in the temporary migration of her family. Or a young husband might decide to hunt in a different region where he had a very good friend, who would be at the same time his wife-exchange partner. Or subsistence strategy might necessitate

2 See also D. Damas 1963:108.

a split. Two brothers might fish salmon or trout or hunt caribou at two different points in order to distribute hunting chances more evenly. Usually however, after a period of separation, the extended family was reunited again.

The co-resident members of an *ilagiit nangminariit* cooperated closely and formed an important economic unit. The economic autonomy of the extended family among the Netsilik was most marked during the summer phase of the annual migration cycle, when it often camped alone near a stone weir or a caribou crossing place. In many such sites it was joined by another extended family, an affinally related nuclear family, or by the family of a wife-exchange partner. Group composition in summer depended on many social and environmental factors, such as the size of the extended family which constituted the core of the settlement, the resource potential of the fishing or hunting site, etc. Together the men built the stone weir, fished salmon trout with leisters, hunted caribou from kayaks, and cached the meat.

At the sealing camps in winter the extended family joined forces with other extended families. It became part of a larger group and in doing so it had to relinquish some aspects of its economic autonomy. During the cold season frequent borrowing took place among members of an *ilagiit nangminariit*. This was an important act in this part of the Arctic coast. As previously mentioned, there was very little driftwood available in the Netsilik area, and consequently very few wooden sledges were made. In addition, the scarcity of dog food obliged the Netsilik to keep very few dogs (on the average three dogs for two hunters). It was therefore essential for a hunter contemplating a distant winter journey to be able to borrow a sledge and some supplementary dogs if he didn't own enough. For such help the hunter turned to his close relatives. No payment was made for such temporary loans, but the sledge had to be returned in good order and with a new shoeing. The borrowing of smaller items, such as tools or weapons, took place in all seasons.

The vital collaborative activities of the extended family hunters were "supervised" by the family headman. He was the father of adult sons or the eldest brother, in general the eldest functioning male in the kinship group. He was referred to as *inhumataq*, or the one who thinks. In summer he gave the signal for the beginning of fishing or caribou hunting, and he decided matters pertaining to migration and camp selection. Yet all these decisions were taken informally and gently, in consultation with the other adult hunters of the extended family, involving long discussions when everyone present could freely express his opinions. In a sense the headman's task was to achieve consensus without hurting the feelings and designs of the other hunters, whose autonomy he respected. The age factor was crucial in the authority structure of the extended family, a headman having greater influence over the younger men of his kinship group than over the older ones. Additional factors could influence these hierarchical relations, such as kinship distance (more distantly related consanguines were supposed to be less submissive) and personality factors. Many cases illustrate differences between stronger and weaker headmen, and there were seasonal variations in the extent and significance of an *inhumataq's* influence. In summer his responsibilities as headman were much more apparent than in winter, when several such leaders camped together.

A case recorded recently but representing a typical situation illustrates the relationship between a strong leader and a younger follower (Steenhoven 1959:24). Akkrak was twenty-nine years old and married. Ulik, his stepfather, was the *inhumataq*. Akkrak said:

> "For hunting I usually follow Ulik . . . I request his thoughts as to far travels; for the rest I do as I please, though sometimes I consult him also for smaller affairs.

If Ulik would disapprove of a far travel planned by me,
I won't go. Such things have happened. Although I
sometimes feel a certain fear, I will go if Ulik tells me
so . . . If I have not much dog food and he tells me to
go deer hunting, even if I feel that same fear, I will go."

Initiative for consultation came frequently from the
younger man, and consequently the leader did not appear to
be giving orders. Moreover, it is evident that Akkrak, in the
example quoted, needed some encouragement and coercion
when faced with a dangerous task. Without pressure from
the leader some hunts probably would never have taken
place. In general, however, the young hunter just "follows"
explicit orders.

In the matter of food ownership and consumption the
extended family also behaved as an economic unit. As with
subsistence co-operation, this pattern was more marked in
summer than in winter. There were no extensive and rigid
rules for sharing caribou meat. Rasmussen (1931:173) men-
tions that the lucky hunter usually gave away the fat hindquarters to be shared by others while keeping for himself
the rest of the carcass including the skin and the valuable
sinews. Closely knit extended families usually kept and used
the returns of their communal hunts. Non-related or distantly related families present at the camp received nothing
or little. Whenever game was abundant, sharing among non-
relatives was avoided, since every family was supposedly
capable of obtaining the necessary catch. In situations of
scarcity, however, caribou meat was more evenly distributed
throughout camp. Any such gift giving usually took place
at the hunting site immediately after the kill.

Camp commensality was another way to share meat, essentially with people outside the extended family. After a
kill it was considered appropriate to set up a feast for all
camp fellows. When two non-related men were stalking
caribou together the lucky hunter would always give the
hindquarters to the other. At the end of the caribou-hunting

season, when time for moving camp came, the unsuccessful
hunters again received portions of caribou meat. Finally in
winter, when the band assembled at the sealing camp, the
hunter who brought a sledge load of caribou meat had to
throw a feast for all his camp fellows.

There were similarly no precise rules for the sharing of
fish caught in summer or autumn. Members of the extended
family, camping together during the seasons of intense fishing, usually made common fish caches, though this depended on the cohesion of the kinship group. If fissive
tendencies were present, individual caches were built.
Camp fellows outside the extended family fished for themselves and kept their catch, though naturally this depended
on the abundance of the salmon runs. Whenever fish was
plentiful, community-wide sharing was considered unnecessary, since any family could secure all the fish it wanted.
In times of scarcity, gifts of fish were made to the needy.
As with caribou meat, feasts of fish were organized at the
midwinter camps.

During the warm season the extended family constituted
a commensal unit as well. Although snacks could be taken
at any time of the day, bigger meals in the morning or in
the evening, essentially when the weather was good, brought
together all the members of an extended family. Two separate groups were formed then, women and children in a
circle eating together on one side, men and older boys forming another group nearby. A single piece of meat or cooked
fish circulated from hand to hand, individuals taking one
bite at a time. In winter, the extended family continued to
function as a commensal unit, but to a lesser degree.
Breathing-hole sealing had a different set of sharing rules
which tended to strengthen the economic autonomy of the
nuclear family. This pattern will be described later.

While the elderly headman co-ordinated the various
activities of the hunters, his wife was responsible for the distribution and consumption of food within the extended fam-

ily. In a sense the old woman performed the functions of a "food controller." Our informant Kringorn described this practice as follows, referring to the extended family of his grandfather in the early 1920s: "When Audladjut's sons came back from the hunt they went straight to their father's tent and brought the meat and skins to their mother. Their mother will cut the meat and give them some." Thus the young couples kept only small amounts of food in their igloos, for intermittent consumption and for their children.

In sum, during the ascending phase of its developmental cycle the extended family was organized around the centrally important bond between elderly father and adult sons. The descending phase witnessed the emergence of the somewhat weaker tie between married brothers. There were in addition two other types of relationships which, although of lesser structural significance, could and did acquire considerable functional importance. These were the ties between nephews or nieces and uncle or aunts and the relations between cousins.

By virtue of patrilocal residence the father's brother and brother's son often camped together. The nephew could observe the close association and daily co-operation between his father and uncle. He frequently and freely visited in his uncle's dwelling. The relationship was not unlike the one between father and son, although in an attenuated form: respect and obedience displayed by the nephew, warm affection accompanied by teasing exhibited by the uncle. As an adolescent boy the nephew participated in the subsistence activities of his adult kinsmen and had ample opportunities to collaborate directly with his paternal uncle. The continuation of this tie depended on the continuation of common residence, which in turn depended on the divisive process operating within the extended family. Even when a split between father and uncle took place, the nephew-uncle bond continued to be recognized, the nephew continued to visit his uncle, and if he wished he could reside with him for prolonged periods.

A similar although somewhat weaker bond prevailed between nephew and maternal uncle. The intensity of this particular kinship link depended on the residential situation. If the maternal uncle lived with his wife's brother, close ties of affection and co-operation were expected to exist between mother's brother and sister's son. This was seldom the situation, since the mother's brother usually resided elsewhere, but in any event, he was recognized as a close relative and his nephew could count on his help and protection when visiting his camp.

Bonds of affection also prevailed between a nephew and his aunts, both paternal and maternal, although aunts generally had more significant relations with their nieces, similar to those between nephews and uncles. Again this depended on common residence. Whenever the two camped together, the niece frequently visited her aunt, performing small tasks she would usually perform in relation to her mother, and she was rewarded with affectionate attention.

One of the most remarkable characteristics of the Netsilik kinship system was the extension of uncles' and aunts' terms to their spouses. Thus the term for the father's brother (*akka*) was also applied to the father's sister's husband, while the mother's brother (*anga*) and the mother's sister's husband were terminologically the same. Terminological extensions were applied also to the females of the first ascending generation: the father's sister term (*atsa*) was used to designate also the father's brother's wife and probably the mother's brother's wife. As a matter of fact, this was the only case within this generation of a term applied to relatives on both the patrilateral and the matrilateral sides. Otherwise the nomenclature clearly distinguished between the two sides.

From the point of view of the young boys and girls growing up within the extended family, these terminological ex-

Tents

Man Carrying a Load and Child

Dog Carrying a Pack

Stone Weir

FISHING AT THE STONE WEIR

ESKIMO EATING RAW FISH

ICE HUT

SKIN SLED WITH HARNESSED DOGS

MEN'S CLOTHING, FRONT

Men's Clothing, Back

WOMEN'S CLOTHING

Igloo

Eskimo Stalking Seal on the Ice

tensions meant a larger number of close consanguines at camp, numerous rewarding kinship ties, and a wider sphere of security. Later, after the extended family had split up, the adult nephew would have a number of elder kinsmen with whom he could alternatively reside and co-operate. The kinship structure provided him with a number of valuable alternatives.

Relations between cousins were no less important, often acquiring greater functional significance than the nepotic link. As a consequence of patrilocal residence, descendants of co-resident brothers grew up together and very close bonds existed among them. The children of two brothers were terminologically described as *angutekattigek,* thus specifically distinguishing the relationship. Boy cousins were much more free toward each other in their behavior than brothers. They constituted the ideal group of playmates. In their play they were joined by other, more distantly related boys of roughly similar age and ceaselessly moved around camp. Again, their activities depended on their age, slowly changing as they grew bigger. Small boys played endlessly in summer throwing rocks, chasing lemmings with sticks and stones, and striking at fish with toy leisters. The favorite pastime at the end of summer was collecting berries or playing with antler and imitating the gait of the caribou. In winter the groups of small boys continued their spontaneous games with the same energy, shooting little arrows, rolling in the drifting snow, or sliding down hills with toy sleds.

The girl cousins, together with some other more distantly related girls, also played in little groups, apart from the boys. Yet their collective games were somewhat less frequent than the boys', girls being more closely associated with their mother's unending activities and having less time to play. One of their favorite games in all seasons was to play house, and in winter they often made cooking utensils of

snow and sat down outside in a circle, imitating adult behavior. Sometimes they played hide-and-seek. The informal
groups of boys and girls usually had a leader (this was
more marked with the boys) and were of course comprised
of children of unequal age, usually between six and twelve.
Thus the younger children had the opportunity to learn
much from their older cousins within their play group, and
this in the typical Eskimo manner—through observation, collaborative performance, and imitation.

There were very few games that brought boys and girls
together. Cross-sexed cousins were called the same as
brothers and sisters, and were treated with respect and slight
avoidance. On the other hand, parallel-sexed cousins were
all called *idloq,* and it was among them that friendliness
and joking prevailed. Terms for cousins were extended to
collateral relatives, yet in behavior first cousins were recognized as such, and more intimate relations prevailed with
these. Later in life, after adulthood was reached, male cousins frequently became good camp fellows. In the absence
of siblings a man could reside on a permanent basis with
one of his cousins and become part of the latter's extended
family. Further, when living in different establishments,
cousins were in the habit of visiting each other. The friendly
and joking relationship that was initiated in childhood often
continued through life.

Relations between grandparents and grandchildren were
marked by ceaseless fondling and joking. As soon as a child
entered the dwelling of his grandparents he attracted their
attention. He was given food and immediately became the
object of loving care, mild joking, and teasing. Although he
was visibly adored by his grandparents, the child behaved
with some restraint and considerable respect. In later years,
when the grandson became an active hunter, he contributed
to the support of his grandparents, together with the other
men of the extended family.

Another important custom was the adoption of small boys
and girls by aging Netsilik women.[3]

Elderly women preferred to adopt a direct grandchild, boy or girl, or a small nephew. They referred to the child as their "walking stick," implying that when they reached the age of senility, the young adopted boy, by then a hunter, would provide for them. In case of a girl, her adoptive grandmother could expect one day to reside with her and live on the meat brought by the girl's husband.

Within the extended family there were certain relations characterized by considerable restraint and even slight avoidance. These involved in-laws, especially the son's wife-husband's father relationship and the brother's wife-husband's brother relationship. These in-laws rarely spoke directly to each other and even in the igloo avoided sitting together. When the two nuclear families resided together the elderly father sitting at one end of the sleeping counter would turn his back slightly to his daughter-in-law sitting at the other end. While the mother frequently engaged in conversation with her daughter-in-law, the father usually abstained from entering the talk. The husband's brothers seemed not to notice the presence of their sister-in-law, rarely turning their faces in her direction. Obviously such overt restraints inhibited any possible sexual attractions.

The many functions of the extended family made it a vitally important kinship group. Within its own organization and authority structure it provided a framework for subsistence co-operation, food distribution, and food consumption. The fact that consanguineal terms were given to the spouses of uncles and aunts, and sibling terms extended to cross-sexed cousins made it appear as a cohesive circle of consanguines to the eyes of the children growing within it. But it was a flexible unit and at any time splits could

---

[3] In Rasmussen's census there are only two cases specifically mentioning older women. He notes that one elderly woman had adopted a young girl, while another was looking after two adopted boys. Both women were part of extended families, their sons providing for them and their adopted children. Since Rasmussen does not indicate the relative ages of the many other adoptive parents mentioned in his census, it is reasonable to assume that the practice was more frequent.

occur which might or might not have been followed by re-
union.

PERSONAL KINDRED

   The personal kindred made up the widest circle of relatives a Netsilik could name, define terminologically, and establish genealogical connections with. It included both the
nuclear family and the extended family and more besides.
This large category of people, without clear limits, was referred to as *ilagiit,* from *ila,* meaning relatives. Ideally all the
consanguineal relatives to whom an individual could apply
a kinship term fell within the range of the kindred. No distinction was made between the relatives on the mother's
side or the father's side—all were rated equally. In actuality
the reckoning of kinsmen was somewhat selective. Very distant relatives a man had never resided with and about whom
he had only heard tended to be excluded from his kindred.
Past co-residence was thus an important determining factor
of kindred composition.
   Although most affinally related (marriage-related) people were excluded, some affines, for instance, the wife's
brother, might have been included on the basis of prolonged
co-residence and close association. Also, following intermar-
riage between relatives, a number of double relationships
resulted, blurring the consanguineal-affinal boundary and
allowing for individuals considered mainly as affines to be
part of one's kindred. Thus, when Anernilik from Pelly Bay
recently drew up a list of the kinsmen he had at the time
of his marriage thirty-five years ago, he named over forty
individuals. Among these were several categories of relatives: first, a group of individuals considered as relatives
mainly through Anernilik's link as adopted son of Atgartuq,
although Atgartuq is also consanguineally related to Anernilik (this group included both of Atgartuq's parents and

Atgartuq's wife's father); second, Anernilik's own family, including some secondary relatives such as the father's father and the mother's parents; third, two affinal relatives; fourth, a class of distant cousins. Anernilik added that at the time, he had heard about some other distant relatives of his but, since he had never seen them, he couldn't mention them. Had Anernilik encountered the latter during some distant journey, undoubtedly he would have included them in his kindred. Thus we may distinguish between the actual kindred of a Netsilik, a circle of relatives with whom he had some kind of meaningful interaction in the past based on common residence, and his potential kindred, consisting of distant relatives whom he had never met but to whom genealogical links could be established.

This distinction becomes significant when we consider the functions of the kindred. First, a bilaterally extended kindred of this kind was not a group in the technical sense of the word. One's kindred never resided together; these were people living in many different localities that no one occasion brought together. Thus, such a kindred had no economic, political, or ceremonial functions of any kind; it was not a discreet social unit, but rather a category of relatives ego recognized in relation to himself and to himself alone. Lacking definite social boundaries and corporateness of any kind, kindreds were overlapping kinship categories, the kindred of the father differing from that of the son, the latter including in his kindred his mother's relatives while the father excluded them. Only the kindreds of unmarried siblings were co-extensive.

The recognition of an actual personal kindred together with its potential extensions was important to a Netsilik in two ways. First, it extended his sphere of personal security, and second, it established a group of women among whom he could select a wife.

5 COLLABORATION

In addition to kinship, the necessity to collaborate in subsistence activities and food distribution was an important
binding force in Netsilik society, bringing people together in
larger residential units and generally making for social cohesion. Collaboration is not only an objective necessity related to the technology and strategy of hunting or fishing
but a recognized behavioral norm. Steenhoven's informants
from Pelly Bay assert that no one may be excused from
hunting except in the case of bodily infirmity. This norm im-
plies the rejection by society of unproductive members and
reaffirms implicitly the necessity for joint effort. All should
hunt. The elderly Kaiaitok added that the most important
means of subsistence should be divided among the inhabitants of the settlement according to certain rules. This expresses the norm of food sharing. Collaboration therefore
covers both food procurement and food consumption, and
we can see that collaboration is deeply rooted in the Netsilik
system of behavioral norms.

Netsilik subsistence activities may be classified by the
extent and nature of collaboration they entail. First, of
course, come the purely individual activities involving the
efforts of an isolated, single individual: stalking the seal in
spring, trapping sea gulls, collecting eggs, fishing for lake
trout, some bow-and-arrow caribou hunting, etc. Second,
there are the non-simultaneous but similar activities of
people residing together, for example, autumn fishing for
salmon trout through the river ice. In this case an extended
family may camp together and every adult will have a fishing hole. The men will go back and forth fishing whenever
they desire, and no co-ordination of effort is necessary.
Third are those activities involving the co-operation of in-

dividuals in a synchronized manner without any division
of tasks. Stone-weir fishing required a group effort to build
the dam, a substantial undertaking. And it was imperative
for all present to enter the central basin simultaneously in
order to equalize fishing returns. Breathing-hole sealing in
winter was a collective activity because of the necessity to
control simultaneously the largest possible number of
breathing holes. In both cases all the members of the fishing
or hunting party performed exactly the same tasks simultaneously. Fourth, activities requiring division of labor and
co-ordination. Such was the case of caribou hunting from
kayaks, where beaters directed the caribou toward a crossing point in the lake to be ambushed by kayakers, who did
all the actual killing.

Although group activities were vastly more productive
than individual efforts, the latter constituted an important
group of alternatives, allowing people to pull themselves
out of temporarily difficult situations by individual action.
And as pointed out, collaboration was by no means limited
to the search for subsistence alone. Many technological activities involved joint efforts (covering kayaks, building
ceremonial igloos, icehouses, sealskin sledges, etc.) and co-
operation was, of course, extended to meat distribution and
consumption.

Both affinal ties and consanguineal bonds were exploited
to ensure collaboration. The important consideration was for
the hunting group to be of optimal size in order to maximize
hunting chances. The residential flexibility so characteristic of Netsilik society allowed for smaller or larger group
formations, depending on the availability of the game and
the particular hunting strategy adopted. In the case of winter sealing, which was the one situation when a kinship unit
could not provide the necessary personnel for a hunt, the
Netsilik solution was to join kinship units together. The vital
importance of sealing necessitated the co-operation of the
largest possible number of hunters. This congregation of

people gave rise to the winter camp, which constituted a socio-economic unit in its own right.

We have no accurate information regarding the average size of winter settlements in the Netsilik area for the traditional period. Rasmussen's general census of the population indicates fifty-four people around Pelly Bay, sixty-six at Boothia Isthmus, thirty-seven at Murchison River, eighty-four at Adelaide Peninsula, and eighteen at Bellot Strait. This last and very remote settlement was mainly a refuge for murderers fleeing revenge and did not represent normal conditions. Rasmussen's detailed census shows a distribution in smaller units: forty people at Pelly Bay, who were soon to be joined by a journeying group of nineteen, another sixteen people at Satoq (Simpson Peninsula), which is near Pelly Bay, twenty-eight at Kuggup Pa (outside the mouth of Murchison River), another twenty-eight at Matty Island, a very small group of twelve on an island west of Matty Island, a large community of thirty on Adelaide Peninsula, and the small community of outlaws at Bellot Strait consisting of nineteen individuals. This detailed census was taken in the spring of 1923 when midwinter conditions were probably drawing to an end and the larger communities breaking up. One should not forget that by 1923 most Netsilik owned guns and that in spring they might have preferred caribou hunting in small groups to breathing-hole sealing from large settlements. Unfortunately Rasmussen does not elaborate on that point. Further, at the beginning of this century a considerable number of Netsilik, over 160 individuals, emigrated to the coast of the Repulse Bay or even farther south to Chesterfield Inlet. These departures undoubtedly had some bearing on the relatively small size of most spring camps in Rásmussen's census.

Therefore it is safe to conclude that the large settlement of ninety people on Adelaide Peninsula was more representative of traditional winter camp size than the very small units at Satoq or Kuggup Pa. It is safe to assume that, at the end of the nineteenth century, an average winter settlement might have comprised between sixty to a hundred individuals. Considering that approximately one out of three individuals was a hunter, twenty to thirty sealers collaborated in each camp. These were large hunting parties indeed.

A winter camp was thus composed of a number of extended families. Elderly Pelly Bay informants recalled that in 1918 four extended families camped together, with a total of over twenty hunters. Despite the fact that the extended families were recognized as discreet kinship units, there were numerous kin-links relating individuals from different extended families. This did not make a single kinship unit of the winter camp, however. The extended families spent the winter together in order to co-operate in seal hunting and not because of extended kin linkages. The large winter settlement functioned both as a ceremonial unit during drum dancing and some major shamanistic performances, and as a commensal unit on festive occasions.

The need to co-operate did not necessarily exclude competition. Among the younger hunters competitive attitudes mostly related to caribou hunting were very strong. The able hunter enjoyed considerable prestige, and in suitable circumstances the men exerted themselves to the utmost. Numerous stories are told about intensely competitive relationships leading to strong jealousies. Competitive attitudes were prevalent also between older men and younger hunters. As Rasmussen states: "A hunter must take into consideration that he can only subject himself and his constitution for comparatively few years to all the strain that hunting demands. Competition is keen and if he has no very special natural gifts and enjoys no unusually good health, he need not be very old before he can no longer hold his own with the young" (1931:140). Although there were cases when violent competition gave rise to quarrels and enduring hostilities, it was not a particularly divisive factor in the community. On the contrary, display of competitive attitudes took place within established patterns of collaboration and by spurring energies contributed to strengthening them.

Independent of kinship ties and the obvious need to establish collaborative alignments in subsistence acquisition, Netsilik society developed numerous patterned dyadic relationships which bound individuals in pairs and constituted an intricate network of reciprocal ties. While some partnerships were very formal and rigid, involving specific rights and obligations which knew of no abrogation, others were somewhat more freely assumed, allowing of choice and alternatives and often considerable ambiguity. <u>Yet it seems that their over-all effect was to more closely relate generally unrelated people and to increase social cohesion both within a given camp and between distant settlements.</u>

The internal organization of the winter sealing camp is reflected by the seal-meat sharing pattern, rigidly maintained at that season. Seal-meat distribution during the dark season depended on an interlocking set of sharing partnerships involving precise and inflexible rules, described in detail by Franz Van de Velde (1956). Since the seal was butchered in accordance with the requirements of the sharing system, it is appropriate to begin by giving an account of the cutting process.

The cutting up of the seal was done by the wife of the hunter who harpooned it on the floor of their igloo. The seal was laid on its back, on top of a layer of fresh snow. First the wife cut off the front flippers with her *ulu*. Next an incision was made longitudinally from the chin to the arms, cutting skin and blubber. Then the animal was skinned, this done with particular care, so as not to damage the skin. The skin was then laid flat on the snow to serve as a plate or container. The removal of the fat layer of blubber followed, leaving the meat carcass looking particularly thin.

The carcass itself was cut longitudinally and the ribs sectioned in half, leaving the abdomen open with all the blood and intestines inside. Meat and blubber were then cut in the fourteen parts described below, each named with precision. In the sharing system, a piece of blubber went with each part of meat.

1. *Okpat* (the hind quarters): cut at the juncture of the spine and the basin. The hind flippers were not attached to it. The corresponding part of blubber was one *naark*, from the abdominal side.

2. *Taunungaitok* (signifying: up to there it is): the high part: all the left ribs with the shoulder, up to the neck. The corresponding blubber part is the *naark iglua*, from the opposite side of the abdomen.

3. *Aksatkolik* (the shoulder): a piece similar to the preceding one minus five ribs. One *awat* is the corresponding blubber part.

4. *Kusak* (the lower belly): the lower part of the spine with the second and third vertebrae and four ribs attached to it. The blubber part is the second *awat*.

5. *Sennerak* (the side): a long piece of meat only, without bones, from the long abdomen. One part of *krittark* blubber goes with it.

6. *Sennerak Iglua:* the other half of the preceding piece. Its corresponding blubber part is another *krittark*.

7. *Kinguserk* (the neck): all the spine without the five lower vertebrae with the meat attached to the neck. Another blubber *krittark* goes with it.

8. *Tamuaniark* (the bite, what your bite is going to be): the fourth and fifth vertebrae with one rib. The corresponding blubber part is *krittausark* (a small *krittark*).

9. *Niakrok* (the head): the head of the seal. The blubber part is the smallest *krittausark*.

10. *Innaluark* (the intestines): the blubber part is an *orsoetusark*.

11. *Tunnerdsuk* (signifying kidney): in fact this part corresponds to the chest bone. With it goes an *orsoetusark* as blubber.

12. *Kramnerk* (the spine): this part consists of the last lower vertebra. The part of blubber is *orsoetusark*.
13. *Senneraernek* (the side): thin long pieces cut in the side of the carcass. No blubber goes with these parts.
14. *Netserta* (the harpooner): this part consists of all that is left in the thorax and abdomen, lungs, the membrane separating the thoracic and abdominal cavities, the stomach, some leftover intestines, also the ends of the front flippers and the skin.

In addition to this fourteenth part, the harpooner also retained the portion of the blubber called *orsogseark*, cut from the back where the blubber is thickest. He also got the fat from the seal's chicks, a poor-quality blubber unfit for use in the lamp, which he gave to his dog. He received practically no meat.

The seal-meat sharing system functioned as follows. Every hunter had a number of sharing partners for each part of seal meat and blubber as previously enumerated. Ideally, there were twelve, and they were chosen by the hunter's mother either shortly after birth or during his childhood. Whenever the hunter killed a seal his wife cut up the animal and gave the appropriate parts to each one of his partners' wives. Since butchering a seal was a woman's task, it was the wives who performed the actual sharing.

A peculiar naming pattern accompanied the sharing partnership. The man who received the *okpat* (hind quarters) was addressed in daily speech by his partner as *okpatiga* (my hind quarters); the man who received the part *taunungaitok* was called *taunungaituga* (my hind part); the man who obtained *aksatkolik* (shoulder) was named *aksatkoliga* (my shoulder), etc. Since the relationships were reciprocal, they resulted in a network of patterned dyadic ties extending over the whole camp and beyond. Sharing partners felt closely attached to each other, conscious of the vital necessity in the dark winter months to live, hunt, and share communally. And although the equitable distribution of

the food supply among camp fellows constituted the ra-
tionale for the partnerships, these also had a social aspect
evidenced in the particular naming pattern which stabilized
friendship alignments and strengthened social cohesion
throughout camp. In order to understand the social importance of the sharing partnership, the manner in which partners were chosen and the duration of the partnerships must
be discussed.

This sharing system was called *niqaiturasuaktut,* a term
derived from *niqaitut,* the name of the sealskin bag in
which the shares were placed and carried away. There were
two classes of sharing partners, the *niqaitorvigit nangminarit* (my own in proper) and the *niqaitorvigit nangminiriungitut* (those who are not my own in proper). The first
were the real sharing partners, usually chosen by a boy's
parents at early childhood. When one of the partners died,
it was customary for his brother to take his place and give
continuity to the social bond. Further, when two adult
hunters were *nangminarit,* they similarly made their sons
partners; the relationship could thus be inherited. And
sometimes when a partner died, a man with the same name
as the deceased could replace him. The important thing was
that the new partner be in a position similar to the old one.
This similarity could be one of descent or of name or of
family; in any of these cases, the Netsilik derived a sense
of continuity and security from the similarity, and the social
organization of the group was thus strengthened.

If a hunter was unable to participate in the hunt, his wife
received his share. *Niqaitorvigit* relationships were life-
long. In the case of a temporary or prolonged absence of a
real partner, his status changed to *nangminiriungitut.* Yet
it was remarkable that this change of status affected only
the partners for shares one to seven. As far as the *nangminarit* for shares eight to twelve were concerned, their
departure brought a definite end to the partnership. It is
clear then that the first seven partnerships were the most

valuable ones, and these seven shares were much larger than the others. As for the thin meat slices of share thirteen, they were given to the children, placed directly in their mouths by the hunter's wife during butchering.

When a *nangminarit* was absent from the camp, it was necessary to replace him by some other hunter present in the winter settlement. This was done by mutual agreement and for a variable duration: for the time the particular seal camp lasted before the next migration to new sealing grounds, or for the whole winter season, or for several hunting seasons. The shares of these temporary partners, however, were slightly smaller than those of the real *nangminarit;* for instance, they did not receive the flippers, which remained attached to the skin and became the property of the lucky harpooner. This practice of finding substitutes to the real partners introduced flexibility in the sharing system. It allowed the real partners to leave camp for undetermined periods of time without breaking the partnership bond. Whenever the real partner returned to the settlement, the partnership immediately became functional again. Second, it insured the continuation of the sharing system itself within a given camp; at any time new sharing alignments could emerge and by the application of old rules integrate non-partners into the local community.

The main characteristic of the sharing system rested in the composition of its personnel. Close relatives and members of the same commensal unit could not become partners. Only distant relatives or non-related individuals were eligible for sharing partnerships. The reason for this was simple. There was no need for close relatives to enter sharing partnerships as, because of their very kinship proximity, they enjoyed each other's confidence and shared food together with no formal arrangements. The situation was different when non-relatives, distantly related people, or several extended families had to live, work, and collaborate together. Suspicion, jealousy, and hostility were often di-

rected toward people outside the extended family. Yet in
the winter it was absolutely essential that several extended
families live and work together in the interest of common
survival. The system of formal partnerships, of which food
sharing was a part, worked to overcome these latent hostilities toward non-relatives and gave the camp social
cohesion. It constituted a permanent set of alliances independent of kinship connections, renewable at each generation, decisively contributing to camp peace.

Of somewhat lesser social significance were a number of
dyadic bonds, some of which gave expression to ambiguous
feelings in an atmosphere of informality while others were
more formal in character.

For some reason, there were men who felt shy and con-
strained in the presence of each other. Their camp fellows
noticed this behavior and loudly commented upon it. This
made the two still more shy; they carefully avoided each
other, refused to talk together, and when in the same house,
turned their backs. They were then called *ibleriit*, or avoidance partners, and refused to pronounce each other's personal names. This generally provoked endless joking among
their camp fellows, who tried repeatedly to mention one's
avoidance partner's name and whereabouts. The result was
increased blushing and shyness. The *ibleriit* relationship
lasted for life and could be inherited within the two extended families by the children named after the elderly
avoidance partners. This is an example of how spontaneous
feelings, in this case sentiments of shyness, could crystal-
lize into formally patterned behavior.

Another formal bond existed between two individuals
with identical names. These were particularly friendly with
each other and frequently exchanged jokes. When after
a long separation they met, it was the custom for them to
exchange gifts of identical objects: harpoons, snow knives,
or stone lamps. Sometimes, different objects were exchanged,
perhaps a marrow extractor for a steel needle. This form of

gift exchange was known as *aviaorosiaktuk,* or trading with one's other half. Both men and women could enter such partnerships. It was important for the gifts to be either identical (knife against knife) or of equivalent value. This gift exchange practice was not carried out to obtain any material benefit, but rather to give expression to a feeling of social solidarity, a sign of enduring friendliness.

Joking partners were particularly numerous among the Netsilik. These were non-related or distantly related men, and the joking relationship was called *akpiusaret.* Often the relationship developed spontaneously among individuals who felt friendly together. Most joking partners were of similar age, although an older man could easily address jokes to a younger one, who would reciprocate in a much milder way. Joking relationships could also be established in a more formal manner. When travelers reached a distant community of strange but avowedly friendly people, the visiting party stopped at a certain distance from camp, waiting for the local hunters to line up in front. Then each one of the visitors would try to find a man of apparently similar height, general appearance, and strength in the local group, march straightforwardly to him, and the two would greet each other in the traditional manner by rubbing noses together. From then on, they were formal joking partners, not only for the duration of the visit but also for any further meeting. Often they also became wrestling partners and exchanged wives as song partners.

The content of the joking relationship usually referred to sexual matters, allusions being made to women one didn't have, or one's sexual potency, etc. Joking usually had a teasing, aggressive tone and was carried out "against" the opponent. There was an effort to belittle the joking partner. Obviously, this was an ambivalent relationship. It should be noted that very close friends avoided overly provocative joking, conscious of the possibility of hurt feelings. As a matter of fact, not infrequently aggressive joking provoked

fist fights, though as soon as the fight was over, friendship
was resumed in the midst of laughter as if nothing had happened. Joking relationships were established between individuals who were neither indifferent to each other nor
very intimate friends. It was a practice that brought people
who were casual friends a little closer together, while at the
same time allowing for the free expression of ambivalent
feelings in a play atmosphere.

Of all the patterned dyadic relationships that the Netsilik
knew, the song partnerships and the wife-exchange practices that frequently went with them were the most complex
and gave rise to the most ambiguous relations. Unfortunately, only sparse information exists on this important
subject, and it is practically impossible to catalogue completely the different kinds of song and spouse-exchange
partnerships. Therefore the following descriptions should be
considered tentative. Both song partnerships and spouse-
exchange relations could lead to song duels, a semiritual
form of conflict resolution, and both had a dyadic, con-
tractual character creating special reciprocal bonds.

There is enough evidence to suggest that song partnerships unaccompanied by wife-exchange practices existed
in traditional times. Such song fellows were called *idloreet,*
or cousins, and frequently were joking partners as well.
They belonged mostly to different camps and were not related. Whenever they met in winter on the flat ice, they
held drum dances together in the large ceremonial igloo.
First, each song fellow had to compose a new song, both
text and melody, and teach it to his wife. The people in
camp were quick to learn about it and spread rumors
concerning the forthcoming event. When the wives had
finished learning their husbands' songs, one of the song fellows would send a messenger to the igloo of his partner
with an invitation to meet him. Then both would go to the
ceremonial house, where all the camp people assembled,

standing in a circle. The song fellows stood in the middle, holding each other by the waist, smiling at the audience, and crying "Hi, hi" as a sign of joy and friendship. They rubbed noses, called each other repeatedly *idluarjuga* (my song cousin), and then one of the wives started singing, with the refrain repeated by a group of women behind her. Her husband danced in a slow pace, beat the drum and shouted "I ai, ai ai." With the end of the first song, the partners embraced again and the first dancer handed the drum to his song fellow, this direct passing of the drum a characteristic trait of the song fellowship. Then the wife of the second song fellow proceeded with her husband's song. These performances took place in an atmosphere of communal enjoyment and laughter.

Often the procedure was less formal and more spontaneous. Song fellows often succeeded each other on the occasion of ordinary drum dances, with the difference that instead of new songs, old chants were used. Generally these were not aggressive or derisive songs, although some slight mockery may have been insinuated. It is important not to confuse this kind of song partnership, expressive of friendly sentiments, with the practice of song duels, which were a form of judicial contest. Song partnerships can be compared to joking relationships with which they seem to have had much in common. They constituted a formal or quasi-ritualized expression of close friendship, while simultaneously allowing latent ambivalences to find a harmless outlet.

Very frequently the two song fellows were so closely associated that whenever they wished, they exchanged wives. The act of exchanging wives was called *kipuktu*, and the partners *aypareet*. A wife-exchange relationship could be initiated in many ways. It may have been the result of an already existing friendship. The wives were usually consulted as to whether they would be willing to have the other man. Generally they agreed. Or a man could conceive an intense desire for a particular woman, propose and obtain an agreement for an exchange from her husband. In this situation there were cases when a strong jealousy expressed by the wife of the man who had proposed the exchange led to a flat refusal to enter such an arrangement, though in such cases the recalcitrant wife was nearly always given a good thrashing by her husband and things proceeded according to his will. It was always assumed that the wife should comply with her husband's will. There were also situations when the wife-exchange process was arranged by the wives themselves. This could be done in two ways. In the event a man wanted to lie with a certain woman, yet he thought himself weaker than her husband and did not dare make a direct overture to him, he would ask his wife to approach the other woman. The latter would discuss the matter with her husband and an agreement was soon reached. In case two wives wanted to exchange husbands, no direct proposition was made, but the possibility was gently suggested with the hope that the husbands would agree, while thinking themselves masters of the situation.

There was no rule as to the frequency and duration of the exchanges. Some took place irregularly, for one night at a time, according to the will of the parties. Others were organized for pragmatic reasons: if a hunter was heading for a long journey and his wife was unable to accompany him, he could temporarily borrow his partner's wife, the assumption being that at some later period the partner would be able to benefit from a reciprocal arrangement. Still other exchanges took place for prolonged periods, many days or weeks at a time.

There was no rule either as to how or when—if at all—the wife-exchange partnership should end. Some of these relationships continued for life, involving occasional co-residence and collaboration in an atmosphere of mutual trust. The bond of friendship was strong and was frequently expressed in the promised marriage of offspring born to the two couples prior to the establishment of the wife exchange. Some cases indicate that after a particular exchange had been repeated a few times, the partners lost interest in it and returned to their spouses full time. In other instances, however, wife exchange led to permanent separations (*avitut*). After temporary arrangements had been organized, the exchanges increased, and the men lost interest in their wives and decided to settle down permanently with their partner's wife. A new marital situation was thereby created, with the children following their mothers to their new houses. If close relatives accustomed to the presence of the previous wife disapproved of the act, they could exert some pressure on the husband to reverse his decision. The final outcome depended on the situation and personalities involved.

Many cases of prolonged wife exchange involving deep emotional involvements ended dramatically, making bitter enemies of the old song fellows and wife-exchange partners. Alleged usurpations of sexual rights sometimes became the subject of malicious gossip, which stimulated sentiments of sexual jealousy and rapidly brought latent hostilities out into the open. Envy and hate replaced friendship and love. Vicious songs of derision were composed in which the opponents were given animal characteristics. Formal song duels marked the end of the once happy partnerships. The song below was sung by Ogpingalik against Takutjartak, and was told to the author by Ogpingalik's daughter Karmatziar in 1960.

> *There*
> *How shall I go to compose this important song*
> *How shall I invent it to help me*
> *I am wholly ignorant*
> *There*
> *Those who have great facility to invent songs*
> *Those who dance with elegance*
> *Those who know the beautiful old chants*

I will get inspiration from them
There
Where one gets caribou skins
To these places I will walk and my thoughts will follow me
Early in the morning I get up
There
Between Oadlerk and Areark lakes I was hunting
There was Takutjartak like a great wolverine
There
Among the tall grass looking for mice to feed himself
I made a noise
You run away
There
With your two eyes you looked at me
Fascinated, astounded
A good large arrow I threw
At your fat ass
It was very annoying for you
You run away fast
There

Part III / MAN AND SOCIETY:

Social tensions

7 FEMALE INFANTICIDE AND MARRIAGE

Case material indicates that Netsilik society did not always function smoothly, in spite of the social bonds created by kinship, collaboration, and partnership. On many occasions, ambivalent feelings permeated interpersonal relations, creating conflict situations. In the absence of any established governmental structure and clear judicial organization, conflict was difficult to control and explosive states rapidly developed. Further, the very high rate of female infanticide traditionally practiced by the Netsilik dangerously reduced the number of marriageable women and was at the root of a number of ambiguous marital practices. And competition for women was vigorous and often led to wife theft and murder.

The high mortality rate and great mobility of individuals in some cases disrupted the extended family alignments and restricted interaction. Socially isolated individuals in this harsh environment considered suicide the only way out of many difficult situations. Certain patterned dyadic relations led to potentially disruptive situations: wife-exchange partners grew jealous and antagonistic, and wrestling partners became overly competitive. Finally derision, the most effective means of social control, while frequently constituting an efficient check on deviant behavior, when carried too far was liable to provoke violent reaction on some occasions and become a source of conflict itself.

Many travelers in the Arctic have noted the prevalence of infanticide among Eskimo groups. Although the rate of infanticide varied with locale, it is clear that girls were more frequently killed than boys. The highest rates of female infanticide recorded were among the caribou-hunting Eskimos of the Barren Grounds, the Aivilingmiut of the west coast of Hudson Bay, and various groups along the Arctic coast. For the Netsilik in the year 1902, Boas noted 66 girls and 138 boys, a ratio of 48 girls per 100 boys. Twenty years later Rasmussen carried out a detailed survey of this custom among the Netsilik Eskimos living at Malerualik on King William Island: "I asked all the women how many children they had borne and how many girls they had put out of the way. I went into every single tent and spoke with every one of them" (1931:140). The list he compiled showed 96 births for 18 marriages, and 38 girls killed. This ratio is in harmony with his 1923 census of the Netsilik tribe as a whole: 259 individuals, of whom 150 were males and only 109 females. Rasmussen concluded: "Despite the high birth rate, the tribe is moving towards extinction if girl children are to be consistently suppressed" (1931:14).

Several different techniques were used to put the newly born female child to death. In winter the infant was placed in the igloo entrance, where she lay screaming until she froze to death—usually not very long. Suffocation was practiced in all seasons by bringing a furry skin over the infant's face. In summer a small stone grave was dug near the family's dwelling and the infant placed inside, where it cried for several hours until it died. Apparently no active killing methods were used. All preparations for infanticide were made by the mother.

Naming had a restrictive influence on infanticide. The Netsilik believed that a personal name had supernatural power closely associated with an individual's personality, and that the dead had a strong desire to reincarnate in newborn infants, irrespective of sex. The dead chose their new infant bodies at the time of birth. If the mother was having a difficult childbirth, she called out various names of dead people in hope of enlisting their help. The name proving the most helpful at delivery was retained, the mother believing that that spirit had entered the infant's body. "I am named Manelaq because when that name was mentioned I came out of mother's womb," said one of Rasmussen's female informants (1931:221). It was essential that infanticide take place prior to naming, since killing a named child might offend the spirit of the reincarnated person, and so the naming of unborn children in hopes of easing childbirth did restrain mothers from practicing infanticide.

The decision to kill a child could be made by the mother, the father, the grandfather, or the widowed grandmother. Most frequently the father made the fatal decision. This was certainly the case with Ogpingalik, a famous bowman, poet, and shaman from Pelly Bay, whose wife gave birth to twenty children, namely ten boys and ten girls. Of the latter, nine were put to death under Ogpingalik's orders:

> None of these was allowed by Ogpingalik to live. When the tenth was born, i.e. Karmatsiark (Kringorn's wife born 1913) Ogpingalik was busy in the sapotit, i.e. in the weir, where the arctic char are speared. For these Eskimos this is one of their most exciting activities in which they can engage with loud enthusiasm. The catch was very good at the moment when the news of the birth reached Ogpingalik. He finished the spearing, then returned to his tent where he allowed Karmatsiark to live. It was then owing to his good mood of that moment that Karmatsiark owes her present happy existence (Steenhoven 1959:50).

Decision-making in regard to infanticide may have been related to the flexible authority patterns within the household. Although routine matters were usually decided by the person in whose sphere of activity the matter fell, in exceptional situations the strongest personality in the household asserted itself. And this was not necessarily the father or the best hunter. Frequently an older woman spoke with conviction, and people listened to her. She might be the one to decide on the fate of a newborn infant. Old Nalungiaq told Rasmussen: "If my daughter Quertiliq had a girl child I would strangle it at once. If I did not, I think I would be a

bad mother" (1931:140). A decision on infanticide was always made within the nuclear or the extended family, without much discussion or hesitation, as shortly after birth as
possible.

Salvation There were two other factors besides early naming which
of child – might save a girl child from infanticide. These were adop-
early tion and demands in marriage. First, although the request
naming for adoption usually took place before birth, any visitor who
adoption heard the cries of an abandoned baby could take it home
demands and adopt it. Second, "promised marriage," a form of spouse
in marriage selection to be described later, might have taken place. Although most young men and women were engaged before
they were born, requests for promised marriage could take
place shortly after the birth of the female infant, effectively
preventing infanticide. Thus unrelated people could influence the decision for infanticide. These requests, however,
benefited other individual families and were not made in
the name of the "community."

What were the reasons for the Netsilik killing such a large
proportion of their female infants? It was evidently not simple "callousness," since the children allowed to live were
dearly loved and cared for. Analyses of case material together with informants' statements indicate that survival
reasons in an extremely harsh environment are to be found
behind this practice. The practice was an adaptive one, for
it increased the chances of survival of the community by reducing the number of non-food-procuring people to be fed.
There were also social reasons for the custom, however, and
in this regard, infanticide was disruptive to the society. The
practice generally fell into one of three major groups.

First are those cases of attempted (or accidental) child
murder that seem to have had purely social causes and were
unrelated to environmental factors.[1] The woman M., for instance, had a boy from her first marriage. When she married

---

[1] The cases discussed were recorded by the author.

her second husband N., the latter decided to kill the child "because he had another father." He did not have time to proceed with the execution (for the child was found abandoned but still alive), and the infant was adopted by someone else.

In another case, the woman Nulianoaq had a small boy who, one day, broke her soapstone pot, a highly valued possession. In her rage the mother stabbed the child with her knife. The child died shortly after.

Second, conditions of extreme ecological pressure may have necessitated infanticide. Kadjak and Iksivalitak were starving while on their way to Pelly Bay. They were dragging their little sled, and they were so weak that they could hardly pull any more. Their adopted son Pupupuk, about eight years old, could not walk any more, so they abandoned him, still alive.

Likewise Apitok was starving with her husband and their little daughter. The hunter could not follow any more and fell behind. Then Apitok, dragging a little sled with the girl on it, joined Itoriksak's family, also on the move. Itoriksak asked Apitok to kill the girl, which she did, although with some hesitation.

The shaman Samik described the following case to Rasmussen:

> Once when there was a famine Nagtok gave birth to a child, while people lay around about her dying of hunger. What did that child want here? How could it live, when its mother, who should give it life, was herself dried up and starving? So she strangled it and allowed it to freeze and later on ate it (1931:138).

To the third category belong the numerous cases of female infanticide that took place shortly after birth, under apparently normal conditions of life. These murders can only be explained as a survival response. Women did not hunt, they were not self-sufficient, and they were less independent than men. The hunter had to feed the girl for many years, and when she grew up she got married and left the family at the very time when she was becoming useful. Further, boys, who would one day become reliable hunters, were greatly desired. If a woman had to suckle a female infant for two or three years she did not have the chance of having a son during that period. A daughter might thus be killed in order to make room, hopefully, for a son.

So infanticide was a flexible practice, not a rigid social rule. The decision to kill was made quickly, in the family, based on several factors such as naming, order of birth, the mood of the family headman, probably the size of the family, and the state of the hunt at the particular season. Above all, infanticide was a flexible practice in the sense that there were alternatives to it—adoption or engagement for marriage.

The Netsilik apparently remained unconscious of the dangers resulting from female infanticide, namely the scarcity of women. Van de Velde (1954:6) describes a group of little girls accompanied by a boy playing in his house at Pelly Bay. The father of the boy remarked regretfully: "If only all these children were males!" Van de Velde added: "Your boy is not even engaged and you would like all these girls to be boys? Where is he going to find a wife then? Boys will have to kill each other in order to get one!" The Eskimo replied with a stupid smile: "*Izagoralluar*" (It is true, despite that . . .).

The impact of the high rate of female infanticide on the sex ratio of the adult population was lessened to a considerable degree by the high mortality rate among males. Despite the fact that in Rasmussen's census not even relative ages are indicated, he counts sixty-six boys to thirty-six girls —a ratio directly reflecting the results of female infanticide. But in the adult population, his tables show seventy-three men and sixty-seven women. It is clear that the imbalance in the sex ratio for children tended to even out as the population got older. This was the result of a much higher mortality rate for males. This high death rate can be explained by the natural hazards of hunting to which the men were subjected (drowning during kayak hunting or river crossing being the most frequent type of accident), by starvation, which seems to have found more victims among men, and by the greater propensity of men to commit suicide.

But in spite of this higher death rate, many young men still reached adulthood to find there was a lack of marriageable women. There were five major ways to get a wife:

(1) Promised marriage was the preferred form of spouse selection. The initiative for such betrothals was taken by the boy's mother or grandmother soon after birth. Often the careful search for a possible bride went on for several years. The mothers of newly born female infants or small girls were approached with marriage proposals; sometimes still unborn infants were promised. As previously mentioned, closely related girls, particularly first cousins, cross or parallel, were preferred as spouses. If a first cousin could not be found, a more distantly related girl of the same generation was looked for. Though no ritual accompanied the marriage agreement between the concerned parties, a small gift was made to the girl's mother.

(2) In spite of the practice of promised marriage, a few girls and a larger number of boys still reached marriageable age without having a promised mate. Their parents could intervene then in the choice of a spouse by accepting or rejecting marriage proposals as the following two cases indicate.

Kanajuq, a young man whose parents were dead, was living in the Aivilik area, northwest of Hudson Bay. He had a promised girl who was residing with her parents in Adelaide Peninsula, very far from the Aivilik country. Tarajajuq, a young man living nearby, approached the girl's parents with a marriage proposal. The parents had not heard from Kanajuq for a long time, and so they accepted the proposal.

Hiniruarjuq's promised husband died. Hiniruarjuq then decided to marry Krabvik, who was residing in a nearby camp. Hiniruarjuq's parents refused to let their daughter leave home where she was considered an indispensable helper. Four consecutive times Hiniruarjuq ran away with Krabvik, and each time she was brutally brought back to her parental home. At a much later date the two families decided to camp together and the marriage took place; residing nearby, Hiniruarjuq continued to help her parents in the domestic chores.

(3) Many marriages took place without the parents' intervention or any coercion. Often adolescent boys found themselves reaching adulthood without a promised wife. Likewise there were widowers and other males who for some reason had lost their wives. These men did not wait for their parents to intervene; they actively searched for a spouse. Some visited the country of the Utkuhikjalik Eskimos along Chantrey Inlet who practiced female infanticide less frequently and had more women available. Many Netsilik people had relatives among the Utkuhikjalik, and finding a wife among them was always a possibility. Some Netsilik men also married among the eastern Aivilik, though such marriages often meant more substantial payments and matrilocal residence for prolonged periods, a situation few husbands enjoyed.

Other marriages involved widows or women who for some reason had abandoned their husbands, as the following case illustrates.[2]

Tinuatluq was Igunaksiaq's wife. She was pregnant when her husband died from an illness. She remarried soon after, but her second husband didn't like the child and was constantly complaining that the igloo smelled of urine. Because he was not pleased with her, he gave Tinuatluq very little food. She became desperate, killed her child, and ran away

[2] The cases described here were all recorded by the author.

to a neighboring camp, where she found another husband. A few months later this third husband was killed by an evil spirit and Tinuatluq married then for the fourth time.

(4) Several cases indicate that <u>men sometimes stole away married women by force.</u> For instance, a man named Kajaksaq and his wife Sarutlu were visiting among the Utkuhikjalik Eskimos. One of these, Tulimaq, had just lost his wife, and he grabbed Sarutlu and brutally dragged her to his igloo. Kajaksaq followed, telling his wife to come back. Tulimaq wouldn't allow her to move, and so Kajaksaq had to return to his native Netsilik country alone.

(5) At least four instances are known involving outright <u>murder of the husband in order to steal away his wife</u>. The following case was recorded by Steenhoven (1959:43):

> More than fifty years ago, my father's father's brother Kakortingnerk killed Sivatkaluk, the son of Konwalark. Kakortingnerk was married to Katikitok, but he wanted (also?) as his own wife Ivilinnuark (Talliitok) who was then Sivatkaluk's wife. It happened south of Boothia Isthmus, at the end of Lady Melville Lake. Ivilinnuark was pulling in front, then came Sivatkaluk, followed by Kakortingnerk and his accomplice Tigusisoktok. Ivilinnuark's child was tied on the sled. (No information about Kakortingnerk's wife Katikitok). Sivatkaluk apparently thought of nothing else but pulling hard. Kakortingnerk, however, his snow knife tied to his wrist, stabbed the former from the back. Sivatkaluk, a very strong man, clasped the knife so as to pull it from the murderer's hand but, since it had been tied, he failed. Tigusisoktok helped to grasp the victim, who was killed. Both victim and assassin were young. The child on the sled cried "anana" to its mother who was in front, pulling the sled with a rope. But she did not hear it and went on pulling. *Probably she did not want to hear it and had asked Kakortingnerk to kill her husband so that she could live with the former.*

It can be seen that <u>although women were scarce, the Net-</u>

silik had many ways to secure a wife. The preferred method was promised marriage with a first cousin, but there were many alternatives, indicating considerable flexibility and adaptability to changing social situations.

Strangely enough, the scarcity of women did not prevent the establishment of polygynous unions among the Netsilik. It was, of course, not practiced by all; only the very best hunters were capable of supporting two wives, and so polygyny was the privilege of the best providers. Rasmussen's census for 1923 indicates three polygynous alignments out of a total of sixty-one marriages.

In the polygynous household, the two wives generally got along quite well, and only rarely were feelings of jealousy expressed overtly. The usual age difference between the two wives made things easier. The first wife was usually much older and the acknowledged head of female activities in the household. She occasionally asked her husband to get a younger woman to join the family to help out with the daily chores, particularly with the grueling skin work. But the younger wife was not treated in any way as a domestic. She had her lamp and belongings and was generally respected by the older wife. Although desire for sexual enjoyment undoubtedly prompted polygyny, economic factors related to the division of labor within the household contributed as well.

Polyandrous arrangements were also known to the Netsilik, probably motivated by the scarcity of women and the related practice of promised marriage. Although Rasmussen's census shows only one such case, recently collected evidence suggests that polyandry must have been more frequent. In a number of households Rasmussen notes the presence of young men with no apparent consanguineal ties to the family. Such young men could have been temporary "second" husbands. Rasmussen writes:

One young man, Angutisugssuk, who lived in King

[margin handwritten note: Two wives generally got along well.]

> William's Land, called a man right up at Repulse Bay
> his father-in-law. Angutisugssuk was then twenty years
> old and unmarried, because his mother-in-law had not
> yet given birth to his "intended." And so for the time
> being he was "second husband" in the house of Tara-
> jorqaoq (1931:194).

While polygynous marriages were relatively stable and
provoked little resentment and jealousy, such was not the
case with some polyandrous alignments. It seems that co-
husbands were frequently jealous of each other concerning
sexual prerogatives and had difficulties in concealing their
sentiments. If the wife expressed a preference for one or the
other, tensions mounted still further, often reaching the explosive stage. Steenhoven (1959:47) has described two
cases of murder resulting from hatred between co-husbands.

[margin note: Two husbands generally did not get along well.]

Around 1935, in Adelaide Peninsula, Arnasluk was sharing his wife Sivorak with Kajorsuq, who was single. Kajorsuq
wanted Sivorak all to himself, so he decided to kill Arnasluq.
The time came when the three were camping alone in a tent
at the caribou hunting place. Arnasluk was in the water pur-
suing a caribou when he was shot by Kajorsuq from behind.
He died there, and Sivorak became Kajorsuq's wife.

Around 1915 (or later) at Pelly Bay, the woman Arnanark
was living in polyandry with Atuvir and Krepingajok. Apparently she inspired the latter to do away with Atuvir, and
so one day he approached Atuvir with his rifle. Atuvir looked
up, saw Krepingajok standing ready to shoot him, then went
on with his work. Krepingajok took pity on him, but
Krepingajok's cousin Kokiark, who was present at the
time, stirred him up. Krepingajok shot Atuvir, and Kokiark
stabbed him twice with a knife. Arnanark had left the tent
before with her daughter. The two men buried Atuvir, then
went inland hunting for a short time; later they returned to
pick up Arnanark and her daughter and fled north to Fort
Ross.

If the lack of eligible women explains the element of flexi-

bility in Netsilik marriage patterns, we have still to understand the preference accorded to the first cousin or any
related female as a spouse. There were three major reasons.
First, the Netsilik assumed that in the case of a promised
marriage at birth or early childhood, the promise would be
more likely kept if it involved close relatives who were the
people to be most trusted. Second, if the boy's and girl's parents were close relatives, there was a good chance that the
two families resided close together, and that the married
girl would camp near her parents and continue to visit and
help them. In this case, marriage for the girl would not mean
a brutal severance of daily relations with her parents and
establishment of an entirely new set of ties with strangers.
Rather it implied the strengthening of already existing
bonds at the level of the *ilagiit*.

But the most important factor contributing to the preference of cousins as marriage partners was a distrust of strangers. All the available data indicate that in traditional times
fear, intense suspicion, and potential or actual hostility permeated relations between strangers. Although such negative
sentiments were usually directed toward complete strangers
from neighboring tribes with whom the Netsilik were only
vaguely acquainted, non-relatives within the tribe or even
within the camp were not always exempted. Suspicion and
fear could lead almost any time to outright aggression
overtly expressed in fist fights and murder, or in more subtle
forms of aggressive magical techniques. Concerning the
more obvious suspicion of non-relatives, Rasmussen (1931:
202) writes: "One would think that in these waste and desolate regions they would feel pleasure when they came across
people who could be company for them; far from it." An old
informant told Rasmussen the following:

> When they broke camp in his grandfather's day and
> moved from one hunting place to another, they drove
> sledge behind sledge, many in company, in a long line,

the first breaking the trail. As there were only few dogs, men and women had to pull too. During such a removal the snow knife was never released from the hand and as a rule a man also had his sealing harpoon with him. A man in the procession could not stop to make water without great risk, for the one who walked in front might easily get the idea that the man for some reason or other would strike him down from behind, and this suspicion alone might be a sufficient cause of bloodshed. They did not trust each other; even if they apparently were the best of friends they could never be sure that the one had not evil intentions. So it is no wonder that they were doubly cautious when meeting strangers.

Rasmussen (1931:203) describes a man's arrival at a strange camp as the man related it:

> Many people came towards me, but without allowing myself to be scared by them I drove right in among them and said:
> "Well, it's only me! I am nobody; if anyone wants to kill me he can do it without any risk at all; I have no one to avenge me."
> They laughed at this greeting, and one of the strangers stepped forward to my sledge and asked:
> "Are you afraid?"
> To this I answered:
> "I am beyond the age when one is afraid of anybody. You see I come quite alone to your village; were I a coward I would most certainly have stayed at home."
> What I said met with much approval, and an old white-haired man then made the following speech of welcome:
> "You are a man, and your speech is that of a man. Stay with us without fear. No one will do anything to you."

Such suspicion and distrust created an atmosphere of insecurity in the camp. Almost any given action could be interpreted in various ways, provoke jealousy, and lead to persecution. Since evil intentions and actions could originate only among non-relatives, parents were reluctant to give their daughters in marriage to strangers. When such a marriage took place, there was always the possibility that the girl who would be taken would have no relatives near at hand to protect her. My informants repeatedly stated: "We were never certain that these people (non-relatives) would not do harm to our girls."

Marital intercourse did not constitute the only form of Netsilik sexual activity. The Netsilik knew of numerous alternate ways to satisfy the sexual urge. As a matter of fact, pre-marital and extra-marital sexual relations were quite common and easily established. Children were allowed great freedom in sexual matters. Rasmussen notes:

> At a very early age children know all about the problems of propagation, indeed to such a degree that copulation enters into their games, they make small tent rings that are usually called places where one plays at copulation. The result is that boys and girls lie together at a very early age, sometimes at ten or twelve, and it does happen that adults will lie with little girls that are not yet nubile (1931:197).

In general, men married or single were willing and quite enterprising in this respect. So much so that cautious husbands often placed their wives in the household of close relatives, protected from adulterous temptations, before leaving on long journeys.

Some men were well known for their sexual enterprise. Their camp fellows were well aware of their intentions, but except for occasional quarrels, there was not much they could do, and this behavior, although it was disapproved of, was generally tolerated. As an example, Ituituq used to go after any available woman, though he was married to Agruta. For some time he tried to associate with the married woman Amauraq, visiting her at nighttime during the ab-

sence of her husband Hindluq. As soon as he entered her
igloo, he would try to rape her. Amauraq complained to her
husband, who loved her very much, but he took no action.
Later Ituituq had an affair with another woman named
Arnarudlu. Every time her husband Inuraq was absent, he
went to stay with her. Inuraq died later on, and people
thought that Ituituq, although he had no shamanistic powers, had killed him with magical weapons. Ituituq quarreled
a great deal, and during his numerous affairs he had to engage in fist fighting with the husbands of the women he
seduced, but he was prudent and avoided getting involved
with stronger men. Another man, Amusa, got this name,
meaning the one who pulls, because of his habit of accosting
absent hunters' wives and trying to copulate with them by
pulling down their pants.

The Netsilik, then, were free concerning sexual matters.
Besides the possibility of engaging in casual affairs there
was also the previously described custom of wife exchanges,
which could afterwards lead to the establishment of quasi-
marital ties. Jealousy was expressed much more often by
men, but there were cases of wives getting angry over the
behavior of their adulterous husbands. Though lovers and
cuckolded husbands often fought with fists, adultery never
led to murder. It was simply not considered important
enough. (One killed to obtain a wife but not to get sexual
access to a woman.)

For a Netsilik man his wife was his most valuable possession. Female infanticide drastically reduced the number of
marriageable women. From an ecological point of view
female infanticide can be viewed as an adaptive custom increasing the survival chances of the community. From a social point of view it may be considered as a harmful practice
which led to an imbalance in the sex ratio, an effort to keep
the marriageable girls within the kinship unit, and a conse-
quent division of the community into many small, mutually
suspicious, unrelated kinship groups.

The Netsilik Eskimo

✳✳   This disharmony between the ecological and social results of female infanticide produced some powerful tensions
within society. Clearly there were no established rules or
processes for the community as a whole which could be
used to resolve this ambiguity. As each man had to find a
spouse by himself in case he was not betrothed in childhood,
so the family unit had to control infanticide and adapt it to
the supportive capacities of the hunter. Both practices were
flexible, and each family had to find its own balance between the need for females and the need to stay alive.

8 SUICIDE AND THE INDIVIDUAL

During the last fifty years, according to the available data, there were about fifty cases of successful or attempted suicide among the Netsilik Eskimos, of which thirty-five were successful and four were unsuccessful. Eleven other individuals expressed their intention to kill themselves, but did not go further for various reasons. For a small population the thirty-five cases of accomplished suicide represent a very high suicide rate indeed, an average of one suicide every year and a half in a tribe of fewer than three hundred individuals.

Males had a greater tendency to suicide than females. The age distribution of the cases shows one ten-year-old boy, five young adults fifteen to twenty years old, twenty-four adults twenty to fifty-five years of age, six individuals over fifty-five and under sixty, and twelve elderly persons over sixty. Married individuals predominate: thirty-four were married and had children, three were married without children, three elderly women were widows, and only five individuals were not married. The comparatively small number of elderly people makes a comparison with Eskimo suicides in other areas difficult, as in these other areas it is generally the older people who kill themselves to avoid becoming a burden to the community. (Such is obviously not the case among the Netsilik.)

There was considerable variation in suicide techniques. In the cases recorded, eleven individuals used guns. Kaokortok aimed at his heart. Tallerk pointed the gun against his chest, hoping to break his spine. The bullet passed through his body, missing the spine, and made a big hole in the snow wall of the igloo. Tallerk, being a shaman, did not even bleed. Ubloreasuksuk killed himself with a bullet in the chest, while Iakka placed the gun under his chin. Avagaidje hoped to hit his brain but the bullet passed through the lower part of his nose.

Twenty-three individuals hanged themselves using skin thongs. Akuardjuk, an elderly woman, did so under a prominent rock. Kangmar, another elderly woman, attached a thong to a stick pushed horizontally into the igloo walls, and hanged herself inside the dwelling. This latter technique seems to be preferred.

There are four cases of strangulation. Inuksak, an elderly man, placed two sticks in the ground and stabilized them with some stones. He tied their tops together with a thong, the end of which he let hang down in a knot for his neck. The structure being somewhat low, he knelt under it and started pulling down, and soon his dead body appeared heavily suspended on the thong. A similar technique was employed by Tunnuq, who strangled herself with a thong attached to the upper end of a peg which she held with both hands. Tallerk, the shaman who did not bleed after he tried to shoot himself, asked the following day to be strangled. He lay on a sleeping bench while two men pulled the ends of a thong knotted around the shaman's neck. They had to pull very hard "because Tallerk was a shaman."

Two cases of drowning are recorded. Kaka, a young woman, decided to put an end to her life by walking over the thin autumn ice on a lake until it broke through under her feet.

The essential characteristic of about half of the number of the suicide cases was a preoccupation with another person at the time the suicide decision was made. Several examples follow:

Irkrowatok, a blind woman who strangled herself, had a son-in-law, a good hunter by the name of Oaniuk, who was accidentally killed during a hunt. When she learned about Oaniuk's death, Irkrowatok said she wanted to kill herself. For about a year, her husband succeeded in dissuading her, telling her: "Don't do it, so that the children may grow up near their mother." Irkrowatok was useful in the household, and she was still a good needle worker. When she strangled herself behind the family sled, her husband said: "This woman didn't have any pity for her children." Her body was left on the sea ice, covered only with snow, because she had not wanted to trouble her people with the preparation of a stone grave.

Oaniuk was killed accidentally during a hunt. Okoktok, a poor hunter, shot him during a caribou chase. Our informant is specific about the unintentional character of this tragedy: "It is certain that Okoktok didn't want to kill Oaniuk, because the latter was a very excellent hunter." As he died, Oaniuk shouted for his gun in order to shoot back at Okoktok, but did not get a chance. Okoktok felt terribly guilty and later, visiting his neighbors, he declared himself ready to be killed. He was told: "You are not a good game; if you want to kill yourself, go out and do it yourself." That is precisely what Okoktok did.

Oaniuk's accidental death also resulted in the suicide of his mother. Oaniuk was Akuarkjuk's only living son. The elderly woman, who was in her tent when she heard about the accident, immediately took a thong and ran toward the place of the tragedy. She saw her son's body lying on the ground and a few moments later hanged herself from a high rock. People saw her running with the thong and knew what she intended to do, but nobody tried to stop her.

Most other suicides came about as responses of individuals to personal disasters. Some examples of these:

Tallerk, the shaman, had been suffering from an illness in the chest. He asked his wife to kill herself in order for him to survive, which she refused to do. Soon after, he committed suicide. Okpik, an adult hunter, Nakungaruk, a young man, and Ubloreasuksuk, an elderly man of high prestige all killed themselves because they were ill. Omaioar's knees became frozen during the winter migrations. An open sore soon developed and Omaioar, a youngster, was unable to walk. It was imperative that the group keep moving, as there was hunger in the band and better hunting grounds had to be found, and so Omaioar asked to be left behind. The people agreed. They made a trench in the snow about his size, and covered it with caribou skins. Omaioar was placed in it in a sitting position, with a little food. A small igloo was built over him. Then the group moved on, and no one returned to see him.

Let us consider briefly the main motives of suicide as given by our informants. About twenty individuals reached the suicidal decision following a disaster affecting a near relative, usually a descendant. Sixteen other individuals took the fatal decision because of a personal misfortune, usually an illness. In six cases we find marital dissatisfaction. Informants were specific that only four elderly persons killed themselves because of old age.

To explain the Netsilik's seeming readiness to commit suicide, three basic reasons must be considered, reasons proposed by anthropologists who have studied the entire Eskimo area. First, there is the well-known ecological explanation. It is said that the harshness of life is such in the Arctic that unproductive individuals cannot remain with the roaming band. Killing of the aged by near relatives or their suicides are seen as accomplishing the same end. Weyer (1932:138), who has summarized most of the available evidence, writes: "The disposing of one who is aged and infirm sometimes seems, indeed, to be more the will of the fated one than of those devoted to him who will live on." But this ecological explanation does not fit the facts for the Netsilik as we know them. First, only four individuals in our records committed suicide specifically because of old age. And considering the disabled and ill, only in the case of the boy with the frozen knees do we find the active collaboration of the group in the suicidal process; our data indicate that on the contrary, the sick person's relatives try to dissuade him from committing suicide. Finally, ecologic or economic factors cannot explain the suicide of a large number of healthy adults and young men.

The second reason for suicide is related to the way the Eskimo looks at life and death. Weyer (1932:248) writes: "In the pursuance of his hunting activities the Eskimo is constantly brought face to face with death, and he grows to regard life as a thing of little account. Like the Stoic who argues, metaphorically, that if the chimney smokes one should get out of the house, the Eskimo justifies suicide, especially if age or infirmity renders one useless and a burden." But this is a dangerous assertion based on analogical thinking: because one has met dead beings he is not afraid of death! It could be just as easily argued that the more one sees of death, the more he learns to value his own life; and so this second explanation is not of much use to us either.

The third explanation seems the most important, and it involves the religious beliefs of the Netsilik. The Eskimos hold the belief that the nature of one's death may influence the destiny of the human soul in the afterlife. The souls of the individuals who suffered a violent form of death, including those who committed suicide, may go to a semi-paradise, one of the three afterworlds known generally by the Eskimos. Rasmussen has recorded similar beliefs among the Netsilik. He has described suicide cases among the Igloolik as well in which religious beliefs seem to have influenced suicidal decisions. One young man killed himself because he wished to live in the underworld where his mother was. Unfortunately, I have no information in my records on the religious factors involved in Netsilik suicidal behavior. My informants repeatedly professed ignorance about any religious factors determining a suicide. Such factors, however, may have been operative. How important they were in the suicidal process perhaps we will never be able to learn.

But all three of these factors, as important they may be,

are not really sufficient to provide us with an understanding
of Netsilik suicide practices. There is a certain uneasiness
among the Eskimos to leave this world when, under certain
concrete conditions, an almost inevitable suicidal tendency develops. The overwhelmed individual who has decided on suicide seems isolated from his social milieu and
from his people. It is precisely this *lack of wider relatedness* that must be analyzed in relation to a number of social
and historical factors to see if one can explain the development of suicidal tendencies.

Major socio-economic changes took place among the Netsilik during the first half of this century, the period when
the suicide cases took place. Numerous families had left the
area, attracted by allegedly outstanding opportunities in the
Repulse Bay and Chesterfield Inlet regions, where trading
posts had been established. These emigrations contributed
to the splitting of many extended families and the corresponding restriction in size of the functioning kinship units
in the Netsilik area. Although the splitting of extended families also took place in traditional times as part of the
developmental cycle of the large domestic units, it was undoubtedly accelerated by new historic conditions. One consequence of prolonged emigration was that many promised
marriages could not take place by virtue of the absence of
one of the promised spouses. As a result, non-relatives or
distant kinsmen were chosen, and many more mates found
themselves moving to a strange social environment. Clearly
the restriction of the kinship units and the resulting disrup-
tion of the preferred marriage pattern were both factors contributing to the severance of vital kinship bonds which might
have existed otherwise.

Further, the generalized use of rifles in the 1920s disrupted the functioning of the traditional collaborative patterns which were closely bound to native technology. With
a high-powered rifle, an isolated hunter could kill caribou
and seals without the aid of his camp fellows. This increased

the geographical mobility of individual hunters and small social units, and strengthened reliance on personal achievement.

And while all these changes were in progress, we must not forget that the traditional disruptive patterns were in continuous operation. The ambivalent character of joking and wife-exchange partnerships frequently led to open hatred expressed in fist fights and drum duels. Having a wife could not be taken for granted at any time; competition for wife ③ ownership was strong and many cases of wife stealing were known. Thus there was a considerable amount of insecurity in the husband-wife relationship. There were also competitive attitudes and feelings of hostility motivated by specific social factors that could even separate brothers. The following is a case in point:

insecurity in the husband wife relationship.

A. was a middle-aged hunter, the father of four daughters; B. was his older brother and the father of a thirteen-year-old boy. A.'s oldest daughter, about sixteen years old, had been promised in marriage to her cousin, the son of B., from early childhood. A. was an excellent hunter, but he kept himself apart from his relatives and camp fellows and was not eager to share his food. He was accordingly considered selfish and was slightly despised, in spite of his outstanding hunting abilities. As he grew older, A. felt an increasing need for a young, strong helper; and so he decided to have his older daughter married to a non-related boy from a different community, provided the young husband would come to live with them as a second provider. The marriage took place, breaking the promise made by A. to his elder brother regarding the union of their offspring. B. was profoundly hurt by his brother's breach of promise but said nothing. The relations between the two brothers became strained, however, and whenever something unexpected happened, it was a cause of mutual accusations. If B. had some skins chewed up by a dog, it was of course A.'s dog that did it. The two brothers began avoiding each other, their families stopped camping together, and the split never ended.

One could present a long list of cases illustrating tensions between kinsmen and between non-related camp fellows alike. Repeated wife beatings and jealousies and hatreds involving brothers and cousins seem to have been numerous. Often these produced the splitting of extended families and the desertion of wives. Maltreated women used to run away from their husbands and seek protection with their kinsmen (when such separations became permanent they were called *avitut*).

In the chase for caribou and musk oxen, during the watch for seals, and in wrestling matches, every man tried to outdo his neighbor, to obtain more food and appear stronger. An element of aggressiveness entered this behavior. One was a strong man primarily in relation to others who were weaker. Society valued a man by his strength. The Netsilik conception of the ideal personality was very similar to the one defined by Mirsky (1937:73) for the East Greenlanders: "The Ammassalik ideal man is one who is outstanding in skill, in strength, in power, a man who expresses his personality fully and without being deterred by economic, social or supernatural sanctions." Often such assertiveness of the self neglected the interests of others. The strong and fearless man felt himself immune from danger, and felt free to deride and make fun of the weaker men. In the mountains south of Pelly Bay, Rasmussen (1932:20–21) met Iksivalitak, a famous shaman, who told him his story:

> In this new country I had a hunting companion, and we often had contests. We were equally fast, equally skillful at hunting, but he was the stronger. We were always alone when we practiced our sports, and my companion, who could not run so far as I can, made use of every opportunity to let me know that he was not afraid of me. And so it happened one day that to prove his superiority he rubbed his muck on me, and that was an

insult I could not forget. When a man does that in our country it is an insult that means that he has an inclination to kill one. The treatment I had received tormented me so much that I could not tell anyone about it. Hatred grew up in me, and every time I met my old companion out caribou hunting it was as if I loathed myself; thoughts that I could not control came up in me, and so one day when we were alone together up in the mountains I shot him.

Jealousies, various resentments, and hatreds, often concealed for long periods, sometimes found an outlet in aggressive magic involving various supernatural beings. One basic characteristic of these spirits, however, was their unreliability and ambivalent nature. When unsuccessful in their mission they could turn back blindly on their masters and bring sickness, death, and destruction to their camp. Interpersonal hostilities thus were further complicated by the supernatural techniques sometimes employed.

We can better understand the isolation of the individual tempted to commit suicide when we see these disruptive, contradictory forces at work in his society. The vital integrative patterns such as extended kinship forms, collaborative practices, and dyadic ties gave cohesion to society, but simultaneously the individual had to cope with historical and internal factors that isolated him from his fellows by restricting the kinship alignments, disrupting the collaborative forms, and introducing ambivalence, suspicion, and hatred into the Netsilik's network of interpersonal relations. These two opposing forces—cohesive factors and disintegrative factors—were in constant conflict with one another, and it is not surprising that a fair number of the Netsilik could not find a secure place in the midst of the conflict. Unable to make a satisfactory synthesis of the various positive and negative relationships he entertained, many a Netsilik found himself—for situational or personality reasons—in greater isolation or fear than the others. He was closely tied to only a small number of relatives, and when one of these died, he had no substitute. He did not seem to be related to any larger social groupings. This lack of relatedness may have been equally applicable to suicide cases resulting from illness or personal disaster. The illness seemed to exhaust the resistance of the Netsilik very easily, and he quickly abandoned hope for recovery, lost sight of all those things which made life worth living, and welcomed death. Admitting Durkheim's generalization that suicide varies inversely with the degree of integration of religious, domestic, and political structures, we can consider Netsilik suicide as belonging to the egoistic type of suicide. ". . . in the same measure as we feel detached from society we become detached from that life whose source and aim is society" (Durkheim 1951:212).

The lesser the degree of integration of religious, domestic, & political structures, the greater the probability of suicide.

Practically any minor or trivial event could produce a quarrel and lead to overtly aggressive behavior, the more so if personality factors provided a suitable setting for it. Though in this regard the Netsilik were no different from any other people, on some occasions they responded rather quickly to aggression, as the following cases illustrate.[1]

Innakatar was an elderly woman with a little adopted girl and a grown-up son who was living as a second husband with a younger woman named Itiptaq in an adjoining igloo. One day Innakatar's little daughter pissed on Itaptaq's bed, wetting the sleeping skins. Itiptaq scolded the girl, who started crying. Her mother didn't like this and started a quarrel with the younger woman. Itiptaq lost her temper and Innakatar answered: "Don't scold my little girl, just come and fight with me." They started hitting each other on the face, just like men. Soon cuts and blood covered their faces as they fought noiselessly on. After a while Itiptaq said: "You are getting in a bad shape, bleeding a lot, I don't want to hit you any more" (meaning that Itiptaq was getting scared and in pain and wanted to find a way to give up the fight). Innakatar, feeling strong, answered: "If I feel anything I will give up, just hit me a few more times." Innakatar was the obvious winner, though both of them were badly cut up around the face.

In another case, Itimangnerk and Utuytoq were joking partners and good friends. One day they were fishing salmon trout at Nuvuteroq on King William Island. They were using the special spring fishing technique which consisted of cutting two parallel rows of holes through the fjord ice and, with leisters in hand, running from one row to the

[1] These cases were recorded by the author.

other as a school of fish passed under. Utuytoq asked Itimangnerk to cut him a fresh fish to eat while he was running between the fishing holes. Itimangnerk, who was also
hungry, cut up two fishes, one from his own and one from
Utuytoq's. The latter thought that both fishes were from his
own catch, and got angry for this very trivial reason. Itimangnerk thought that Utuytoq was only joking and
laughed. Utuytoq took the argument seriously and hit Itimangnerk on the chest. A real fight followed, until they were
separated by Mangalukut, who was fishing nearby.

Obviously quarrels of this sort could and did arise among
the Netsilik at any time and apparently for most insignifi-
cant reasons. Though in many cases such quick explosions
were probably the expression of already existing tensions, in
other situations the reaction seems quite spontaneous. Almost always after the exchange of blows, however, peace
was re-established and the enemies of a minute before
parted good friends.

Mockery or derision was one behavioral trait among the
Netsilik that frequently provoked resentment and hostilities.
But derision was special because, while it caused resentment
and anger, at the same time the threat of derision caused
a fear of being laughed at and so it acted as a kind of control, keeping deviant behavior in check. The consequences
of incessant mockery could lead to violent reactions, as we
saw in the case of Iksivalitak mentioned in the last chapter.
He killed Amarualik because the latter was constantly making fun of him. This was an unusually extreme reaction,
however, and usually mockery provoked only a derisive answer from the other party; and any real enmity established
most often found expression in fist fights or formal song
duels. Excessive boasting was another form of indirect aggressive behavior. It was not really aimed at anyone in particular, but it diminished the social and manly importance
of the others by enhancing one's own prestige.

Impinging upon sexual privileges, failure to give a girl

promised for marriage, wife stealing, jealousies implicit in wife exchanging, ambiguities in polyandrous alignments— in sum, competition for sexual access to women in all its multiple forms—constituted another important factor leading to conflict. It is clear that the settings in which these jealousies and competitions arose depended on the highly variable total social situations. Other jealousies led also to strife. The more successful hunters were often surrounded by feelings of jealousy which were skillfully concealed and found expression in secretly performed sorcery. Fast kayakers were especially likely to be envied, and slower hunters used to throw evil spells on their kayaks. Many cases from the Netsilik area have been recorded illustrating these feelings of envy. The following was observed by Rasmussen (1931:200):

> An elderly man, Itqilik, discovered quite by chance that an old woman at the village had for a long time been stealing salmon from his son's catch and hiding the fish in a grave. She was jealous that his son was a better and luckier fisherman than her own, and so she was trying to kill him by magic; for it is believed that a man will quickly die if any of his hunting spoils come in contact with the dead or dead men's possessions. Yet all the time the old woman was plotting against the life of the young man, her relations with both him and his father were of the most cordial kind.

According to recent observations it was during midwinter, when the people were most weary of the long nights and intense cold, that malicious backbiting was most frequent. One often heard then that such-and-such a neighbor always had more food, had caught more foxes, more bears, etc. Certain persons, particularly women, were naturally of a more jealous nature than others. They would keep quiet for long periods and then all of a sudden one night they would give free expression to their envy in front of some trusted person.

There is a general rule among the Netsilik and, as a matter of fact, among most Eskimo groups, that no undue appropriation of important natural resources should take place by individuals or families. People have the right to hunt wherever they wish and nobody is entitled to exclude others from a hunting area that he himself is using. Any infringement upon this basic rule is bound to provoke strong resentment and sometimes leads to strong reaction. The following case, which is probably legendary and impossible to date, illustrates this point.

An elderly man, N., used to camp alone with his wife and three grown-up sons at Oadliq, a crossing point for caribou west of Pelly Bay and an excellent hunting area. One day when N. was alone in his tent three hunters arrived there with their kayaks to catch caribou. They were coldly received by N., who told them: "Nobody should come here unless they want to look at the sky" ("looking at the sky," meaning to lie dead on the ground with the face turned up to the sky). The people said nothing, but went down to the lake shore where they waited until N.'s sons returned and then killed them. N. went insane with anger and ran about screaming, until the three hunters killed him also. After these murders the lake was open for hunting to everybody.

There is another general rule among the Netsilik according to which all able-bodied men should contribute to hunting, and the returns of the hunt should be shared according to established custom. Any activity in exception to this rule was bound to provoke criticism, various forms of conflict, and frequently social ostracism. Such an exception was the lazy hunter, whom the Netsilik called *nuniurut*. They were not usually less skillful than the others—on the contrary, some *nuniurut*, when necessity demanded, were very good in the chase—but they were incurably lazy. While the temporarily disabled hunter was generally helped with gifts of food, nobody liked sharing with the *nuniurut*.

Innaksak had a grown-up son by the name of Tutyaq who

was married to the daughter of Kablalik. They all lived together with Tutyaq's grandmother, an assertive woman
well in control of food distribution in the large family.
Kablalik was a stranger to the area, having come to live with
the group when his daughter married Tutyaq. He was a lazy
man, generally disliked and despised. His situation was
aggravated by the fact that, being a stranger, he was igno-
rant of the local hunting grounds and had to depend closely
on the others for whatever hunting he did do. Having established camp on the sea ice one evening, the women of
the group separated from the men for the evening meal as
custom demanded. Tutyaq invited Kablalik, who didn't have
any food, to join Innaksak's igloo for a meal. Then Tutyaq
went to visit his grandmother, who was with all the other
women. The grandmother was furious when she learned
that Tutyaq had invited Kablalik to eat, and in her rage she
hit Tutyaq with her snow beater. She then went immediately to Innaksak's igloo and started quarreling with Kablalik. Innaksak remained passive until Tutyaq arrived on the
scene, when his father started scolding him very sharply.
Tutyaq attempted to answer but another older man stopped
him and the quarrel finally died out.

It is evident from this case that lazy hunters were barely
tolerated by the community. They were the objects of backbiting and ostracism for a long time until the opportunity
came for an open quarrel. Stingy men who shared in a nig-
gardly manner were treated similarly. Sometimes the social
position of a lazy hunter could save him from overt community hostility. Such was the case of Higak, a thief, incurably lazy, and a bad hunter besides because of his poor
vision. He was avaricious and almost everybody hated him;
but since he was a shaman, people feared his protective
spirits and avoided hurting him, although nobody gave
him any food. Higak eventually established a strange partnership with Krasovik, an excellent and highly successful
hunter, in which Higak sent his protective spirits to help

Krasovik hunt, in exchange for which Krasovik shared his
catch with the shaman.

These were the most usual causes of conflict—mockery,
jealousy, laziness, and minor misunderstandings. Once a
conflict situation had been created and left unresolved, secondary causes for quarrels often arose. The social atmosphere of fear and suspicion previously described constituted
an excellent ground for the seeds of hostility and persecution to grow in. This process was considerably aided by the
Netsilik ability to conceal malicious intentions and hostile
feelings in order to prevent possible reprisals by magic and
sorcery. On the surface camp life proceeded smoothly, but
hidden tensions were such that the slightest incident could
set off aggression at any time. A traveler among the Arviligjuarmiut described the following situation to Steenhoven
(1959:73):

> I. traveled on Kellett River together with A., S., and
> some others, who on their sleds had been visiting their
> caches. The weather was beautiful and we walked to
> and from each other's sleds, while the sleds were moving
> all the time. A. was seated on the back of S.'s sled and
> the latter sat in front of him. A. was eating a fish. I was
> driving my sled behind his. One moment when S. was
> turning towards his dogs or so, I saw A. suddenly make
> a lightning stab with his knife at S.'s back—a would-be
> stab, to be sure. Then he immediately looked around
> himself. But I looked already in another direction. S. is
> the son of I. and it was known that A. and I. did not get
> along well. It was my impression that this stab had been
> prompted by an altogether subconscious impulse and
> that A. only became aware of it after he had done it. I
> believe he could just as well have really stabbed S. out
> of these subconscious feelings of resentment.

Theft, although cheerfully practiced in relation to
strangers, practically never occurred among camp fellows.
Household objects were few anyhow and their owners well

known, which made theft in the camp virtually impossible to conceal. There are cases, however, of property destruction, obvious expressions of hatred. Two recent cases involving the destruction of another's cache were recorded by Steenhoven (1959:37). The first case took place at Thom Bay, where two unrelated children had demolished the household cache of an absent family. Apparently this had been done because the owner of the cache had once refused food to the children's families when they were hungry. In the second case two related children totally destroyed the household cache of an elderly man during his absence from camp. The motive here seems to have been related to the jealousy the children's fathers were known to feel for the privileged position occupied by the victim in the community. In both cases children acted as their fathers' emissaries, allowing the adults to later disclaim any responsibility for the act.

Murder was the most extreme form of aggression among the Netsilik. It was committed in two ways: physically, by knife or gun, or supernaturally. Killing with magic was by no means the prerogative of shamans only. The Netsilik knew of a whole arsenal of aggressive magical techniques available to practically anybody. Many deaths were therefore attributed to revenge by evil spirits. Here we shall analyze only physical murder, as described by Steenhoven. The desire to steal a certain woman was the most frequent cause for attempted or successful murder. Ambivalences inherent in some polyandrous arrangements leading to murder would be included in this general category. Motives related to an individual's prestige in the community reflected by excessive mockery, bullying, or resentment constitute another category of causes for murder.

Among the seven relatively recent murder cases recorded by Steenhoven (1959:46) five contain information on the killing technique employed. Two men were shot from behind, apparently unaware of any plans afoot to kill them;

one was shot while asleep; another was stabbed in the back with a knife while driving on a sledge; still another victim knew his murderer's intent yet did nothing to forestall it. It is remarkable indeed that all the men but one were killed from behind and by surprise. Murderers were evidently careful to avoid a struggle. Further, with one exception, all the murderers were men, although some might have been influenced by women. As for the exception, it was the woman Merkreaut, who shot her sleeping husband, apparently because she did not want to live with him any more.

With the probable exception of the murderess Merkreaut, all other six cases indicate that the decision to kill was slow and deliberate. The potential murderers waited for the appropriate moment to come, then killed with determination. The following case further illustrates the premeditated nature of most murders.

Pre-meditated

Ikpagittoq was married to Oksoangutaq's sister. They were Netsilik and in the spring they lived on the west coast of Pelly Bay, where they hunted seals. Not far from their camp lived Saojori, a particularly strong man from the Aivilik country, with his two wives. Saojori, although a stranger in this area, frequently boasted that he feared nobody and that no man would dare attack him. Ikpagittoq encouraged Oksoangutaq, who was single, to kill Saojori and take his wives. So one morning the two brothers-in-law walked to Saojori's tent and were told by his wives that Saojori was hunting seals. The two men went out and found Saojori on the ice at the very moment when he was about to catch a seal. Saojori guessed the evil intentions of his visitors, and so he held the seal with one hand and kept the other free to grab his knife if he needed to defend himself. The visitors apparently were very friendly and helped to drag the seal to the shore, where Saojori extracted the liver for a quick meal. Then he went down to the beach to wash his hands, still holding his knife between his teeth, ready for defense. As he knelt down at the water, Ikpagittoq attacked him from behind, trying to throw him to the ground. A struggle developed, while Oksoangutaq stood by watching until the embattled Ikpagittoq shouted at him, "You said you wanted to kill this man, what are you waiting for?" Oksoangutaq stepped up and pushed his knife into Saojori's neck, killing him on the spot. After the murder the two men went inland to hunt caribou; on returning home, they sent Oksoangutaq's sister to Saojori's tent to inform his two wives about the murder. One of the wives was very frightened and ran away with her child. Oksoangutaq had no trouble catching her, and made her his wife. This woman, being an Aivilik, some time later expressed a desire to return to her country and visit her parents. Oksoangutaq agreed. When they reached her father's igloo, she invited her new husband to come in. After some hesitation he walked in, holding his knife in hand. Apparently two Aivilik men had planned to kill him, but they didn't succeed; and Oksoangutaq returned safely to Pelly Bay.

Oksoangutaq's decision to kill was taken calmly, motivated by self-interest and executed at the appropriate moment. Strangely enough, in all the historical cases recorded not a single instance of successful physical revenge occurs, although intentions for revenge are clearly expressed by close relatives of the victim even years after the murder has taken place. There are, however, numerous cases of revenge by supernatural means, though the evil spell may take a long time, sometimes years, before reaching the culprit and accomplishing the original intention of revenge. No specification is made as to the nature of the murderer's death. He may drown, starve to death, or die from sickness; invariably his death is attributed to the spirits charged with the mission of bringing revenge.

The community, in reaction to an accomplished murder, appears on the surface to be remarkably calm and somewhat indifferent. Witness the affable reception of the murderer Oksoangutaq in Aivilik. It is, however, likely that this apparent indifference hides deeper feelings. Clearly the idea of revenge existed, not as an absolute obligation, but definitely as a possibility and a right, albeit a vague one. As an informant put it recently: "It takes away even one's sleep—this fear and tension because of possible revenge." And there was a special camp area, Fort Ross, extremely isolated in the northern part of Boothia Peninsula, where murderers fearing revenge often went to stay for a few years after the homicidal act, waiting for passions to calm down. Now, the community could not passively watch a murder followed by a revenge which in turn could provoke a third homicide and lead to a chain reaction. Every murder signified the loss of a highly needed seal hunter. The community had to intervene and did so. Earlier we mentioned the murder of Sivatkaluk by Kakortingnerk: "Some time later, when they arrived at the camp of Iksingajok, who was Sivatkaluk's father's brother's son, there was a quarrel, and Iksingajok challenged Kakortingnerk to fight (for life or death) with bow or knife, *but this was prevented*" (Steenhoven 1959: 43).

A stranger in the camp, particularly if he was traveling with his wife, could become easy prey to the local people. He might be killed by any camp fellow in need of a woman. In ancient times such assassinations led to the formation of revenge parties consisting of the relatives of the victim, resembling war expeditions. The following story was told recently by Irkrowaktoq, a middle-aged man from Pelly Bay;[2] he affirmed that the case took place before the arrival of Sir John Ross's ship in the area.

Ugak was an elderly Netsilik who had land around Boothia Isthmus. He had three sons: Kujaqsaq, Anarvik, and Neruqalik. Around Pelly Bay there lived a group of Arvilik whose headman was Kukigak. His son was Anganuak. The feud seems to have started with the murder of old

[2] It was retold by Itimangnerk (Irkrowaktoq's brother) to Steenhoven (1959:55–57). Fragments of it appear in Rasmussen (1931:440, 444–45).

Ugak by Kukigak's people. The Netsilik were outraged, and they formed a revenge party which set off for Pelly Bay. They were known as excellent archers and practiced their marksmanship all the way along the road. As the Netsilik party approached Kukigak's hunting grounds, they saw his son Anganuak at a distance watching a breathing hole. They decided not to kill Anganuak, who then ran ahead to warn his camp. Kukigak immediately sent his two sons away in the opposite direction, toward the Aivilik country (presumably to escape death). When Kujaqsaq reached Kukigak's camp he sent his mother ahead to tell the Arvilik people that his party had come to fight. The old woman did so and Kukigak answered: "They will not fight." The woman pointed out: "They have their weapons ready." Kukigak answered: "They will not use them." In spite of which both groups started preparing for the fight. Kukigak didn't have special weapons for fighting, so he got his caribou-hunting gear together. A young man originally from the Netsilik country had been living with the Aivilik, and Kukigak invited him to fight with them, but he refused to fight his relatives. The two groups lined up to face each other, and the first to fall was a sick Arvilik man who had a large opening on his clothing right in the middle of the chest. An arrow hit him there and he died immediately. Then Kujaqsaq saw his father-in-law in the Arvilik group. The old man cried: "I don't want to kill my son-in-law!" Kujaqsaq answered, "If you don't want me to kill you, then get out of the way." And the old man left the battleground. A massacre followed, many Arvilik men died, and Kukigak was mortally wounded. Dying, he said, "When we kill one man we don't kill any more, you people don't want to listen to us." Kujaqsaq answered: "I remember when you were ten men to kill my father, so don't say anything like that." Kukigak was then brought to his igloo, where Kujaqsaq's mother visited him, commenting: "What is wrong with the people, when they meet, they always fight." Kukigak asked one of

[margin annotation] Revenge parties

his two wives to give the old woman a bag full of precious iron objects, possibly as a request for mercy. Kukigak's last wish was to be buried at Kangerk, in a big stone grave, and for all his people to play around it (meaning to camp in this same area, which would indicate that he had had an honorable death).

We have fragmentary information on smaller revenge parties that were formed in the general Netsilik area against the Aivilik and the Garry Lake people living inland. The degree of detail in some of this case material may reasonably be considered as historical truth. As Rasmussen remarked, the Eskimos pride themselves on good memories and are particularly trustworthy in storytelling (Rasmussen 1931:23). Consequently we can safely draw a certain number of conclusions. Physical revenge in traditional times did exist following the murder of defenseless strangers. The feuding groups were usually distantly located. The revenge party was organized by a headman (generally a close relative of the victim) and consisted of his kindred, organized as an action group. There was a formalized pattern for intergroup fighting, involving a messenger, preparations, distribution of the people in two rows facing each other, the choice of valuable opponents, preference given to bows and barbed arrows, etc. The objective of the revenge party was not just to kill the original murderer but members of his kindred as well. In a sense the members of the kindred shared responsibility for the murder.

Why then the absence of physical revenge in the recent historical cases described by Steenhoven? First, it seems that most of these murders involved camp fellows. In this instance, a community could not allow internal feuding, which could result in the loss of vitally needed seal hunters, leading to hardship for everyone in the group. Second, with the introduction of firearms, individual families could get by much more easily, and so the murderer could flee to Fort Ross and remain there for a prolonged period, thus escaping revenge. Third, by the early 1920s, the Royal Canadian Mounted Police had made their presence felt. The police discouraged feuding, and pursued the murderers themselves, often satisfying the desire for revenge in this way.

The Netsilik used various strategies to control or resolve conflict. These were either ambivalent and temporary or decisive and permanent. Gossip falls into the first group. My recent field observations indicate that every Netsilik individual was surrounded by a circle of gossipers who watched his behavior and were ready to comment on it. This undoubtedly helped to check deviancy. Yet it sometimes happened that a man was so provoked by malicious backbiting that he reacted aggressively, answering gossip with gossip or engaging in evil magic. In this case, the means that were supposed to check misbehavior just generated more trouble. Mockery and derision worked the same way. Fear of derision might have stopped an individual engaged in aggressive action, but if he was pushed too far, there was always the chance that he would retaliate and initiate a derisive action of his own, with dangerous consequences. This could also hold true for the fear of magic. Two men who were quarreling might stop short, each afraid that the other might become so angered he would perform some secret act of aggressive sorcery. This same fear, however, might lead either party to assume that the other already had resorted to a magical attack of some sort, leading him to go ahead with magical activity of his own in retaliation. Thus fear of sorcery, instead of resolving the conflict, simply makes it covert.

The Netsilik knew of a number of rather formalized techniques for peacemaking that were positive in the sense that usually they brought conflict into the open and resolved it in a definitive manner. These techniques were fist fights, drum duels, and approved execution.

Any man could challenge another to a fist fight for any

reason. Usually they stripped to the waist and the challenger received the first blow. Only one blow was given at a time, directed against temple or shoulder. Opponents stood without guard and took turns, the contest continuing until one of the fighters had had enough and gave up. This seemed to settle the quarrel, for, as one informant put it: "After the fight, it is all over; it was as if they had never fought before."

As well as its use in the wife-exchange practice, the song duel was a ritualized means of resolving any grudge two men might hold against each other. The songs were composed secretly and learned by the wives of the opponents. When ready, the whole group assembled in the ceremonial igloo, with a messenger finally inviting the duelists. As was the case with all drum dancing, each wife sang her husband's song in turn, while the latter danced and beat the drum in the middle of the floor, watched by the community. The audience took great interest in the performance, heartily joking and laughing at the drummers' efforts to crush each other by various accusations of incest, bestiality, murder, avarice, adultery, failure at hunting, being henpecked, lack of manly strength, etc. The opponents used all their wits and talent to win the approval of the assembly. Here is an example of a derisive song collected by Rasmussen (1931:342–45):

> A certain Ilukitsoq Arnarituat from Itivnarssuk (Back's River region) had in a song accused Nakasuk of being a poor hunter. Nakasuk, who is the leading man, whom everybody at the villages at Iluileq relies on, hits back by first ironically painting himself as a bad hunter, that his wife has to beg for food and clothing from her neighbours. Then he chastises and mocks his opponent for sexual excesses and impotence, and concludes with a description of how he once, quite alone and sitting on the ice, had held a bearded seal on his harpoon line and killed it.

I will now put together
What is to be my song which nobody wants to sing
Thus—they were only pitiable
The women—these
Who on the neighbours had to run
Like women whom a provider were forced to lack.
This is what I would like to recall:
He it was—my big song-fellow
Because he tried to get at me.
He—my big song-fellow (Ilukitsoq)
Properly forestalling me—prating about everything he could
    think of
Pattered out words—sang a song of derision
At the festival house here—by the side of it;
His eyes were not boldly raised—how was it he behaved?
When I happened to hear about him—I almost made you
    better than you are
For the sake of your helpfulness—once
I, who am not accustomed to help
Men—in the right way.
And so I think I now can answer
In the festival house's room
When I sing mockingly—when I doughtily begin to patter
    out the words
I can usually answer—for I am one about whom nothing is
    heard
As I am one devoid of anything untrustworthy.
What was it? On the sea's ice
For your daughter-in-law Teriarnaq—yonder
You conceived immoral desires
And yearned for her.
You are one with brief thoughts—and your thoughts never
    go to
Your wife, poor Akta;
(Your penis) That, to be taken with the hand, that, fondly
    desired
When it really felt a yearning it needed no help
And certainly, it could at that time—
But towards your wife—the desired one

You had to have help from Savinajuk—there,
Your great helping spirit there
He had to help you, when you were really going to;
When I heard this of you—I did not think of you as one
I need fear!
But what was that? At Itivnarssuk over there on the land
People say that your sister Inugpanguaq
On your way at night
Was felt by you, indeed, was squeezed by you!
When I heard that of you, I did not feel much inclined to
    remember you
In that way—I used to look out for
Arnarituat from Winerfik's summit
I used to look out for him
And wished he would appear at last—through
Aimarqutaq bay there
On his way to our land—and not simply rest content with
    sending songs of derision
To Imeriaq's bay—I tried to cross his path.
But I suppose you had no one to go with you—of kinsmen
Or women who are pretty.
At Putuggut and Nuvavssuit islands
At Arfangnak islands and Umanaq's sound
A big bearded seal through its breathing hole I got hold of
No hunting companion (was there) down there
It was Arnarituat's vainly tried for, that there
Which I got hold of there
Quite alone, sitting—out there!

Contests involving derisive songs constituted remarkable
efforts to resolve conflict in several ways. First, this was a
formalized procedure involving preparation and a controlled succession of actions. Apparently free rein was given
to the expression of aggressive feelings, yet they have to be
molded in verse form. Second, conflict is brought out into
the open, with society present to act as arbiter. But society
did not act as a judge, separating right from wrong or con-
demning culprits or absolving innocent individuals. Most of

the derisive songs recorded by Rasmussen contained no reference to private grudges. It was rather the whole personalities of the opponents that were evaluated through their performances. The more biting and witty the song, the better was the reaction of the audience. Society stimulated the free expression of aggressive feelings. Song duels thus undoubtedly had a cathartic value for the individual opponents, and in this particular sense conflicts became "resolved." Sometimes one or both of the opponents at the end of a song duel continued to feel enmity. When this was the case, they often decided to resume fighting, this time with their fists. This definitely settled the matter.

Execution or approved homicide was another important *Execution* technique used to control socially undesirable aggression. From time to time there was trouble with insanity, an individual starting to behave in an increasingly strange and dangerous manner, physically menacing and hitting other people. Or sometimes dangerous sorcerers became old and bitter, and took to performing malevolent magic against even their close relatives. These people seemed to hate everybody and to have no mercy even for children. Obviously they constituted a serious threat to the peace of the camp, and a stop had to be put to their vicious activities. Often shamans used their supernatural helpers to neutralize an evil sorcerer. There are two historic cases of approved physical execution. The first was recorded by both Rasmussen (1931:30–31) and Steenhoven (1959:53–54). The latter version is more detailed and is reproduced below. The informant is Kringorn, born in 1905 and living at Pelly Bay:

> Around 1922—I was about sixteen years of age—we were living in a large winter house near Lake Willerstedt. I recall the following camp members: my grandparents Aolajut and Kukiaut; their younger son Krimitsiark, who always accompanied his parents; their oldest son Kokonwatsiark; their younger sons Abloserdjuark and Arnaktark; Igjukrak, who was Aolajut's

cousin and married to the latter's sister Nujakrit; Igjuk-rak's two sons-in-law Nerlongajok and Magnerk. All were accompanied by their wives and children. There were also non-relatives in the same camp, but I was early adopted by my grandparents. My father Kokonwatsiark (alias Ubloriaksugssuk) was the "oldest" of the camp. I was early adopted by my grandparents and I lived therefore under the supervision of my uncle Krimitsiark. It was around the darkest time of the year and the camp was preparing to move from the lake, where they had been fishing, on to the sea to hunt seal. The women were busy sewing clothing and thawing meat to be consumed during the journey.

Krimitsiark and Magnerk had already helped Arnaktark to pack forward some six miles, and Magnerk stayed with him there, so as to keep an eye on him; for Arnaktark had suffered the last months from psychic disturbances for the first time in his life. But after two days, Arnaktark disappeared and Magnerk set out to find him. But he failed to locate him and returned to the main camp to inform the family, upon which Kokonwatsiark and Abloserdjuark started searching, also without success. Shortly after, Arnaktark must have returned to his igloo and that same night he stabbed his wife Kakortingnerk in her stomach. She fled on foot with her child on her shoulders, and after arriving at the main camp she told what had happened.

They started to fear that he might stab again at someone they loved, and they discussed what should be done. The discussion was held among family, and it was felt that Arnaktark, because he had become a danger to them, should be killed. Kokonwatsiark said that he would carry out the verdict himself and the others agreed. Old father Aolajut was not supposed to do it, because Arnaktark was his own son; but if Kokonwatsiark for some reason would not have done it, the next oldest, Abloserdjuark, would have offered himself to do it. After the decision was taken, Kokonwatsiark notified the non-relatives, because they also were afraid. All agreed that there was no alternative.

Then the entire camp broke up: Aolajut, Kokonwatsiark, Abloserdjuark, Nerlongajok and Igjukrak traveled to Arnaktark's igloo, and Krimitsiark led the others and the women and children along another route to the new camp at the coast. Upon arrival at Arnaktark's place, the latter was standing outside, and Kokonwatsiark said to him: "Because you do not know very well any more (have lost control of your mind), I am going to 'have' you." Then he aimed at his heart and shot him through the chest. Then they moved on to join the others at the coast. His grave is yonder, towards the end of Willerstedt Lake.

The second case was recorded both by Steenhoven and myself, though from different informants. My version is presented below. A few preliminary details had been already gathered by Rasmussen (1931:143–44), who noticed that the old woman Krittark was heartlessly treated by her son-in-law Mikaluk (Arverk). She was poorly clad and often dragged behind when the sleds moved ahead. Apparently Mikaluk could not do better, since he had barely enough clothing skins for his wife and children.

According to my informant, Nakasuk was Krittark's daughter. Nakasuk had two co-husbands, the young Mikaluk and Tingerjak, who was older and had decided to leave the household to marry another woman. Krittark also had a son. Krittark literally hated everybody; she made trouble all the time, using her powers as a sorceress. She stabbed her own son with a knife through the wrist. She used to remove the amulets from the children's clothes for no apparent reason. Repeatedly she cut small pieces of fur from people's clothing and hid these in graves, trying to cripple them. Her daughter finally became frightened when she thought that her mother might bewitch her husband Mikaluk, and so she decided that Mikaluk should kill Krittark. It happened in

winter during a migration. Krittark lagged a short distance
behind, then sat down to rest, her back turned to the sled.
At that very moment Nakasuk asked Mikaluk to kill the old
woman, which he did, shooting her through the head. Krittark's spirit later became an evil ghost and tried repeatedly
to take revenge and kill Nakasuk. Several years later
Nakasuk saw a fish with a big head in a lake. She thought
this was her mother's spirit bringing death to her, and she
died a year later.

Both cases indicate that gratuitous aggressiveness and insanity could not be tolerated indefinitely. There came a
point when drastic measures had to be taken, even if it
meant execution. (The fatal decision was taken informally
within the circle of relatives present in the camp.) It seems
that non-relatives abstained from getting involved, and if
the situation became too dangerous, they preferred to move
away. The execution was always carried out by a close relative. This was considered a duty and had the advantage of
avoiding any possibility of revenge. There were thus extreme instances when, in the absence of established courts
and rigid judicial procedures, the kindred could act in an
informal manner to judge and impose the death sentence
when necessary. It should be emphasized, however, that the
kindred's capacity to act as arbiter was applicable only to
the most critical situations when camp peace could not be
maintained by any other means.

There was one other very important strategy for conflict
resolution or, better, for conflict avoidance. This strategy
consisted simply of withdrawal. Whenever a situation came
up in which an individual disliked somebody or a group of
people in the band, he often pitched his tent or built his
igloo at the opposite extremity of the camp or moved to
another settlement altogether. This is common practice even
today. A reading of the topographical distribution of the
dwellings in a large camp reveals not only the alignments
of kinsmen living close by, but also the affinities and hos-

[margin handwritten notes:]
Decision:
informal
by rela-
tives

One other
important
strategy:
with-
drawal

tilities of the camp fellows. People who like each other stay together, those who do not live apart. An additional detail is significant in this respect. If for any reason two families who are not on friendly terms have to camp close by, the openings of their dwellings will face in opposite directions, indicating that there is no intercourse between the two families. The opposite is true if the families like each other. Dwelling distribution therefore becomes a very good guide to the social preferences of a Netsilik community. As old quarrels are mended and new hostilities arise, fresh alignments emerge. It is by no means an uncommon sign to see a family pack its belongings and move from one part of the camp to another to adjust to its friendship alignments.

In dealing with aggression in the Netsilik community, the whole field of social control was characterized by flexibility. Highly variable personality and situational factors make it impossible to establish any arbitrary connections between wrongdoing and sanction. But this does not mean, as Steenhoven supposed, that "formal anarchy" prevailed. Netsilik society did have behavioral norms, mostly concerned with the broad interests of the community as a whole. There were definite obligations with regard to food procurement and food sharing. Freedom of access to important natural resources was also essential. When camp stability was endangered by individuals who disregarded these community interests, or upset the social balance by disruptive aggressive activity or by evil sorcery or insanity, the community did take action—even to the extreme of execution, if it was needed.

When conflicts occurred, social control was, above all, flexible.
Behavioral norms concerned the interests of the entire community.

Societal Obligations:

① Food procurement
② Food sharing
③ Free access to natural resources

Part IV / MAN AND THE SUPERNATURAL

10 ELEMENTS OF NETSILIK RELIGION

Purpose

Religious beliefs and ritual observances had a great influence on Netsilik social life and formed the intellectual basis
of its culture. Religion explained the world's past, present,
and future states, helped control numerous crisis situations,
influenced interpersonal relations, and reduced fear. Essentially the relation of society to nature was mediated by a
series of symbolic representations and actions increasing an
individual's feeling of security in a hostile environment.

It is impossible to give a detailed account of Netsilik cos-
mogony, myths, legends, and religious practices in a single
chapter.[1] In the following section only a brief outline of the
main elements of Netsilik religion will be presented, followed by an analysis of the principal functions of local ritual
observances. Particular attention will be given to the specific nature of the relations between individuals and supernatural beings and among the supernaturals themselves. It
will become clear that while most relations with supernaturals were ambiguous and flexible, certain classes of religious
observances were extremely rigid and knew of no alternatives. Further, the influence of certain supernaturals affected
individual behavior alone, while the power of others concerned society as a whole. And while certain religious activities were thought to be beneficial to the people, others were
distinctly malevolent in nature. This dichotomy proves to
be the basis of Netsilik morality. Throughout this section the
term "religion" will be used in its broadest sense, including
such diverse elements as collective religious representations,
individual sorcery practices, certain native classification systems, etc.

---

[1] For a comprehensive description of these the reader is referred to Rasmussen's full treatment of Netsilik intellectual culture (1931:190–443).

The Netsilik believed that both the vast, cold universe and their individual camps were inhabited by supernatural beings of many different kinds. Most important were the human souls, of which there were three species: personal souls, name souls, and ghosts of deceased men and women. In addition, people were surrounded by amulet spirits with important protective powers. Animals also had souls, some incarnated and some free floating and ghost-like. Shamans had the ability to harness many of these ghosts for specific tasks as personal protective spirits. Another category of supernaturals that inhabited certain areas of the country included various monsters, giants, and dwarfs, mostly anthropomorphic in nature. Above these various lesser spirits there reigned three major deities: the sea spirit Nuliajuk, the weather god Narssuk, and the moon spirit Tatqeq.

The Netsilik obtained their manly strength mainly from their souls. The human soul was thought to consist of a mysterious yet extremely powerful force. It contained the life force of a human being and gave him the power to act energetically and with determination. The soul strengthened the hunter's capacity to withstand hardship, enabled him to make quick and appropriate decisions, and was generally the source of all will power. Further, the soul gave a man his identity. The soul contributed to good health and animated a man's whole body. It was assumed that a man's soul was similar to his physical appearance both in size and in facial characteristics. Generally the soul resided in the hunter's body, occupying it in its entirety. In some cases of shamanistic acts, however, mention is made of very small human souls, about two inches in height, that evil sorcerers could pull from under their sleeves. These small souls could be given instructions and sent out to enter men's bodies, bringing them great misfortune or death. The belief in these reduced souls was not very widespread in the Netsilik area, however. Netsilik women also had souls, though little is ever mentioned about them.

Though the personal soul was the source of health and energy, it was also vulnerable to attack by evil spirits and malevolent shamans. All physical sickness resulted from evil spirits hurting the human soul by taking abode in the patient's body. The Netsilik knew numerous techniques to protect their souls from these harmful influences. One such practice was to have the soul removed from the body at the very moment of birth. This was done ceremonially by a shaman, who placed the soul under the soapstone lamp of a close relative of the infant, preferably the mother, where it remained forever, free to grow to full strength. The distant location of the soul confused aggressive evil spirits, who were unable to find it in the body they wanted to attack, and so their action was rendered ineffectual.

Human souls, called *inoseq* (in the liking of man), were considered immortal and continued their independent existence after the death of the body. If the various taboos associated with death were properly observed, the soul migrated peacefully to one of three afterworlds, where it remained forever. When a breach of a death observance occurred, the soul became an evil spirit, blinded by anger. Instead of leaving for the happy land of the dead, it stayed near camp and might strike indiscriminately against any living person, including relatives. The presence of such evil ghosts was revealed by shamans before, during, or after a disaster. Numerous techniques were used in defense against the invisible attacks of ghosts, the most reliable being the shamanistic practice, to be described later.

Quite distinct from the ordinary human souls were the name souls. Personal names were thought among the Netsilik to possess a personality of their own characterized by great power and a distinct ability to protect the name bearer from any misfortune. In fact they acted as guardian spirits, highly beneficial to humans. It was therefore in the interest of individuals to acquire as many names as possible, and sometimes a person accumulated up to twelve names and

more. No distinction was made between male and female
names, which were used indiscriminately. Personal names
were drawn from a variety of categories: inanimate objects,
animals, domestic activities, etc. One Netsilik woman was
called successively 1) pack ice; 2) the little one whose feet
are cut; 3) leister; 4) butterfly; 5) the one who is partial to
woman's genitals; 6) the little one with the bib; 7) the one
who has been beaten with a piece of wood; 8) the one who
has just shit; 9) the round one; 10) the admirable one; 11)
the coarse stitch; 12) the unlucky one.

Hunters valued having many names because of the additional manly strength they gained, while women thought
that the many name souls they themselves possessed would
make their offspring healthier. The first name soul was acquired sometime before birth and was of special importance.
This was associated with the name a woman chose for her
baby when having a difficult childbirth. As already explained, the mother in labor called out various names; if
birth was speeded following the mentioning of a particular
name it was assumed that this name soul had entered the
infant's body and successfully speeded delivery. Thereafter
the child would bear that name. This indicates a belief in
reincarnation exclusively concerning name souls and not
personal souls. It was rigorously forbidden to kill a newborn
infant who was already named.

Three particular animals were distinguished by the power
of their souls: seal, caribou, and bear. As with human souls
after death, the hunter had to pay homage to the animal he
killed by observing a number of rigorous taboos. A failure in
any of these observances could turn an animal soul into a
crooked spirit, a bloodthirsty monster. Particularly dangerous in this respect were bear souls. Numerous instances of
shamanistic behavior indicate a special association between
evil shamans and bear souls. The Netsilik lived in perpetual
fear of wandering animal ghosts, since they depended for
survival on regularly killing game animals. The very food

*Food could become a source
of evil.*

which was absolutely essential for the survival of society became a source of evil.

Death taboos for dealing with animal souls were the main strategy by which hunting animals became a safe activity. ——— It was thought that the soul of a killed seal for which all death taboos had been properly observed would be greatly pleased by the received attention and would reincarnate in another seal body with the intention of letting itself be killed again by the same hunter. In this sense a careful hunter continuously hunted the same animal. The death taboo about seals not only prevented the soul of a seal from turning crooked by helping it reincarnate, but also insured continuous successful hunting.

[margin note: Reincarnation of animal souls to aid in hunting.]

[margin note: AMULET] Another very important group of spirits was connected with the various amulets carried by men, women, and children alike. The physical appearance of the amulet was of little significance. The amulet received its supernatural power from the resident spirit exclusively and not because of any physical properties. Practically any small object could serve as an amulet. In the very large collection of Netsilik amulets gathered by Rasmussen (1931:269–70) at camps near the Magnetic Pole, small parts of various animals were particularly numerous. Pilarqâq, a young man, carried six amulets: seal teeth sewn onto the band of the hood of his inner coat, which brought luck when sealing; the head of a tern, sewn into the back of the neck of his inner coat, which made him a clever salmon fisher; an ermine sewn to the back of his inner coat, which made him a good runner; two miniature snow beaters, sewn to the inner coat at the height of the shoulder blades to protect him against evil spirits; a small kayak cleaner that belonged to a deceased kayaker famous for his fast rowing, to give Pilarqâq the same skill.

Most amulets were attached to the owner's coat to protect him wherever he traveled. Special belts were also worn outside the coat with numerous amulets hanging from it, including little models of flensing knives and snow knives,

[margin note: Amulets attached to coat to aid when travelling]

rows of seal teeth, metatarsal bones of foxes, bear teeth, etc.
While most men or women carried up to half a dozen amulets, there were exceptional cases when persons wore a very
large number of amulets. The boy Tertâq owned no less
than eighty amulets. Amulets were given to boys and girls
by their mothers and considered strictly personal property.
Only the owner could benefit from their supernatural
power. They were never exchanged or given away. Women
did not wear their amulets for their own benefit, but to help
the children they would bear. And amulets did not lose
their power with time. On the contrary, amulets increased
in strength as they grew older, getting more and more powerful as they were inherited by successive generations.

3 functions: There were three functional categories of amulets. The
① Sub- first was related to subsistence: amulets in this group were
sistence intended to bring luck to the hunter. Almost all amulets in
this category concerned specific species of game animals,
with caribou and seal appearing most frequently, followed
by salmon trout and bear. This of course reflects both the
economic importance of the seal and the unreliability of
caribou hunting. There were a few amulets to render the
game tame and some which made the hunter invisible at the
caribou crossing place. Still others were supposed to help in
fast running and paddling while at the chase or to ensure
good aiming with the bow. Almost all amulets were specialized in this way, with only a few considered as general helpers in any kind of hunting.

② Virility   The spirits attached to the second category of amulets
protected or strengthened various manly qualities not connected with specific hunting abilities. The most general of
these aims was to ensure that the owner remained a real
man, a proper and stern human being endowed with good
health and substantial strength and vigor. More specific objectives were long life, good bearing, a strong stomach,
strong shoulders, powerful arms and fists, protection against

headaches, and ability in craftsmanship, fighting, and song
dueling.

The third category of amulets concerned relations be-③ Super-
tween men and the supernaturals themselves. These amu- natural
lets made the owner clever at shamanizing, protected him relations
against evil spirits, and gave him visions.

As pointed out, most amulets had narrow functions which
applied to specific situations. The point of reference was always the hunter. Various amulets provided the owner with
supernatural help in case of environmental pressure (hunting, fishing) in relation to himself (good health, strength,
etc.) and in reference to the supernatural world (protection
against evil spirits). Amulets whose functions related the
owner to another person were very rare. Amulet spirits
clustered around each person like a ring of supernatural
protectors and helpers. They were individually owned and
aided only their owner.

Apersaq

Another important class of supernatural beings were the
shaman's own protective spirits, called *apersaq* (helpers)
or *tunraq*, the general term designating spirits. Some of these
the shaman acquired during his initiation, others he obtained during later practice. The shaman called his spirits
before a trance with the help of a special song, and could
ask them to perform any number of different tasks. The
following is the list of the spirits owned by Iksivalitak, the
last practicing shaman among the Netsilik:

1) Kingarjuaq, big mountain, about three inches long
   and one inch high, with black and red spots. The
   shaman could remove this *tunraq* from his mouth,
   where it was in the habit of staying, and make it run
   on his hand.
2) Kanayuq, sea scorpion, residing also in Iksivalitaq's
   mouth, whence it could show its ugly head.
3) Kaiutinuaq, the ghost of a dead man.
4) Kringarsarut, the ghost of a dead man, big as a
   needle, with a crooked mouth and one very small ear.

5) Arlu, the killer whale, white, very big.
6) Kunnararjuq, a black dog with no ears.
7) Iksivalitak, the ghost of the shaman's grandfather.

A great variety of things could count as a shaman's helping spirits: human beings, ghosts, animals, elements of nature such as the sun or moon, and a number of monsters and
bizarre beings. Their common characteristic was that their
energy could be harnessed for the benefit of the officiating
shaman.

The Netsilik believed that their country was peopled by a
multitude of strange beings, mostly human-like but inevitably endowed with very characteristic supernatural personalities. In size they varied greatly, some being enormous
monsters while others were dwarfs. While most had no real
ethical characteristics, some were particularly bloodthirsty
and dangerous to humans, and others were relatively indifferent to humans. The following is a list of some of these
supernatural beings in the order described by Rasmussen:

> *Ijerket* (peculiar eyes) live in mountain crevices. They
> generally look like humans except for their winking
> sideways with their eyes. They are extremely fast run-
> ners and are able to overtake caribou and catch them
> alive.
> *Ignersujet* (related to fire) are beings who look almost
> exactly like humans except that the rims of their eyes
> are very narrow and they never sleep.
> *Narajet* (big bellies). They are like men, distinguished,
> however, by their shamanistic capabilities and glutton-
> ous character: at one single meal they can eat a caribou
> cow and its calf. They are also fast runners and excellent
> hunters of caribou.
> *Taglerqet* are shadows, moving fast, with human fig-
> ures. They live and hunt like Eskimos but are invisible
> and cannot be seen until they are dead.
> *Ivigtut* (the fidgety ones) are associated with a big
> stone near a river at Iluileq. Despite their human figures

they have the peculiar ability to disappear into the big stone if seen by people. There is the belief also that they feed on stone.

Totalet (seal men) resemble both humans and seals.

Totanguarsuk is the spirit of the string figure. It is a very dangerous being that attacks women and those who indulge in excessive playing with string figures.

Amayersuk is another dangerous being. It is a giant woman with a big space in her back. She steals children.

Nakasungnaikut have no calves or shin bones. This makes them crawl instead of walk. They are extremely dangerous man-eaters.

Inugpasugsuk lived in times past. He was a giant who caught salmon with his hand and killed seals with a stick. He was both afraid and fond of humans and took great pains not to harm them.

Nanorluk are giant bears with a great liking for human flesh. Their jaws are so large that they are capable of swallowing whole men, who suffocate in the bear's belly.

Inuarugligarsuit are dwarfs living up in the mountains. They have human figures and live exactly as Eskimos. The game they hunt is also tiny, their bears no bigger than lemmings. When seen by Eskimos, these dwarfs have the peculiar ability to grow in size up to the height of ordinary human beings.

Many stories and legends were associated with these strange beings. Hunters on the trail could see their fresh tracks, follow them, and just as they were about to reach them, see the supernatural creatures disappear on the horizon. All Netsilik however lived in great fear of some of these evil monsters, especially during the dark winter months. Shamans were frequently called to protect people from being devoured.

Above all these lesser spirits were the three deities: Nuliajuk, Narssuk, and Tatqeq. Nuliajuk, a female deity living in the depth of the sea, was considered the mother of all animals and the mistress of both the sea and the land. The

following story was told to Rasmussen (1931:225-26)
about how Nuliajuk came to be:

> Once in times long past people left the settlement at
> Qingmertôq in Sherman Inlet. They were going to cross
> the water and had made rafts of kayaks tied together.
> They were many and were in haste to get away to new
> hunting grounds. And there was not much room on the
> rafts they tied together.
>
> At the village there was a little girl whose name was
> Nuliajuk. She jumped out on the raft, together with the
> other boys and girls, but no one cared about her, no one
> was related to her, and so they seized her and threw her
> into the water. In vain she tried to get hold of the edge
> of the raft; they cut her fingers off, and lo! as she sank to
> the bottom the stumps of her fingers became alive in the
> water and bobbed up round the raft like seals. That was
> how the seals came. But Nuliajuk herself sank to the bot-
> tom of the sea. There she became a spirit, the sea spirit,
> and she became the mother of the sea beasts, because
> the seals had formed out of her fingers that were cut off.
> And she also became mistress of everything else alive,
> the land beasts, too, that mankind had to hunt.

Since as an orphan girl Nuliajuk had been rejected by the
camp people, she had no particular liking for mankind. She
possessed enormous power and could make game disappear
right from under the sealer's harpoon. This she did with the
help of her innumerable spirit assistants who could also
raise storms to prevent successful hunting. When she wanted
to, she could also be generous and provide the people with
necessary game, and so it was essential to soothe her occasional angers. This was achieved by skillful shamans diving
to her sea abode, or by observing all the taboos concerned
with animal souls and the proper separation of different
kinds of food. Rigorous taboos were essential in this respect, since Nuliajuk had an immediate knowledge of any
breach of taboo. As the supreme deity, she was most con-

cerned with the proper observation of taboos and the controller of all such rules.

(2)   Narssuk, the giant baby, was the weather god, master of
the wind, rain, and snow. His father, a double-toothed monster of enormous size, had fallen in battle with another
giant. His mother, too, was killed, and Narssuk was left an
orphan. Although an infant, he was so large that four women
could sit on his penis. Eventually he went up into the sky
and became a wicked spirit detesting mankind. He was
wrapped in caribou skins tied with thongs. Whenever
women kept silent about their menses, Narssuk's thongs
loosened, he became free to move, and blizzards swept the
country. Then shamans had to fly up in the air and fight
against the enormous strength of Narssuk. If they succeeded in tightening the thongs, Narssuk was immobilized
and good weather followed.

(3)   Tatqeq, or the moon spirit, was a deity of no great power
and was generally well disposed toward mankind. There is
the general belief that in ancient times the sun and the
moon were brother and sister and lived on earth like ordinary humans. But they had an evil mother who wanted to
murder them. Aware of this, the children killed the mother,
fell incestuously in love with each other, passed up to the
sky, and became the sun and moon. While there were no
particular beliefs concerned with the sun, the moon was assumed to bring luck to the hunter and fertility to women.
For this reason, women were not allowed to sleep exposed
to the moon, as it was believed they would become pregnant.

This completes the list of the major classes of supernatural
beings the Netsilik believed in. Looking back, we can make
certain generalizations. First comes the fact that many
spirits were personally owned by the people and generally
at their service: souls, name souls, shamans' protective
spirits, amulet spirits. Even the relationship between persons
and animal souls and monsters was direct and concerned

Narssuk (giant baby) god of weather; master of
wind, rain, & snow; detested mankind

Tatgeq moon spirit; liked mankind; brought
luck to hunters & fertility to women

only the parties involved. It seems that only the major deities performed functions of collective concern involving society as a whole. With the exception of name souls and amulet spirits, almost all supernatural beings were either openly evil and dangerous or could become such, and these would include human souls that became evil ghosts, animal souls, and shamans' own protective spirits, who could change nature and become bloodthirsty monsters.

Clearly, evil spirits and supernatural beings of uncertain intentions seem to have vastly outnumbered the good souls; even the two major deities were inimical to mankind. The Netsilik thus lived in perpetual fear of sudden attacks by malevolent spirits. Their fears reflected the assumption that spirits controlled both the natural world and the major events in human life. Nuliajuk and animal souls were responsible for the presence or absence of seals and caribou. Narssuk could raise a storm at any moment and render hunting impossible. Some evil spirit could strike blindly and bring sickness and death in camp. The action of spirits had some bearing on almost every facet of social life and survival activity; it is not surprising that the Netsilik were so concerned about them.

Actions of spirits had some bearing
On every facet of social life and
survival activity.

11 NETSILIK COSMOLOGY

The Netsilik Eskimos knew a number of relatively short myths explaining the origin of the world and the state of things in primeval times. Although many of these beliefs are obscure and are not altogether complete in their explanation of the world order, they did provide the basis for much of the way the Netsilik viewed life.

It is convenient to divide the Netsilik world view and its associated cosmological notions into four major parts according to chronological order: creation myths with indications of how the universe came to be; beliefs pertaining to a particular race of beings, the Tunrit, who immediately preceded the arrival of the Netsilik in their present country and taught them all the hunting skills necessary to survival; the way the Netsilik presently consider their position in the world; and the complex beliefs held about afterlife, the different classes of shadowy worlds where human souls migrate after death. The following is a synthesis of several separate versions of the creation. It should be remembered that there are many incoherencies in mythical thought, that actions are not always placed in a logical order, and events may seem to precede or follow each other in a disordered manner.

[margin note: 4 parts of world view: Creation, people, present position in world, & after-life.]

[margin note: CREATION]

The earth was the original element. It is the one thing that has always existed. At first there was darkness or a kind of twilight all around, and when man first appeared, he lived without sunlight. There were no animals to hunt then; man did not have to suffer for his livelihood, but there were no pleasures either. Then came the incident when men rejected Nuliajuk, the orphan girl, by pushing her into the sea from the kayak raft. She sank to the bottom of the ocean and became a goddess, and it was she who created all the animals and obliged humans to hunt, toil, and rejoice. She imposed also all taboos on people. During these times, there was no difference between humans and animals. They lived promiscuously; a person could become an animal and vice versa. Both people and animals spoke the same tongue. Words had great power, and anything uttered could produce immediate physical effects. The fox said: "Darkness, darkness, darkness," implying its liking for the dark, when it could steal from humans' caches. And the hare said: "Day, day, day," preferring light in order to better find a place to feed. The word of the hare was stronger, light was created, and from then on day and night alternated.

There was not much game, and people had to travel great distances to catch enough food to stay alive. That was made easy, however, by the use of magic words. As soon as people wished it, their whole camp was transported through the air to the new place. Forests grew on the bottom of the sea, which is where driftwood comes from even now. After a sea storm, branches of wood get detached from this underwater forest and are carried to the beaches.

There were still no women on earth. They came into being only after a dreadful deluge. Incessant rain flooded the land and great destruction followed. All the animals and men died, with the exception of two shamans, who copulated together, one of them becoming pregnant. Their children grew up, and among these were girls.

It was during these times also that giants fought and people ridiculed Narssuk, the monstrous baby who later gained control of the weather, so important to the Netsilik. The stars, like the incestuous sun and moon, were people who for one reason or another had gone up in the air and become celestial bodies. Many evil spirits also went up into the air as a result of broken taboos, and they made human life very dangerous.

This brief summary of Netsilik creation myths points to certain basic assumptions. First, creation was conceived of not only as having come out of nothing, but as a process of increased differentiation and separation from the original chaotic condition. Second, humans as they first existed, although possessors of powerful magic words, were thought to have led a dull, tasteless, and sleepy life. It was when suffering and pleasure both appeared that human life acquired meaning. Third, human wickedness seemed to be the source of evil: malevolent spirits and the taboos established to control them came into being as a consequence of wrongdoing by man. Fourth, the creation of the visible world, the major deities, and lesser spirits took place simultaneously with the establishment of the moral order characterized by good and evil and the taboos that related to them. In a sense the creation myths did not separate clearly between the three and point to the natural, the supernatural, and the moral orders as a whole that existed as such since the beginning of time. *RACE OF PEOPLE*

The more recent legendary past of the Netsilik was concerned almost exclusively with a kind of Eskimo-like people called the Tunrit. These were the original inhabitants of the Arctic coast area, and it is they who, according to legend, rendered the country habitable. According to the Netsilik the Tunrit were not Eskimos, although they spoke a language similar to the one used by the Netsilik. The Tunrit were very big, strong people, very good natured and timid. They did not wear caribou-fur clothing but preferred bear skins. They had no sledges and, unlike the Eskimos, built stone houses and large stone graves. Most of their camp sites were along the sea beaches from which they hunted whales, walruses, and seals with kayaks. What they liked most, however, was musk-ox and bear hunting. Their skills were superhuman and they were peculiarly capable of throwing spears with their feet. Although they were peace-loving creatures, they fled to the east and the north when the Netsilik arrived. Apparently no great fights took place between the two tribes, and the Netsilik remained very

[margin note: gifts of Tunrit]

grateful to the Tunrit for many essential things. It was the Tunrit who invented hunting caribou from kayaks with bows and arrows. They were also the first to use the leister. More important, however, was the fact that the Tunrit built the stone cairns that led the caribou to the special crossing places and constructed the stone weirs for fishing. The Netsilik believed that in these essential activities they themselves were just continuing what the Tunrit had established already, and that they were in a sense the heirs of the legendary Tunrit. Despite the fact that legend and prehistory are closely connected here it should be repeated that according to local beliefs the Tunrit were superhuman, somewhat quasi-mythical creatures, and in this respect belong to the pantheon of Netsilik supernatural beings.   *[margin note: PRESENT WORLD]*

As for the more recent Netsilik world view, one thing is clear. To the Netsilik, life was dangerous. This is the basic assumption underlying the way the Netsilik saw the physical world around him and the supernatural forces behind it. An old woman told Rasmussen (1931:213): "For up here where we live, our life is one continuous fight for food and for clothing and a struggle against bad hunting and snowstorms and sickness." Skill in hunting, perseverance on the chase, and continuous endurance were qualities that helped to overcome the dangerous environment, but there were supernatural spirits behind the natural world which had to be contended with as well. It is a perilous visible world controlled by unreliable supernatural beings that is most characteristic of the Netsilik world view, a world of double danger. This is clear from the testimony of Qaqortingneq, an old camp leader. Rasmussen asked him, "What is it you desire most of life?" He answered:

> "I would like at all times to have the food I require,
> that is to say animals enough, and then the clothes that
> can shield me from wind and weather and cold.
>   I would like to live without sadness and without pain,
> I mean without suffering of any kind, without sickness.

And as a man I wish to be so close to all kinds of animals that in the hunt and at all kinds of sports I can excel over my countrymen.

All that I desire for myself I desire also for those who through relationship are near to me in this life."

"What will you do to attain all this?"

"I must never offend Nuliajuk or Narssuk.

I must never offend the souls of animals or a tonraq so that it will strike me with sickness.

When hunting and wandering inland I must as often as I can make offerings to animals that I hunt, or to the dead who can help me, or to lifeless things, especially stones or rocks, that are to have offerings for some reason or other.

I must make my own soul as strong as I can, and for the rest seek strength and support in all the power that lies in the name.

I must observe my forefathers' rules of life in hunting customs and taboo, which are nearly all directed against the souls of dead people or dead animals.

I must gain special abilities or qualities through amulets.

I must try to get hold of magic words or magic songs that either give hunting luck or are protective.

If I cannot manage in spite of all these precautions, and suffer want or sickness, I must seek help from the shamans whose mission it is to be the protectors of mankind against all the hidden forces and dangers of life."

(Rasmussen 1931:224-25)

AFTERLIFE

The real life of the daily present runs parallel at any given point of time to a supernatural life that existed long before a person was born and will follow him after death. Nalungiaq told Rasmussen (1931:315): "The world is not only that we can see. It is enormous, and also has room for people when they die and no more walk about down here on earth." The Netsilik held firmly to the belief that people who had not turned into evil ghosts after death went to one

of three afterworlds well known to shamans, who had
visited them. Two of these places were very similar in the
conditions they offered to the dead and differed only in
location.

(1) *Agneriartarfik*, or the village one can always return to, is
located high in the sky. There is plenty of game at all times,
the caribou in particular roaming in great herds. Hunting
is invariably very good, and whenever the dead become
tired of caribou meat and wish a different food, the moon
spirit helps them down to the sea where they can kill seals.
The country is beautiful up there, the weather good, and the
dead continuously happy. They play at all sorts of games,
everything is happiness and fun, and in all respects it is a
land of pleasure. (The people who go there are the clever
and energetic hunters, especially those who have died violent deaths. As for women, only those with large and beautiful tattooings have access, this because they had the
courage to endure the suffering involved in the tattooing
technique.) The dead remain there forever at the age that
they were when they died. Thus there is an evident advantage in dying young, as one remains young forever.

(2) *Aglermiut* is an underworld located very deep under the
tundra. Living conditions for the dead are as good as for
those living in the sky. There is plenty of caribou, and salmon fishing is very rewarding. The dead live there in joy and
abundance. The seasons are reversed from those on earth—
whenever there is winter among the Netsilik, there is summer in the underworld. The same good hunters and tattooed
women who go up into the sky can live here.

(3) *Noqumiut* are called the dead who live in a different underworld, located just below the crust of the earth. They
always sit huddled up with hanging heads. Their eyes are
closed. Their only food is the butterfly, which is caught when
it comes too close to the head of a dead man. The *noqumiut*
are perpetually hungry, idle, and apathetic. Lazy hunters

(marginalia, left side:)
Good place; One remains forever at age one died.

Good place; like the One above.

Sad place; under crust of earth.

go here, along with the women who would not endure the suffering of getting tattooed.

Clearly there are some striking relations between the quality of personal behavior on earth and individual destiny in one of the afterworlds. Energy, endurance, fearlessness for young men and the ability to endure suffering for women are the qualities most rewarded in the afterlife. Laziness, idleness, apathy, and refusal to accept pain are punished. It is not surprising that beliefs related to afterlife closely relate to basic Netsilik values.

Good behavior is rewarded in the afterlife. Bad behavior is punished.

The religious activities of the Netsilik can be divided into two main levels of complexity: first, the relatively simple and very numerous minor rituals such as magic words, various observances, taboos, and elementary forms of malevolent magic and, second, the highly complex body of shamanistic practices. Whenever relevant in the following description, the social implications of symbolic action will be emphasized.

A large number of magic formulae for beneficial purposes were known to the Netsilik. They were addressed either to the various spirits or to human ghosts and souls of dead animals. They were considered personal and very secret property, transmitted from father to son or purchased from a shaman. Their powerful and generally mysterious nature was enhanced by the special language of the shamans with which they were composed. Since nobody was allowed to hear them, they were uttered either early in the morning when one's housemates were still asleep or far in the country, away from camp and fellow hunters.

A definite characteristic of magic words was their specificity of purpose. Each formula was applicable to one subject only. There were magic words for better hunting in strange lands, for help in caribou hunting, musk-ox and bear hunting, fishing arctic cod and salmon trout, to cure sickness and heal wounds, to facilitate birth, to make dogs hardy while chasing bears, to give boys strength in competitive games, etc. Rasmussen (1931:280) recorded this formula to bring luck when hunting caribou:

Great swan, great swan,
Great caribou bull, great caribou bull,
The land that lies before me here,

Let it alone yield abundant meat,
Be rich in vegetation
Your moss-food
You shall forward to and come hither
And the sole-like plants you eat, you shall look forward
  to
Come here, come here
Your bones you must move out and in,
To me you must give yourself!

Evidently magic formulae performed very similar functions to amulet spirits, though the latter seem to have had a more continuous power. Both were employed to give supernatural help to people in need.

TABOOS

The Netsilik knew and rigidly observed a very large number of taboos and rituals. The strict taboo system indeed constituted the cornerstone of their religious life. There were basically two broad categories of taboos, the first concerning hunting activities and game animals (seal, caribou, bears, salmon), the second relating to the critical phases of a person's life cycle (birth and death) and certain physiological functions such as menstruation.

There were a number of observances that had to be made in connection with seal hunting in midwinter and particularly with seal butchering. A freshly killed seal was never to be laid on the dirty igloo floor. This was because the animal soul would be offended by resting on a place where women had been walking. It was therefore necessary to bring in fresh clean snow for the seal to lie on. Further, it was assumed that even dead seals would be thirsty, and so some water had to be poured into its mouth. This gesture of kindness and respect to the soul of the animal would encourage it to reincarnate into another body and, out of

gratitude, allow itself to be killed again by the same harpooner. This observance was therefore believed to have a
greatly beneficial effect and bring luck in seal hunting.

As long as an unflensed seal lay on the igloo floor no
woman could sew or do any other work. A similar taboo
applied to men, who could not work on stone, wood, or
iron. It was thus essential to proceed with butchering as
soon as possible. Further, all old blubber had to be taken out
of the house through the window when a freshly killed
seal was brought in. And at the sea ice camp, seal meat
could be cooked only over the blubber lamp and not by any
other method. And when people moved camp in midwinter, the skulls of the seals caught at the old site were laid
on fresh snow, pointing in the direction the migration was
going to follow, this with the assumption that their souls
were going to accompany the people to their new hunting
grounds.

The souls of caribou were thought to be particularly delicate and necessitated special care. While caribou hunting
was going on, it was strictly forbidden to do any stretching,
scraping, or sewing of clothing furs. Scraping caribou skins
was particularly dangerous at that period. Scraping could
wound the animal soul, and if the grazing caribou happened
to witness the suffering of one of their kind, they would be
much less willing to be caught. When a caribou was killed
during the great herd migrations, it was forbidden to cut its
ears off by the root, as otherwise the soul of the animal might
turn into an evil spirit. Caribou meat could not be cooked
over a driftwood fire, nor could driftwood be used for even
kindling a fire over which caribou meat was to be cooked.
The soul of the caribou was very sensitive at its leg skins,
and so no stranger, but only the hunter's wife, could work
them. Another major taboo related to caribou bones. Although many exceptions and variants were known, the general rule was that no marrowbones were to be broken until
all the caribou had left the country. And it was absolutely

forbidden to eat caribou killed with the bow and arrow on the same day that seal meat was eaten. Further, at the caribou hunting camps it was forbidden to sleep with seal meat in the tent. And of course, no work on caribou skins could be done during the dark winter months. The counterpart of this rule was that in spring, no sewing of sealskins could take place until all the snow had melted and the caribou had grown their new coats.

The soul of the bear was considered to be particularly dangerous and powerful, and numerous exacting observances were necessary to counter any revengeful intentions its soul might have had at the end of the hunt. It was believed that after the bear had been killed, its soul remained on the tip of the hunter's spear for four or five days. During this period, to avoid the soul's turning into an evil spirit, the following had to be done: the skin had to be hung inside the house and surrounded by various implements, all man's or woman's work was forbidden, including sledge shoeing, and presents to the soul of the bear had to be placed on its skin.

Taboos associated with salmon seem less numerous. Just as the caribou hunting places were considered holy, there was a general taboo on both men's and women's work at all stone weirs. For any minor sewing or repair work on leisters that had to be done, people left the river and hid behind a large rock. No pregnant women were allowed to approach the weir.

These were the most important taboos and observances related to hunting various kinds of game animals. Now we shall consider the practices and taboos related to the personal life cycle.

The various observances connected with childbirth were exceedingly numerous and lasted for a whole year. As soon as a woman felt birth pangs, a small igloo was built for her where she was confined in solitude for four or five days. She gave birth there without any assistance. Occasionally an elderly woman was allowed to be present to help with the naming of the child, but not with the actual delivery. Nobody was allowed to touch the woman, who was thought to be extremely unclean and impure. If difficulties occurred a shaman was called to officiate. The mother actually delivered the child while in a kneeling position. The infant glided down directly into a hollow on the snow platform and was not wrapped in skins. The mother severed the navel cord with a special flint knife that she held in her left hand. The infant was then wiped with a special skin that would later be considered a powerful amulet. Soon after birth the baby was placed into the *amaut,* or the big pouch on the back of the mother's coat.

After her initial period of rigorous isolation in the small snow hut, the mother entered a second phase of less strict separation. A larger, more comfortable igloo was built for her, where she remained for another month. She was allowed to receive female visitors occasionally and when going out always carried a scraper and a snow knife. She could eat only food caught by her husband and could have no intercourse with him. This period of relative isolation was followed by a whole year during which a new series of taboos had to be observed. Although the mother moved freely around camp, she ate only early at morning and late at night, kept her drinking bowl bottom upward, avoided eating raw meat, etc.

Death was surrounded by an equally important group of observances. If the death taboos were broken there was always the danger that the soul of the deceased person would turn into an evil spirit and bring misfortune to the camp fellows, and so these taboos were carefully heeded. Immediately after death there was a period of four or five days, depending on whether the deceased was a man or woman, during which a rigorous work taboo applied to all members of the household. It was assumed that during this period the soul remained with the body. The other camp fellows meanwhile would not comb their hair or cut their nails, stopped cleaning soapstone lamps and feeding dogs, and avoided sledge driving. At the end of the mourning period two close relatives would drag away the body on a sledge and leave it on the ice without any covering. In summer, while inland, a stone was placed by the head and another at the feet. The Netsilik never built stone graves. With the "funeral" completed it was believed that the soul of the dead had departed for the afterworld. Usually most of the dead person's belongings were left near the body, unless he had divided them up among his family before death. Immediately after the funeral, camp was moved to a new hunting place. This ended the required death observances for the camp fellows, but for a whole year a brother who had lost a sister or a sister who had lost a brother abstained from plucking the hair of any land or sea animal.

As with women after childbirth, menstruating women were considered polluted. They were obliged to inform the community about their condition and remained confined in their houses, avoided song feasts, never mentioned game animals by their names, etc.

The preceding list of taboos could be almost indefinitely lengthened. Why did the Netsilik burden their lives with so many restrictions, some of which were obviously very cumbersome? What is the significance of the taboo system in relation to Netsilik religion considered as a whole? What is the social meaning of these taboos?

No simple or single answer can be given to these questions, but the Netsilik taboos had certain common characteristics that can help us discover their principal functions. First, there were the very important rules separating land from sea animals. As Rasmussen notes (1931:179): "caribou hunting and sealing must be kept quite distinct . . ." It has been mentioned that no work on caribou skins was allowed at the sealing camps. It was strictly forbidden to eat lake trout, a land animal, on the same day that one had eaten seal meat. Land and sea animals were kept separate with

reference to hunting, utilization of parts, and food consumption. All these observances were really ways to confirm sym-
bolically the separation of the world into two halves: land
and sea. This dichotomy was very much in harmony with
the character of the Netsilik migration cycle, characterized
by a dual form of ecological adaptation. (In a sense these
separation taboos were a symbolic expression of the dualistic life the Netsilik had to lead.)

   Second, the majority of taboos concerned activities of
the greatest importance to society, namely hunting and childbirth. The survival of society depended on both. Further,
and it is possible here to include death, these were issues
largely beyond the control of individuals. The hunter on the
chase was never certain of a kill. Mothers obviously entertained fears about the survival of their newborn infants and
death could occur practically any time. (The taboos thus appear as symbolic provisions destined to control the uncontrollable and to reduce the level of anxiety generated by
uncertainties.) Of course if things turned really bad the shamans could be called upon for help. Their intervention
however was occasional and generally depended upon invitation. The application of taboos was of a different order. It
was compulsory, no exception was made, and concerned
everyone. It was in this respect that the systemic and rit-
ualistic character of the taboo was most important. The
taboo system was the first automatic defense mechanism
against uncontrollable and unpredictable dangers. Taboos,
then, could function as important psychological control
measures for the reduction of anxiety.

   Third, taboos were important because the breaking of
taboos provided the Netsilik with an understandable reason
for tribal misfortunes. Inadvertently or out of weakness,
someone breaks a taboo. This angers some evil spirit who
brings disaster to a camp fellow, all under the watchful eye
of Nuliajuk. The shamans then have to be called with their
helping spirits to exorcise the harmful spirit, and everyone

[Handwritten margin notes:]
Why Taboos?
① Taboos Symbolic of dualistic life of Netsilik ←
② Taboos assured Survival of society ←
③ A way to control the uncontrollable & conquer uncertainties. ←
④ Psychological control measures for anxieties ←
⑤ Breaking One gives a reason for trouble. ←

feels better about whatever the misfortune was. Strangely, in the Netsilik religious order, the taboo system, which is in a sense the underwriter of the supernatural order, becomes the very source of evil. It is as if despite continuous efforts to keep things in good order, society fails to control itself at a certain point and generates evil. Here lie the ethical aspects of the taboo system. The ethics of taboo do not concern interpersonal relations, however. They refer to individual misfortunes or group disasters or more generally to the relations between society and the supernaturals.

Fourth and most important are the essentially religious aspects of the taboo system. Rasmussen noted that at certain important caribou hunting places and stone weirs some very exacting and different taboos had to be observed, which gave the areas a kind of holy status. It is easy to conclude that many hunting taboos reconfirmed locality sacredness. The majority of hunting taboos referred to the souls of animals, the objective being to appease their anger and ensure future success in hunting. Hunting taboos and animal souls were closely connected, with the result that the observation of the first constantly strengthened the belief in the second. As for childbirth and menstruation taboos, they centered around the notion of impurity, particularly female impurity. These taboos guarded society from any danger of pollution. When pregnant and menstruating women were confined to their tents at the caribou hunting and fishing places the sacredness of these was thus preserved. Taboo breaking was immediately related to the action of evil spirits and their supreme controller Nuliajuk, and required the intervention of the shamans. The taboo system worked to strengthen religious beliefs by making the spiritual world omnipresent.

SHAMANISM

The shaman, or *angatkok,* occupied an important position in Netsilik society. Although in daily life he behaved like an ordinary hunter, he was generally respected and feared for his supernatural powers. The preparation of young shamans took place as follows.

The *angatkoks* were in the habit of observing the behavior of boys, to discover if some bright young man had received the call. Once selection had been made, the formal training started. Initially the novice joined the household of an elderly *angatkok*-teacher, where he observed a series of special taboos, such as abstaining from eating outdoors, from eating liver, head, heart, or intestines, and from having sexual relations. The novice, assisted by a spirit, slept intermittently and began having visions. Then he moved to a separate igloo where, during a period of several weeks, he was taught the secret vocabulary together with necessary shamanistic techniques and obtained his paraphernalia (a headdress and a belt) from his parents. Finally his teacher presented him with a protective spirit (*tunraq*), and they officiated together. Initially the *tunraq* was the master of the novice, and only gradually did the young *angatkok* learn to control it. Eventually, as he gained experience, the novice became a full-fledged shaman, possessing a competence and strength apparently equal to that of his master.

Shamans had control of only one class of spirits, the *tunraqs*. They continued to acquire *tunraqs* throughout their lives, usually as gifts from other shamans or by the spirits' own volition. Relations between *angatkoks* and *tunraqs* were by no means simple; they showed considerable ambivalence, because of the ethical characteristics of certain spirits and their relative autonomy of action. If it is generally true that most powerful shamans were well in control of their *tunraqs*, there were other *tunraqs* that were very independent. Such was the case with the spirit called Orpingalik, who used to attack his master Anaidjuq suddenly from behind and pull off his genitals; the unfortunate shaman, after much yelling, had to recover these during a trance (Balikci, 1963:382–83).

As mentioned before, many classes of malevolent supernaturals could bring misfortune to people. Besides the evil ghosts, *tupiliqs* were another important group of evil-intentioned spirits. Round in shape and filled with blood under considerable pressure, they could cause terrible sickness. The *tunraqs* themselves were more dreaded, however. When a shaman dispatched one of his spirits on an aggressive mission and the *tunraq* failed to achieve its task, it became a "reversed spirit" or *tunraq kigdloretto*, a bloodthirsty being, blinded by frustration, totally out of control, who generally turned against his master and relatives and brought sickness and death into their camp. Under these circumstances, other shamans had to intervene and with their more powerful *tunraqs* harness the *kigdloretto*.

Sickness was always caused by evil ghosts and spirits, usually angered by a breach of taboo. These attacked the patient in group formation and took abode in his body. The shaman was then called to chase them away. In a typical performance the shaman, adorned with his paraphernalia, crouched in a corner of the igloo or behind the sleeping platform and covered himself with a caribou skin. The lamps were extinguished. A protective spirit called by the shaman entered his body and, through his mouth, started to speak very rapidly, using the shaman's secret vocabulary. While the shaman was in his trance, the *tupiliqs* left the patient's body and hid outside the igloo. The shaman then dispatched his protective spirits after the *tupiliqs;* and with the help of the benevolent ghost of some deceased shaman, they drove the *tupiliqs* back into the igloo through the entrance. The audience encouraged the evil spirits, shouting: "Come in, come in, somebody is here waiting for you." No sooner had the *tupiliqs* entered the igloo than the shaman, with his snow knife, attacked them and killed as many as he could; his successful fight was proven by the evil spirits' blood on his hands. If the patient died, it was said that the *tupiliqs* were too numerous for the shaman to kill, or that after the séance, additional evil spirits attacked the patient again.

The main para-shamanistic technique, called *krilaq* (head lifting), was widely practiced in the Netsilik area. The *krilasoktoq* (practitioner of *krilaq*) did not require any special training and was much weaker than a regular shaman; his technique, although involving the manipulation of spirits, lacked a trance. His spirits, *aperksaqs* (helping spirits), were weaker than the *tunraqs* and not his personal "property." Head lifting was performed generally on the *krilasoktoq's* wife or on his own leg or on a stone. A thong was tied around the hooded head of the woman; then the *aperksaqs* were called. The *krilasoktoq* pulled on the thong; an easy answering pull meant a negative answer from the spirits, a heavy pull a positive one. The helping spirits, which were the ghosts of the practitioner's deceased relatives, were called in the following order: father, mother, brother, grandparents, sister. Typical curing consisted of questioning the helping spirits in order to discover the broken taboo that had caused the sickness. This accomplished, the evil spirits were supposed to leave the body of the patient. The *krilasoktoq* repeatedly assured the patient that he was getting better. *Angatkoks* apparently never practiced *krilaq*; they disdained the lack of sharp vision and the dilatory action of the *krilasoktoq*.

Angatkungaruks (lesser shamans) constituted a third class of curers. Their para-shamanistic technique involved identifying the evil spirit and localizing it in the patient's body. They were helped by some of the weaker *tunraqs*, though they never possessed them. The *angatkungaruk* would sit calmly near the patient and after many hesitations

declare that he saw the evil spirit and that the latter was
leaving the patient. Because of the *angatkungaruk's* lack of
keen vision and inability to control powerful supernaturals,
the diagnostic treatment and his encouragements to the patient had to be often repeated. This variety of shaman received no special training, practiced the *krilaq* technique
very rarely, and was incapable of foreseeing future events.
Different from the shamanistic and para-shamanistic techniques described so far was a form of magical practice called
ilisiniq. It is probable that numerous persons engaged in this
evil art in order to bring calamity, paralysis, or death to a
secret enemy or to a person disliked or envied. Many manip-
ulative techniques were known, most of them based upon
connecting something associated with the enemy to the
dead or to menstrual blood: animal bones brought in by
the enemy might be stolen and placed in a graveyard; the
enemy might be touched with the mitt of a dead man; some
fur from a graveyard might be obtained and placed in the
kayak of a fast kayaker in order to slow him down; menstrual
blood might be mixed with the seal meat brought in by the
enemy, etc. Some practices were simpler: breaking the
bones of the enemy's seal or spitting in front of him. It was
essential for all such acts to be accompanied by mental
wishes specifying the evil aim desired. The role played by
spirits in *ilisiniq* remains obscure, mainly because of lack of
information. Rasmussen noted for the Igloolik Eskimos that
tupiliqs were used in evil witchcraft (Rasmussen, 1929:143).
Among the Netsilik, however, *ilisiniq* appeared as a rather
mechanical or peripheric shamanistic art. As was the case
with *tunraqs*, *ilisiniq* acts could sometimes backfire and
harm their very practitioners.

Such were the basic Netsilik techniques for manipulating
supernatural spirits with regard to curing sick people. But a
classification based only upon the objectives ostensibly pursued by shamans—curing, putting down storms, calling the
animals to be hunted, providing help in obtaining a mate,

[margin note: Practicing evil on an enemy]

etc.—obscures any understanding of the relations between the shaman, as an individual, and the group. Shaman-group relations can be understood by examining the shaman's efforts at manipulating the social life of his people. Accordingly, the practices of the shaman will be discussed below in terms of his attempts to control a) environmental threats endangering the group; b) individual or group crises; c) interpersonal relations; and d) his own prestige among his people.

Shamanistic control was frequently used to maintain a balance between people and environment, particularly in cases of disaster. Shamanistic practices to attract game belong to this category. Whenever game was unavailable, the *krilasoktoq* was asked to discover, with the help of his spirits, where the animals were located, while the *angatkok's* *tunraqs* more actively directed the game toward the hunters. Frequently a breach of taboo brought the community to the verge of famine, and the shaman had to invite people to make confessions. His spirits informed him in advance of a breach of taboo, but it was essential that culprits confess of their own volition before the shaman could see about increasing the food supply.

[handwritten margin note: Shamanistic Control ① To keep a balance between man & nature]

Shamans could control thunder and put down snowstorms. They accomplished this either by dispatching a *tunraq*, or, in a trance, tying thongs around the child-like weather god Narssuk. Shamans could even stop the cracking of the ice, as is illustrated in the following case.

> At the winter sealing camp, built on the flat ice, a young girl had a hole in her boots, repaired them, and thus broke a sewing taboo. There soon followed an extraordinary snowstorm, and the ice started cracking and breaking, endangering the whole camp. The people, terrified, gave presents to the *angatkok* and begged him to stop the oncoming disaster. The seance took place in the *kagske*, the large ceremonial snowhouse, after putting down all the lamp lights. The *angatkok*, in trance,

cried, "It is coming," pointing to a young caribou (a
spirit) he saw running about. Everybody except the
young girl started confessing, admitting breaches of taboo. When the spirit came near enough to be seen by
the girl, she admitted her fault, and the ice cracking
stopped.

②To
control
individ-
ual or
group
crises.

Shamanistic acts could control individual or collective
crises not necessarily stemming from the physical environment. Crises were generally brought about by breaches of
taboo which angered the spirits and caused them to attack
humans. All cases of curing may be grouped under this
category. A sickness should not be considered, however, a
purely individual misfortune; it was a collective crisis. Such
is the dependence of people on each other in an extremely
harsh environment within a small community that a hunter
in bed means probable hunger for the family and lessened
chances for the group to catch food; likewise a sick wife
leaves the husband with nobody to cook the meat and mend
his clothes.

Evil spirits and various classes of monsters might try to
attack the people. The whole community often lived in
dreadful fear, surrounded by malevolent beings. The intervention of several shamans then became imperative. Rasmussen described such a case for a Southampton Island
community (Rasmussen 1929:144), and several additional
cases are known for the Netsilik area.

Harpoons, ice chisels, and iron needles were important
tools, highly prized and difficult to replace. Loss of any of
them created a crisis calling for the shaman's help. Harpoons
and ice chisels often fell into the sea through seals' breathing
holes. The shaman recovered them either by jumping supernaturally into the water through the narrow ice hole, in
front of a credulous audience, or by tying them with a thong
lowered through the breathing hole; the helping spirits did
the rest. Lost needles were directly found by *tunraqs*.

Numerous shamanistic acts and *ilisiniq* practices were

meant to control interpersonal relations. All aggressive acts, ③ To
even involving the shaman himself in a competitive or control
otherwise hostile relation, belong to this category; here, inter-
too, we can include his supernatural aid in selecting a mate personal
and in achieving blood revenge. relations

Interpersonal tensions came about for many different reasons. Jealousy, however, seems to have been the most frequent motivation for aggressive shamanizing. Some illustrative cases:

> Irqi was the mother of a grown son, a very poor seal hunter. This boy's meat-sharing partner, Krasovik, used to catch many seals. Krasovik was a much faster runner. Irqi grew jealous and made *ilisiniq* against Krasovik. The latter, protected by powerful amulets, got only some pains in the legs. The aggressive act turned against the witch and killed her son.

> Having lost a child, Irkinoark grew jealous of another woman's child and made *ilisiniq* against the boy. The aggressive act turned against her and she felt sick. An *angatkok* told her she had done something very bad. Despite her admission of having done so, she died, became an evil ghost, and as such managed to bring sickness to the envied boy. The latter was cured by a shaman.

> Kaormik was a better bear hunter than Amaoligardjuk's son, so Amaoligardjuk, a shaman, became jealous and sent his *tunraq* polar bear against Kaormik. The bear scratched the left side of his face severely but failed to kill him. Amaoligardjuk added after: "This man is hard to kill!".

A certain external difficulty may irritate an individual and lead him to aggression.

> Atkrartok, a shaman, and Nulialik were traveling together on rough ice. Nulialik became irritated because of the difficult journey and apparently wanted to turn

back, to which Atkrartok objected. A fight with knives
ensued; they decided to stop using knives but to continue fighting with supernatural means. Nulialik did
ilisiniq against the shaman, believing that his opponent
was trying to kill him with his *tunraq*. The evil act
turned against Nulialik and killed him.

Constant quarreling may be a cause for supposed shamanistic aggression.

Inaksak, an ambitious *angatkungaruk,* and Qagotak, a
shaman, both very bad tempered, were constantly quarreling. Qagotak was in trance one day, officiating, when
Inaksak saw under Qagotak's feet a dark shadow. Inaksak thought this was his own soul Qagotak was trying
to steal from him in order to make him sick. Fortunately,
being an *angatkungaruk,* Inaksak knew how to defend
himself.

In traditional times, as was previously noted, the high in-
cidence of female infanticide caused a considerable sex-
ratio imbalance to exist. This made for great difficulties in
finding a wife. Steenhoven (1959:40) notes several cases of
the murder of husbands by men who wanted to steal their
wives. Such murders could be accomplished with supernatural means.

Kaumadluk, a shaman, desired Inuksak's wife. So Kaumadluk decided to kill Inuksak. He did so with the help
of his *tunraq,* who turned over Inuksak's kayak; the latter drowned. Unfortunately for the murderer, his victim's wife did not want him and married another man.

In the following cases evil shamanizing was used to
avenge frustrated lovers.

After the death of her husband, the shaman, Arnapak
moved with her sons among the Kagnermiut, where she
wanted to marry again. The young man she had her eye
on had no desire for her, presumably because of her age.
Arnapak decided to take revenge by sending her *tunraq*

caribou to attack him and he was killed. The people saw this and also noticed that Arnapak was smiling; they consequently realized what had really happened. Shortly after, the Kagnermiut put Arnapak and her sons to death by shooting them with arrows from behind.

Some shamans considered lying with a particular woman as a necessary part of a shamanistic act. The audience assumed this was a desire of the *tunraq*. Often, however, the shaman's propositions were rejected.

The people asked Igarataitsok to stop a particularly violent snowstorm. The shaman first desired to lie with two girls. The father of the first agreed immediately, but the husband of the second said: "A *tunraq* can not copulate with women."

This attitude was not general with all shamans. Informants agreed, however, that a shaman who desired a particular woman would readily threaten her with imminent sickness in order to attain his aim.

It was important for shamans to discover cases of incest, which could be a source of calamity.

Avataut, son of the woman Nuutlaq, was sick for a whole winter. Both a *krilasoktoq* and an *angatkok* tried to discover the cause of this sickness, without much success. The patient and his mother refused to admit their sin. Ivaiarak, the shaman, finally said, pointing to both: "Your wife and your husband." Nuutlaq violently denied the charge. The *angatkok* repeated the accusation several times, with the same result. Avataut, near death, said: "I waited for somebody to speak, but nobody did, so I better say something before I die." And Nuutlaq added: "Oh, I remember. I love my son so much that when he asked me I slept with him once." Despite the confession, Avataut died.

Steenhoven (1959:61), after analyzing several Netsilik murder cases, failed to see any evidence of blood revenge in the historic data. But Steenhoven's cases refer exclusively to physical murder. I collected some cases in which murder was committed by supernatural means for the purpose of blood revenge.

> Kotirjoaq and her husband were quarreling. The latter became angry at his wife and in his anger hanged himself. Kotirjoaq remarried soon to Neharaisok and had a baby. Armadluq, the first husband's mother, decided to avenge her son's death, and with her *tunraq* she killed Kotirjoaq soon after the birth of the child.

> Moraq, a dangerous shaman, killed the brother of Itiitoq, another shaman, with his *tunraq* polar bear. Itiitoq decided to avenge his brother's death. When the two met, they had a friendly conversation; they both went to sleep in their igloos. In the middle of the night Itiitoq said to his daughter: "Wake up. Moraq is out of his bed." Indeed Moraq was lying on the ice floor of his igloo; he had been immobilized there by Itiitoq's *tunraq* at the moment when Moraq wanted to go deep underground and attack Itiitoq, while asleep, from below. Moraq's wife went to implore Itiitoq to help her husband. At that moment Itiitoq got frightened, believing that if he killed Moraq, the latter might become an evil ghost and bring disaster to his family. So he decided to let Moraq live.

The fourth major category of shamanistic activities includes the large number of shamanistic performances, the obvious or hidden objectives of which are to control the shaman's own position in society, to enhance his prestige. Fights between shamans as a test of supernatural strength have this end in view.

> Utaq was a *krilasoktoq* and Inutsaq an *angatkok*. They were wrestling partners and frequently engaged also in friendly competitions with *tunraqs* in tests of supernatural strength. One day, after a bitter quarrel, Utaq dreamed that Inutsaq's *tunraq* polar bear was on a mis-

sion to kill him. Utaq immediately dispatched one of his own helping spirits to stop the *tunraq,* which, over-powered, became a *kigdloretto.* Utaq made a polar bear out of snow and turned it against Inutsaq. The blood-thirsty evil spirit turned back and later killed its own master.

Iksivalitak and Isargataitsoq were both great *angatkoks.* In the sealing camp Iksivalitak boasted about his super-natural powers, and sent his *tunraq* in the form of a dark monster under the breathing hole attended by Isar-gataitsoq, who, after some hesitation, refused to strike it. Then by supernatural means Isargataitsoq stuffed his opponent's breathing hole with seaweeds.

Other cases of shamanistic competition lacked this aggressive element.

Two shamans of different camps had a competition in flying with the help of their *tunraqs.* The one who flew higher and passed over the other had the power to ground him. After many circumvolutions one shaman was immobilized on the ground. "If I leave him on the ground, he will freeze to death. So I will bring him up again," decided the victor.

Atkrartok, a shaman, asked Neptaroq, a *krilasoktoq:* "Do you think I can pass through this tea cup?" Follow-ing a negative answer the shaman first pushed his head through the cup, then his whole body, and finally disap-peared underground with a rumbling noise. He came back the same way.

The shaman was capable of performing strange and won-derful acts upon his own body, and this always in front of an audience. Iksivalitak used to shoot himself with a gun, Qagortingnerk removed his own leg, other *angatkoks* pre-ferred to pierce themselves with spears and grow beards in a second. People who claim to have seen such performances still speak with awe and admiration about the ability of these shamans.

Finally, there is the large class of outstanding shamanistic achievements, such as journeys to the underworld, travels to the moon, or meetings with strange monsters, which fill the pages of Rasmussen's reports. These were feats of the most important shamans, to whom they brought considerable prestige, and by the time Rasmussen visited the Netsilik area the shamanistic art was already in decay, and probably very few shamans could claim such successes.

Fusion of good & evil elements in the Netsilik shamanism.

The most striking characteristic of Netsilik shamanism and associated beliefs was the fusion of good and evil elements. Although the Netsilik distinguished clearly between an evil shamanistic act from its positive counterpart, the same shaman was capable of performing both. Thus, although most shamans were considered good, at some time in their career they committed aggressive acts; and even the very few reputedly evil shamans were considered bad only during particular periods. A considerable ambivalence or blending of ethical qualities characterized the protective spirits and ghosts themselves. Good spirits and ghosts could evolve into malevolent beings, and an opposite change could affect evil spirits. This intermixing of good and evil had important social consequences.

The possibility of nearly any Netsilik's supposed ability to influence supernaturals for aggressive purposes contributed much to the interpersonal suspicions and hidden hostilities of their society. The cases cited in this chapter show the wide variety of reasons why people decided to use aggressive magic, and also how carefully malicious intentions were concealed behind amiable attitudes. On the surface, camp life proceeded peacefully, while secretly vicious attacks were going on back and forth with the help of supernaturals. "An action, apparently the most innocently meant, and not worthy of a second thought, may be the cause of remorseless persecution" (Rasmussen, 1931:200).

Possibility of one person influencing supernaturals for aggression contributed to the latent hostilities of the society!

The individual lived in an atmosphere of suspicion and fear, dreading both the possible secret attacks of his camp fellows and the spirits who might initiate an evil action on their own.

If shamanism was practiced as a kind of social control, its ethical ambivalence meant that it was not always very effective. Certainly the society used shamanism often in a conscious effort to enforce norms or re-establish harmonious relations between environment, people, and supernaturals. If many cases fulfilled such an aim, however, the aggressive acts surveyed here show that the ready recourse to supernatural helpers sometimes actually worsened social relations and intensified interpersonal hostilities. The shaman rarely had full control over the spirits; they could acquire autonomy, attack some individual blindly, and create new enmities altogether, with quite an opposite effect than that desired by the society. Thus, in the imbroglio of fears and accusations, not only existing enmities found free expression but entirely new hostilities could emerge.

The second major function of Netsilik shamanism was perhaps more successful than the social control function. For the Netsilik, the shamans were the people who brought the world together. Environment, spirits, the afterworld, social life—all of those elements were brought together for them into one meaningful whole. Both the components and the acts of shamanism indicate that for varying aims a multiplicity of elements were fused during the shamanistic performances. Elements of nature, the animals of land and sea, snowstorms and thunder, cracking ice, etc., were brought under the shaman's power. The world of the dead was also present during a séance: deceased relatives were utilized as protective spirits, and evil ghosts fought. Society was also represented, and in two ways; often an audience participated directly in the shamanistic performance, and all shamanistic practices involved the presence of at least part of the community. Basic religious beliefs were also included in the shamanistic complex. In varying situations and for different purposes the shaman integrated these diverse elements into a dynamic unity. In his role as integrator, in a stream of symbolic effusions, the shaman gave meaning to a multiplicity of situations which would have remained inexplicable to society without his intervention (Balikci 1963: 395).

Shaman's role was a very
* important one in Netsilik
society.

CONCLUSION

Throughout this work I have tried to concentrate on what appeared to be the most significant and original aspects of Netsilik culture and social life. Many secondary traits were deliberately left aside, and in this sense the present ethnography of the Netsilik Eskimos is far from being complete. An effort was made to describe separately the essential aspects of the relationship between the Netsilik and their environment, the ordering of their social life, their principal religious symbols, and their ritual activities. And as one studies these people and looks at their technology, their social organization, and their religion, one consideration stands out as consistently most important: survival. Essential aspects of Netsilik life and culture seem to address themselves in some way to the problem of the survival of the individual and the group in an extremely hostile environment. Let us review the principal points raised in the preceding chapters in the light of this central theme.

The sophisticated and highly specialized technology of the Netsilik is the most visible cultural elaboration allowing for a successful utilization of the available natural resources. Without the sealing harpoon, double-pronged leister, kayak and spear, or bow and arrow, no game animals could have been killed with the efficiency peculiar to the pre-firearm Eskimos. Then, too, there was clearly an exciting pleasure factor connected with inventiveness and problem solving that compensated partially at least for the inevitable hardships that the Netsilik endured.

Likewise, the Netsilik kinship system was admirably suited to the hunting way of life. Despite the fact that extended families were not rigidly structured, they did exist, with the result that the nuclear family was only in exceptional cases forced to fend for itself. Boys had the opportunity of acquiring their technical and general knowledge from a number of older relatives. The system was remarkably flexible. At any given time, a nuclear family could break away and join another group. Affinal ties could be exploited and substituted for consanguineal bonds. Kinship and affinal alignments often provided the organizational framework for necessary collaborative activities, of which there were many. The list of the various collaborative forms among the Netsilik is truly impressive. They extended to the fields of food acquisition, distribution and consumption, borrowing, help during crises, etc. There is no doubt that the extent and flexibility of collaboration were vital factors in Netsilik survival. Yet because of its very flexibility, the kinship system had to be supplemented by additional binding mechanisms. These were the numerous patterned dyadic relationships which established social bonds primarily between non-kinsmen. The most important such mechanism was the seal-meat-sharing pattern, remarkable indeed for its rigidity. Collaborative forms determined by biogeographic or technological factors, consanguineal and affinal ties, and the patterned dyadic bonds, all worked together to produce a complex network of relationships which made for the social cohesion the Netsilik needed to hunt and live together.

The problem of survival has to be viewed differently, however, when social phenomena having a more direct bearing upon local demographic conditions are analyzed. The very high rate of female infanticide is the crucial consideration here. It produced an extraordinary imbalance in the sex ratio of the tribe and naturally directly affected the distribution of women in society and the very nature of marriage. There is little doubt that under conditions of continuous ecological pressure, a certain amount of female infanticide had an adaptive value, but the Netsilik seem to have practiced it to excess, to a point where there simply were not enough women to go around. As long as women could be brought in from the westerly neighboring tribes, the sex imbalance for adults could be kept within certain limits. If the flow of women had stopped, however, then probably as Rasmussen predicted, the tribe would move toward extinction if it kept up its practice of excessive female infanticide. And there was another harmful effect: it provoked rivalry among males for the possession of women, who were in short supply. Wherever competition led to the elimination of the weaker males, the stronger won the women, did the procreating, and society benefited. Among the Netsilik, however, this competition was sometimes so extreme that things went awry, and the better hunters ended up being stabbed in the back.

We can look at suicide in a similar way. The suicides of older people who did not contribute sufficiently to community survival can be considered as adaptive. But many of the Netsilik who committed suicide were younger people, capable wives and hunters. It appears that it was the weaker person, incapable of withstanding ostracism, derision, hate, ambiguity, or neglect that killed himself. In this sense, suicide operated as a mechanism making for the elimination of the socially weaker persons. In sum, if both female infanticide and suicide worked in favor of the survival of the fittest, then the term "fittest" refers here not only to hunting capability but also to capacity to live actively in society. This assertion, however, should be considered as a hypothesis, the available data remaining insufficient for drawing definite conclusions.

In religious symbolism, survival preoccupations are strongly visible. The human soul as a source of strength and the name soul, the numerous amulet spirits, the magic words, the taboo system, and many shamanistic acts aimed at ensuring success in hunting or at eliminating various dangers such as bad weather, sickness, etc. Yet evil existed, and it was through the agents of the supernatural world that the source of misfortune was to be found. Malevolent ghosts and monsters acting independently could attack humans almost any time and bring disaster. And disaster did occur occasionally, despite all the admirable adaptive strategies employed by the Netsilik. Rasmussen was told by an elderly informant that in the winter of 1919, seven people had starved to death near Cape Britannia. The following year, sixteen men, women, and children had died of hunger in the vicinity of Simpson Strait. This makes nearly 10 per cent of the tribal population. No wonder dreadful memories haunted the minds of the people. This is what Qaqortingneq told Rasmussen (1931:137) about Tuneq, a middle-aged Netsilik:

> One winter, many years ago, hunting was a failure. Day af-
> ter day went by and nobody had anything to eat. People
> died of hunger or froze to death, and the quick lived on the
> dead. Then Tuneq suddenly became disturbed in his head.
> He began to consult the spirits, and it was not long before he
> began to do so through his own wife. He used her as a me-
> dium: *qilaq*. He did it in this way: he tied a line to one of her
> legs and made her lie on the platform; then he tugged at
> her leg and let the spirits answer through her leg. He did this
> often, and it was not long before he said he had received the
> answer that he was to save his own life by eating his wife. At
> first he only cut small pieces from her clothing and ate them,
> drinking water with it to help him to swallow it. People who
> saw him say that he behaved like a man possessed of a wild
> and evil spirit. Bigger and bigger were the pieces he cut from
> her clothing; at last her body was quite exposed in many
> places. The wife knew that the spirits had said her husband
> should eat her, but she was so exhausted that it made no im-
> pression on her. She did not care. It was only when he began
> to feel her, when it occurred to him to stick his fingers in her
> side to feel if there was flesh on her, that she suddenly felt a
> terrible fear; so she, who had never been afraid of dying,
> now tried to escape. With her feeble strength she ran for
> her life, and then it was as if Tuneq saw her only as a quarry

that was about to escape him; he ran after her and stabbed her to death.

After that he lived on her, and he collected her bones in a heap over by the side platform for the purpose of fulfilling the taboo rule required of all who die. He was going to hold death-taboo over her for five days. But people say that the ghost of his wife often walked through her own bones, Tuneq waking up at night as the bones he himself had gnawed began to rattle. Sometimes they moved up and down, and it happened that the man sitting up on the platform would be hauled off during the night by some invisible power. And when he then suddenly awoke there was no one in the snow hut, only the bones lying over by the side platform, rattling.

SLOW CULTURE CHANGE BETWEEN 1920 AND THE EARLY 1960s

When Knud Rasmussen in 1923 journeyed through the Netsilik
country, most of the Inuit were already in possession of muzzle
loading guns acquired from a trader established near Repulse Bay,
northwest of Hudson's Bay. These old guns were not very effective;
they were hardly better than the bow and arrow. The very day
Rasmussen left the Netsilik area, a boat arrived carrying
construction materials and supplies for the first Hudson's Bay
trading post to be built in that remote part of the Arctic. That
same season the Netsilik Inuit acquired both high powered rifles
and steel traps.

In 1936 a Catholic missionary established the first mission near
the mouth of the Kugardjuk River, on the east coast of Pelly Bay.
In a very short time, the Netsilik band around Pelly Bay converted
to Christianity.

These two factors, the acquisition of rifles and steel traps and
the arrival of the missionary produced profound social, economic
and ideological changes among the Netsilik affecting the whole
of their culture. Let's examine now how the Pelly Bay band reacted
to these acculturative pressures around the 1950s.

Seal hunting at the breathing holes with the harpoon implied
definite collaborative patterns; all able bodied men had to hunt
together or starve together. Following the introduction of the rifle
an entirely new sealing method was adopted; seals were hunted

at the ice edge, that is in open water, in the northern part of Pelly
Bay where strong currents do not allow the winter ice to
consolidate. The hunter stood right at the ice edge and as soon
as a seal surfaced to breathe it was shot in the head and pulled
from the water with a canoe. This hunting method was highly
efficient and a single hunter could kill several seals in a day. With
an increased supply of seal meat the Netsilik were enabled to keep
large dog teams pulling bigger and heavier sleds made from
imported wood. This greatly extended the mobility of the Netsilik
and the range of their hunting expeditions. Consequently, group
hunting at the breathing holes in winter was gradually abandoned.

Caribou hunting was also affected by the introduction of rifles.
The Netsilik did not have to lay in ambush anymore waiting for
the migrating herds to reach the crossing places. At any season,
summer or winter, the hunters could reach the tundra for caribou
and with the new fast rifles exterminate whole herds. Intensive
caribou hunting took place practically everywhere in the Canadian
North and very rapidly the caribou population declined drastically.
As a result, in the 1950s there were almost no caribou to be hunted
in the Pelly Bay area. As for musk-oxen which were relatively
easy to kill even with spears, they vanished completely from the
arctic coast region and became an endangered species protected
by federal laws.

The introduction of nets greatly increased the efficiency of
fishing. Although the Netsilik continued to gather at the stone
weirs, in early summer and late fall they preferred to fish with
nets which were strictly individual property. Ingenious methods
were devised even for net fishing under thin autumn river ice.

Fox trapping with steel traps never became a strategic activity
among the Pelly Bay band. In other arctic communities where
the Hudson's Bay Company had established fur trading posts the
Inuit spent most of the winter trapping intensively, using up to
200 steel traps per hunter. At Pelly Bay trapping remained
subordinate to hunting. When my informant Itimangnark, went
seal hunting to the deep ice edge, he placed five or six traps along

his path. On his way back he checked the traps and collected the foxes.

The missionary built in the 1940s a small stone church and an adjoining trading post. At his store he purchased fox pelts, seal skins and polar bear skins and sold ammunition, canvas for tenting material, duffle for clothing in replacement for caribou furs, tea, tobacco and various sundry items. Since no boat could reach Pelly Bay, all imported supplies, now vital necessities, had to be brought in on sleds from the Repulse Bay settlement on the western coast of Hudson's Bay. Bigger items like wooden canoes were purchased at the HBC store at Spence Bay and carried to Pelly Bay on sleds.

These changes in the technological equipment and subsistence activities of the Pelly Bay Inuit had far reaching effects in other aspects of culture. First, the settlement pattern of the band was profoundly transformed. Anciently, the band stayed together at the winter sea ice camp while in summer the families spread over the tundra in small units. Following the establishment of the mission center, most Pelly Bay families settled around the mission with only men going alone on hunting trips. Thus the nomadic existence came gradually to an end. Second, with rifle in hand, every family head became economically self sufficient. The traditional collaborative patterns disappeared together with the seal meat sharing partnerships. Every hunter owned the game he brought home. The social integration of the band was greatly weakened and the individual family emerged as the basic socioeconomic unit in all seasons. The final result was an atomization of society. Third, with fur trapping and increased reliance on imported goods, the Pelly Bay band was integrated into the market economy and became dependent on the local store.

The most drastic changes in the field of social organization were introduced by the Catholic missionary. Following regular preaching and continuous personal influence, the missionary succeeded in suppressing all practices of female infanticide and senilicide. This quickly brought to a balance the sex ratio between men and women. All young men could find wives and there was no need to steal women or to murder a husband in order to marry his widow. The missionary firmly established monogamous marital stability as a rule and eliminated polygyny together with all illicit sexual arrangements. Very quickly these Inuit learned to behave as good Christians.

In the areas of religion and myth, the changes were equally profound. Taboo was the first block of local belief to collapse. It is true that the innumerable taboos observed by the Netsilik were a heavy load to bear. They quickly abandoned most ritual prohibitions, apparently with no regret. Considering that the taboos were the cornerstone of local religion upon which most beliefs in supernaturals, ritual actions, and shamanistic practices rested, the whole religious structure collapsed. Amulets disappeared, the old myths were forgotten, and shamanism was considered as a devilish activity. And since the drum was vaguely associated with the office of the shaman, all drum dances were suppressed by the missionary. Yet in traditional times the shaman provided an explanation of things extraordinary together with some form of leadership in moments of crisis. These functions were taken over by the missionary who became the community leader in matters social and religious. The Inuit attended Mass every day and recited prayers regularly. Although the Netsilik were unable to grasp the deep significance of Catholic dogma and ritual, the intellectual atmosphere in the community became gradually and rigidly enframed by the periodicity of Catholic ritual.

It is clear that during this period of relatively slow yet profound sociocultural change, practically all aspects of culture were affected. The acculturative process was planned by the missionary who consciously followed a blueprint for action. The main reason for the missionary's success was due to the fact that there were no other resident Euro-Canadians in the settlement. As principal agent of social change, the missionary was able to proceed selectively; he accepted innovations only as far as they fitted his program. Undesirable external influences could be rejected. In the mid-1950s, a DEW line station was established, not far from the missionary settlement. Other than improving communication, this had only minimal impact on the acculturative process, since the Netsilik were discouraged to fraternize with the station residents. The missionary cumulated the functions of religious leader, trader, teacher, and government agent. His authority remained unchallenged until the middle 1960s.

RAPID CULTURE CHANGE SINCE 1965

Until the late 1950s, the Canadian government had remained markedly indifferent to the fate of these Inuit. It is true that in many northern settlements RCMP constables were stationed. The mounties 'conducted a patrol to outlying camps once a year, distributed some medicine to the sick, and issued relief in small amounts to the destitute. Although the official reason for the RCMP being there was to apply the law, there were hardly any criminal cases to be investigated. For all practical purposes, the Inuit were considered to be wards of the HBC and the missions.

In the 1950s, the Canadian government established the Department of Northern Affairs. One of the major aims of the new Department was to integrate the northern people into the mainstream of Canadian life. The Inuit were to be provided as soon as possible with most of the basic opportunities, amenities, and services enjoyed by southern Canadians, namely a variety of salaried jobs, decent and warm housing, electricity, a regular water supply and some kind of sewage system, fully equipped schools, medical facilities, and an amiable administration to guide the people on the road to civilization. Vast sums of money were invested by the government in achieving these objectives. Let's examine now the results of this dynamic policy in Pelly Bay.

In 1963, the decision was taken to construct a federal day school at Pelly Bay, comprising one classroom for all elementary grades, plus living quarters for the teacher and his local assistant. The building was quickly erected at great cost, since all building materials had to be air freighted. Two electrical generators were added. In the next two years, the whole area around the old mission site was transformed into a construction camp, at least during the summers. The old missionary was replaced by two young priests who together built a new mission house. Finally the government provided building materials to the Inuit for the construction of family houses consisting of three bedrooms, a kitchen-living room, and a toilet. The project was successful and, within two summers, there was not a single igloo to be seen at Pelly Bay. Soon a nursing station appeared together with a large general store, several warehouses, and a community hall. An all-weather airstrip was an essential addition to the construction and development program. The material basis of the community changed drastically and the Pelly Bay settlement, seen from outside, increasingly resembled a modern city suburb.

The social changes that took place at the same time were no less important. The day school probably was the one single institution that affected most deeply the life of the Pelly Bay Inuit. All boys and girls between the ages of seven and fifteen attended the elementary grades combined within one classroom unit. Courses were conducted exclusively in English and included, besides language instructions, rudimentary notions of calculus, geography and science. Soon another classroom was added and a second teacher arrived to teach the upper elementary grades. Students who wished to pursue their general education further were sent to boarding school at Inuvik, in the Western Arctic, and boys who wanted to be trained in one of the trades went to various southern vocational schools.

Continuous instruction in English contributed to make English the preferred language of communication among youngsters. With fluency in the dominant language followed a new openness for things of the donor culture. Various new mannerisms, clothing styles, games, food tastes, and numerous other behavior patterns belonging to the dominant culture acquired prestige in the eyes of the younger generation and were eagerly borrowed. Particularly fascinating appeared to be the technical gadgets which are a distinctive peculiarity of Euro-American culture. The young Inuit began accumulating tape recorders, record players, radios, motorcycles, snowmobiles, and so on. The generation gap at Pelly Bay quickly became a cultural gap, with the younger generation speaking English and aping the American way of life while the older generation continued to speak only Inuktitut and tried to understand (with difficulty) the new way of boys and girls. It should not be forgotten, however, that the school was responsible for *unveiling* the mysteries of civilization.

The Inuit's appetite for imported goods proved to be truly insatiable and the new store was very important in satisfying this new demand. The new store, however, was no ordinary commercial establishment. It was a cooperative endeavor sponsored by the missionaries. It was indicated previously that the HBC never established a trading post at Pelly Bay and, consequently, the local mission had to engage in some trading activities. Following the recent developments, the old mission store proved to be wholly inadequate and an entirely new operation had to be envisaged. The Inuit settled upon the cooperative formula and created a local co-op, to be owned and managed by the Inuit and for the Inuit. A young Inuk from a neighboring community was appointed manager and several local men found employment there. The Co-op proved to be a highly successful enterprise, bought the locally made carvings and shipped them out for sale, imported a great variety of goods for sale in the store, and obtained from government the contracts for water supply to the family houses and refuse collecting. Most importantly, the Co-op acquired a four-engine airplane, a DC-4, to fly in supplies and fuel oil, a vital commodity since all buildings were oil heated and oil was used to operate the electrical generators. In a sense, the Co-op was the principal economic integrator of the community and the mediating agency between the community, the government, and the Euro-Canadian economic system in all matters of commerce and economic enterprise.

Despite the increased integration of the Pelly Bay community in the modern economic system, hunting and fishing were not abandoned. These subsistence activities continued, although in a different manner. Strangely enough, in recent years the caribou population in the Pelly Bay area had greatly increased. This was due primarily to the fact that no inland Indians and Inuit hunted the caribou any more in the Barren Grounds and near the tree line. Left to themselves, the caribou reproduced rapidly and appeared in increasingly larger numbers near the shores of Pelly Bay. Further, since snowmobiles were introduced, sledge driving declined to the point of being completely abandoned. The sledge dogs consequently disappeared from Pelly Bay. Caribou hunting with snowmobiles was a quick affair. Two hunters with two snowmobiles could leave the settlement in the morning, drive quickly inland to where caribou might be found, locate a small herd, shoot several caribou, load them on small sledges pulled by the snowmobile and drive back home the same day. And since there were no dogs to be fed, all the meat was consumed by the people. Some hunters even sold caribou meat to the Co-op which was later purchased by the permanent job holders in the community. With a good supply of caribou meat, seal hunting with rifles was gradually neglected. There were several reasons for this. First, everybody preferred caribou to seal meat, caribou meat being considered more tasty and tender. Second, seal oil had become useless since there were no dogs to be fed and no soapstone lamps to be kept aflame. Third, the ice edge where seal hunting was conducted was much further away than the near caribou hunting grounds.

Fishing continued intensively as before, with nets. Fishing at the stone weir was completely abandoned; nets, however, were placed both along Kellet River in the fall and all around the settlement in the shallow waters of Pelly Bay. Fresh or frozen salmon trout remained thus an important source of food.

Salmon trout abounded in such large quantities in the Pelly Bay area that the regional administrator decided to establish a commercial fishery, providing the paint and paying the Inuk tenant a fee to paint the house he was living in. The family had to pay only a nominal rent of $14 a month. The Inuit could rely on a steady supply of caribou meat and fish for food and, occasionally, some seal meat. Clearly the living conditions of the Pelly Bay Inuit had improved enormously with each family enjoying obvious material security and comfort. Yet the general desire for additional material acquisitions grew considerably and an increased cash income was regarded as something essential. Many young and even older men found employment locally: keepers for the school, the nursing station, and the generator plant; workers at the Co-op or at the airstrip; truck drivers for garbage removal and water delivery; seasonal construction workers on various buildings, and so on. Many women and several men became very active carvers of small soapstone figurines while older men like Itimanguark engaged in the reproduction of traditional artifacts such as harpoons and kayaks for various museums and private collectors. And, of course, family allowances and old age pensions remained as a steady source of income. With cash in hand, the Inuit could buy expensive clothing, snowmobiles, gas, and gadgets of all sorts, as well as some imported foods such as bread, eggs, and fruit.

Disease was not to be feared either. The resident nurse visited periodically all the local families and was constantly available for any emergency situations. In case of difficulties, the nurse could telephone the doctor in the regional hospital and call for an airplane to evacuate the patient. A boy, six years old, had his fingers caught and scratched between the two school doors. He was evacuated by plane for X-rays and further treatment. It is clear that even minor injuries (which in the past would have been barely noticed) get immediate attention at present.

In the field of sociopolitical development, besides the Co-op, two new organizations have been established in recent times: first, the Housing Association which was created under government auspices to collect rents and supervise the maintenance of the buildings (a salaried Inuk secretary was appointed to supervise the daily administrative tasks of the association), second, the Hamlet Council which set the Pelly Bay community on the road to self-government. Acquisition for Pelly Bay of Hamlet status was a project promoted by the missionaries who encouraged the relative administrative autonomy of the community. The local population voted (secret ballot) for the election of six councillors, one of whom is president and the second functions as vice-president. The missionary became the financial manager of the Hamlet Council. All debates of the Council are public, yet decisions are taken secretly. The main function of the Council is to serve as administrative intermediary between the Territorial government and the local community. In a sense government officials cannot take direct action in Pelly Bay without prior submission of an action plan to the Hamlet Council for approval. It should be noticed that the Hamlet Council cannot overrule the Housing Association which supervises government property.

What is the position of the new missionaries in the new environment? The old missionary, by virtue of his being the only resident Euro-Canadian, cumulated many functions and was the real leader of the community. His successors apparently had lost numerous functions, namely trading, treating the sick, local administration, welfare, and essentially teaching. They seem confined to their primary functions of preaching, saying Mass, and looking after the spiritual needs of the people.

It is clear that the material base and social conditions of the Netsilik have changed drastically. On the whole, these Inuit have demonstrated once more their extraordinary adaptability to changing circumstances. They do like their new way of life, the warm house, the speedy snowmobiles, the education the children get at school, the opportunities for money making, the films shown at the community hall, and the modern dances every Friday evening. Melancholic thoughts about the traditional way of life are not often heard, although complaints are made about adolescents not listening to their parents. The young people seem particularly at ease, they speak the language of the dominant society and are the first to benefit from the government's generosity. And they don't have to marry the traditionally promised spouses; young people are free to make their own marital choice.

Pelly Bay is not a truly "autonomous" community. It depends on government subsidies and services. If the government stopped its regular supply of oil, igloos would have to be constructed immediately. In a sense, the Co-op and the Hamlet Council have the task to handle and distribute governmental funds, goods and services. Under the auspices of iocal administration, the Pelly Bay Inuit have become wards of the government.

BIBLIOGRAPHY

AMUNDSEN, ROALD
1908 *The North West Passage.* 2 vols. London.

BALIKCI, ASEN
1961 "Suicidal Behavior Among the Netsilik Eskimos," article No. 35, *Canadian Society: Sociological Perspectives,* B. Blishen, ed., Chicago: The Free Press of Glencoe.
1962 "Some Acculturative Trends Among the Eastern Hudson Bay Eskimos," *Aktendes 34. Internationalen Amerikanistenkongresses.* Wien (1960).
1963 "Shamanistic Behavior Among the Netsilik Eskimos," *Southwestern Journal of Anthropology,* 19:380–96.
1963 "Le régime matrimonial des Esquimaux Netsilik," *l'Homme,* 3:89–101.
1964 *Development of Basic Socio-Economic Units in Two Eskimo Communities,* Bulletin 202, Ottawa, National Museum of Canada.
1966 "Ethnographic Filming and the Netsilik Eskimos," *Educational Services Incorporated Quarterly Report,* Spring–Summer 1966:19–33.
1967 "Female Infanticide on the Arctic Coast," *Man* 2:615–25.
1968 "The Netsilik Eskimos: Adaptive Processes," article No. 8, "Man the Hunter," R. Lee and I. DeVore, eds., Chicago: Aldine.
1973 "The 'Hunters' Ecology," *Nature in the Round,* Nigel Lalder, ed., New York: Weidenfeld and Nicolson.
1975 "Reconstructing Cultures on Film," *Principles of Visual Anthropology,* P. Hockings, ed., Hawthorne, NY: Mouton de Gruyter.

1978 "The Netsilik Inuit Today," *Etudes/Inuit/Studies*, Vol. II, No. 1.
1984 "The Netsilik Eskimos," *Handbook of North American Indians*, Vol. V, Smithsonian Institution.
1985 "Ethnographic Film and Museums," *Museum, UNESCO*, No. 145.
1988 "Anthropology, Film and the Arctic Peoples," *Anthropology Today*, April.

BIRKET-SMITH, KAJ
1928 *Five Hundred Eskimo Words*, Reports of the Fifth Thule Expedition, Vol. III, No. 3, Copenhagen.
1940 *Anthropological Observations on the Central Eskimos*, Reports of the Fifth Thule Expedition, Vol. III, No. 2. Copenhagen.
1945 *Ethnographical Collections from the Northwest Passage*, Reports of the Fifth Thule Expedition, Vol. VI. Copenhagen.
1959 *The Eskimos*. London: Methuen.

DAMAS, DAVID
1963 *Igluligmiut Kinship and Local Groupings: A Structural Approach*, Bulletin 196, Ottawa, National Museum of Canada.

DURKHEIM, EMILE
1951 *Suicide*, Chicago: The Free Press of Glencoe.

KLUTSCHAK, HEINRICH W.
1881 *Als Eskimo unter den Eskimos*, Wien.

KROEBER, A. L.
1953 *Cultural and Natural Areas of Native North America*, Berkeley: University of California Press.

MARY-ROUSSELIERE, GUY
1965 *"Jeux de ficelle chez les Esquimaux de Pelly Bay,"* M.A. dissertation, Université de Montréal.

MIRSKY, JEANNETTE
1937 "The Eskimo of Greenland," *Cooperation and Competition Among Primitive Peoples,* M. Mead, ed., New York: McGraw-Hill.

NELKIN, DOROTHY
1976 "The Science-Textbook Controversies," *Scientific American,* April.

PONCINS, GONTRAN DE
1941 *Kabloona,* New York.

RASMUSSEN, KNUD
1929 *Intellectual Culture of the Iglulik Eskimos,* Reports of the Fifth Thule Expedition, Vol. VII. Copenhagen.
1931 *The Netsilik Eskimos,* Reports of the Fifth Thule Expedition, Vol. VIII. Copenhagen.

ROSS, SIR JOHN
1835 *Narrative of a Second Voyage in Search of a North West Passage,* London.

VAN DEN STEENHOVEN, GEERT
1959 *Legal Concepts Among the Netsilik Eskimos of Pelly Bay, N.W.T.,* Ottawa: Northern Co-ordination and Research Centre, Department of Northern Affairs and National Resources, NCRC-59-3.

VAN DE VELDE, FRANZ
1954 "L'infanticide chez les Esquimaux," *Eskimo* 34:6–8.
1956 "Les règles du partage des phoques pris par la chasse aux aglus," *Anthropologica* 3:5–15.
1958 "Toponymie Eskimo de la région de Pelly Bay," manuscript, Mission catholique, Pelly Bay, Northwest Territories, Canada.
1959 "Liste des instruments Netsilik pour la chasse à l'aglu," manuscript, Mission catholique, Pelly Bay, Northwest Territories, Canada.

WEYER, E. M.
  1932 *The Eskimos*. New Haven: Yale University Press.